38.00

Microprocessors in
Instrumentation and Control

Microprocessors in Instrumentation and Control

S. A. Money
TEng (CEI) MIElecIE MBCS

McGraw-Hill Book Company

New York   St. Louis   San Francisco   Montreal   Toronto

Library of Congress Cataloging-in-Publication Data

Money, Steve A.
   Microprocessors in instrumentation and control.

   Includes index.
   1. Automatic control.   2. Microprocessors.
3. Engineering instruments.   I. Title.
TJ223.M53M66   1985   629.8'95   85-23652
ISBN 0-07-042707-0

1234567890   DOC/DOC   8932109876

ISBN 0-07-042707-0

First published in Great Britain by
Collins Professional and Technical Books in 1985.

First American edition published by McGraw-Hill in 1986.

Printed and bound by R.R. Donnelley & Sons Company.

Contents

Preface

In recent years the widespread availablility of microprocessor devices has made the production of versatile and reliable data acquisition and digital controller systems practicable. Earlier designs for such systems were usually relatively inflexible and bulky because they required large numbers of small scale integrated logic devices. Although digital controller schemes could be implemented by using a minicomputer, the arrival of the microprocessor has meant that controller units can be made compact and independent of a central computing facility. In this book some of the principles and techniques involved in designing microprocessor-based systems for use in data acquisition and control applications are explained.

In the first chapter a brief review is made of the principles of operation of the basic hardware elements of microprocessor systems. Then, Chapter 2 goes on to examine some of the principles involved in programming the CPU to perform its required tasks. One of the more important tasks of the CPU is that of performing logical and arithmetic operations. In Chapter 3 the principles of arithmetic operations using a microprocessor are examined. This includes an introduction to the principles of floating point arithmetic and functions such as differentiation and integration which are required in the implementation of digital control systems.

To be of any practical use a microprocessor system must be able to communicate with the outside world and in Chapters 4 and 5 we examine the techniques involved in transferring digital data to and from a microprocessor system. Chapter 4 deals with parallel input and output schemes and includes a discussion of the popular IEEE 488 General Purpose Instrument Bus scheme which is used on many current laboratory instruments. Chapter 5 looks at the serial mode of transfer for digital information using both asynchronous and synchronous data formats.

For data acquisition and control systems many of the inputs and outputs will be in analogue form and Chapter 7 examines the techniques involved in converting signals from analogue to digital and from digital to analogue form. Some aspects of the software required for setting up and testing analogue input and output channels are also discussed.

Data acquisition when using a computer type system inevitably involves taking discrete samples of the input signal and this can present problems with 'aliasing' where the sampling process can cause false signals to be generated which, to the microprocessor, are indistinguishable from genuine input signals. This problem is discussed in Chapter 8 which also examines some of the programming principles involved in setting up a data acquisition system using a microprocessor.

In the past most automatic control systems have used analogue feedback techniques to implement the controller function. With the available computing power of the microprocessor it becomes possible to consider implementing the control function by using digital techniques. This allows the development of more flexible control schemes where the characteristics can be readily altered by merely inputting new data into the microprocessor equations. The basic principles of implementing such systems are discussed in Chapter 9.

For many microprocessor applications, the computing operations must take place in real time. To make effective use of the CPU some means is required by which its normal program sequence can be temporarily interrupted to deal with an external event that must be processed immediately. This can be achieved by making use of the 'interrupt' facilities provided on almost all available microprocessor devices. The principles of operation of such hardware interrupt schemes are covered in Chapter 10.

A microprocessor by itself is virtually useless until it has been programmed to perform some desired task. The writing of the program for a microprocessor is generally called software development and includes the overall design of the program sequence, the writing of the actual program code and, finally, the testing of the software and correction of any errors in operation. This task may be performed by using a low level mnemonic language which generates individual instructions for the CPU, but a much better approach is to use a high level language which allows the programmer to concentrate on the program action without needing to get involved with details of the operation of the CPU. In Chapter 11 the principles of software development and the use of some of the more popular high level languages are considered.

Ultimately the microprocessor system must consist of some hardware which performs the required functions demanded by the program software. In the early days of microprocessors this involved designing the hardware from scratch around a set of integrated circuits. Today it is possible to obtain ready-built modular circuit boards which will provide the various elements likely to be required for a microprocessor-based system and this makes the design of the hardware system a much simpler task. For many applications it is possible to make use of one of the many personal or small business computer systems to implement the required microprocessor based project. Some of the principles that need to be considered when choosing the hardware are discussed in Chapter 12.

S. A. Money

Chapter One
Basic Principles

In recent years the development of microprocessor devices and microcomputers has made possible the design of more versatile equipment in the fields of electronic instrumentation and control. In the past such systems used analogue circuit techniques designed to perform a limited range of functions. With the development of integrated circuit devices in the 1960s and the introduction of a wide range of integrated digital logic devices, it became practical to introduce digital techniques into instrumentation. The advantage of using digital techniques is that a higher degree of precision and a wider range of functions can be incorporated into an instrument or controller unit.

The physical size of the digital electronics package can become quite large when standard integrated circuit logic devices are used. By using more complex custom-designed integrated circuits the number of devices needed can be reduced to permit a more compact instrument package. For applications where the number of units to be produced is small the use of custom-designed circuits can become very expensive and this approach is not economical unless the equipment is to be mass-produced.

An alternative approach is to replace the custom-designed circuits by using a microprocessor and a few standard support chips. The advantage of using a microprocessor is that it is a general purpose device which can be manufactured in vast numbers at low cost and then programmed for use in a wide variety of different instrument or control applications. As a result, the electronics equipment may consist of just a few complex integrated circuits forming a compact module with the added advantage that the operation of the system can readily be tailored to satisfy the user's particular requirements.

Many domestic appliances today incorporate microprocessors as part of their control system. Some of these use a relatively simple control scheme which carries out a pre-programmed sequence of operations. In a washing machine, for instance, the water has to be heated to some pre-set temperature, then the drum is rotated for a pre-set washing period, the heater is turned off and a rinsing process is carried out and finally perhaps a spin-dry operation may be performed. In early automatic washing machines the sequence of actions was governed by a motor-driven switch assembly and water temperature might be controlled by a simple thermostat switch. Modern machines, however, are required to provide a wide variety of different washing programmes and to cater for these a mechanical switch system becomes very complex and expensive to produce. A microprocessor-based control system will allow the user to pre-set a wide variety of wash programmes and may also be used for temperature control and to provide various other monitoring functions at very low cost.

In a video recorder a microprocessor usually controls the complex sequence of actions needed to thread the tape and run the tape transport mechanism. Here the microprocessor controls the sequence of actions as well as monitoring tape speed, tape tension, end-of-tape sensors and other operating parameters, and will automatically modify the operation of the system to compensate for any changes in these parameters. More recently, microprocessors have been applied to functions such as control of the operation of an automobile engine. By using a microprocessor it is possible to optimise the engine's operating conditions to give improved fuel economy, smoother running and better overall performance than earlier engine designs which used rather crude analogue control schemes.

In the laboratory most of the older instruments use some form of analogue measuring technique with the results displayed on meters or charts. Such systems tend to be relatively inflexible and require careful operation if accurate results are required. By using digital techniques measuring instruments have been made more precise in operation and easier to use. Instruments incorporating a microprocessor can be made very flexible and may include features such as automatic range selection to suit the signal being applied.

The results measured, perhaps in an experiment, usually need to be analysed in some way in order to obtain the desired information. In the past this has involved the manual collection of a large number of instrument readings which are then fed to a mainframe or minicomputer system for analysis and production of printed results. By using modern data acquisition systems together with suitable measuring instruments, it is possible to collect the experimental data automatically and record it on a medium such as magnetic tape. After the experiment this recorded data may be read directly into a computer for analysis, thus saving a considerable amount of time and manual effort. If a microprocessor-based instrumentation system is used it becomes possible to perform some or all of the required analysis as the experiment progresses, thus saving time and the need to have access to a large computer system.

In process control we have basically a larger scale version of the type of system used in a device such as a video recorder. In processing some raw material such as steel or plastic, a number of different operations may be required in sequence in order to produce the final product. Each step of this process may in itself be relatively complex and require the monitoring and control of a variety of parameters. Here the entire process may be controlled by a single large computer but it is often more effective and more economical to use microprocessors to control individual stages of the process with perhaps another microcomputer governing the whole system.

Microprocessor systems such as those in domestic appliances are usually dedicated to the particular tasks that they have to perform. They can be manufactured in large quantities and as a result will usually be much cheaper to produce than a general purpose controller device or computer. For laboratory work and for some forms of industrial control and monitoring, one of the popular home computer systems based around a microprocessor can be a useful tool. These machines have the advantage of providing general purpose computing facilities at low cost and are relatively easily programmed by users who are not experts in computer programming. For one-off experiments this type of machine, when combined with some simple interface circuits, can provide adequate results and be more economical to use than a more dedicated set of laboratory instrumentation.

In this book we shall be looking at the operation of microprocessor devices and some of their applications in the fields of instrumentation and control.

Digital logic and signals

In the real world we find that physical quantities such as length, weight, etc. can vary over an infinite range of values. For instrumentation or control purposes these physical parameters are generally converted, by means of a suitable transducer, into an electrical voltage or current that is proportional to the physical parameter being measured. These electrical signals are called 'analogue' signals.

The analogue signals can be manipulated in various ways by using amplifiers and filters and the results may be displayed on meters or plotted. It is even possible to build a computer using analogue signals. The main problem with analogue systems is that it is difficult to maintain high accuracy and stability in the analogue processing circuits. Analogue schemes also tend to be relatively inflexible and the circuits usually need to be rewired to a new configuration if a change is made in the calculation or analysis that is to be performed.

An alternative to the analogue approach is to make use of simple electrical circuit elements which have only two possible states namely on and off. Such a device can represent only the numbers 0 and 1 but by using the combined states of a set of these simple switch circuits we can represent any desired number. Thus if we take three switches there are 8 possible on/off combinations as shown in Figure 1.1 and these may be used to represent the numerical values from 0 to 7. Increasing the number of switches to four gives 16 combinations, whilst five switches permit 32 possible combinations. In

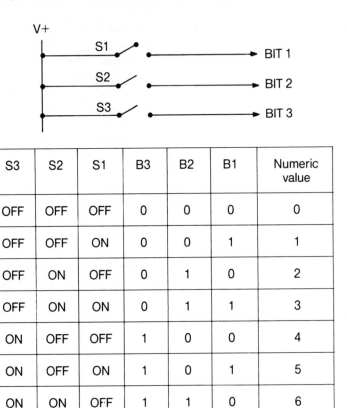

Fig. 1.1 Use of combinations of on/off states to represent numbers.

S3	S2	S1	B3	B2	B1	Numeric value
OFF	OFF	OFF	0	0	0	0
OFF	OFF	ON	0	0	1	1
OFF	ON	OFF	0	1	0	2
OFF	ON	ON	0	1	1	3
ON	OFF	OFF	1	0	0	4
ON	OFF	ON	1	0	1	5
ON	ON	OFF	1	1	0	6
ON	ON	ON	1	1	1	7

fact each time a new switch circuit is added to the group the number of possible combinations doubles.

Because each switch has only two possible states the system is called 'binary' (scale of two). Each switch represents one digit of the complete number and is called a 'bit' (binary digit). The two states of the bit are normally referred to as '0' and '1'. In the more familiar decimal numbering system each digit has ten possible states ranging from 0 to 9 and the digits, working from right to left, indicate units, tens, hundreds and so on. In the binary system each digit is either a 0 or a 1 and they represent, from the right-hand end, units, twos, fours, eights and so on, as shown in Figure 1.2.

The set of bits which makes up a binary number is generally called a 'word' and in microcomputers the word length may range from 4 bits for a small dedicated device up to 32 bits for a large general purpose microcomputer system. The typical word lengths found in practice are 4, 8, 16 and 32 bits although one or two early microprocessors did use a 12-bit

BIT 7	BIT 6	BIT 5	BIT 4	BIT 3	BIT 2	BIT 1	BIT 0
2^7	2^6	2^5	2^4	2^3	2^2	2^1	2^0
128	64	32	16	8	4	2	1

Weighted value of bits

Example

$101100 = 32 + 8 + 4 = 44$

Fig. 1.2 Numerical weighting of bits in a binary number.

word length. The word length determines the range of numbers that can be operated upon by a single processor operation. Thus an 8-bit word may represent numbers from 0 to 255, whilst a 16-bit word expands the number range giving values from 0 to 65 535.

Basic microcomputer architecture

As a start, let us take a look at the general organisation of microprocessor and microcomputer systems. In effect a microcomputer is simply a digital computer system which has been implemented using a small number of complex integrated circuits. In some cases all of the vital functions are built into a single integrated circuit.

The organisation of a typical digital computer system, whether it be a microcomputer or a large mainframe system, follows the basic pattern shown in Figure 1.3. At the heart of the system is the central processor unit or CPU which contains the complex logic needed to carry out arithmetic and logic functions and to control the timing and sequence of operations in the computer system.

In addition to the CPU, a computer system needs some form of memory. This is effectively an electronic filing system which allows items of information in digital form to be stored away for later use. One important function of the memory is to hold a list of instructions, called the 'program', which tells the CPU what to do. The memory is also used to hold the data that is to be processed and the results produced by processing the data. In small dedicated microcomputer devices the program and data sections of the memory may be separated but in systems designed for general purpose applications it is usual for both the program and the data to be held in a common memory unit.

If the computer is to be of any practical use it is important that some

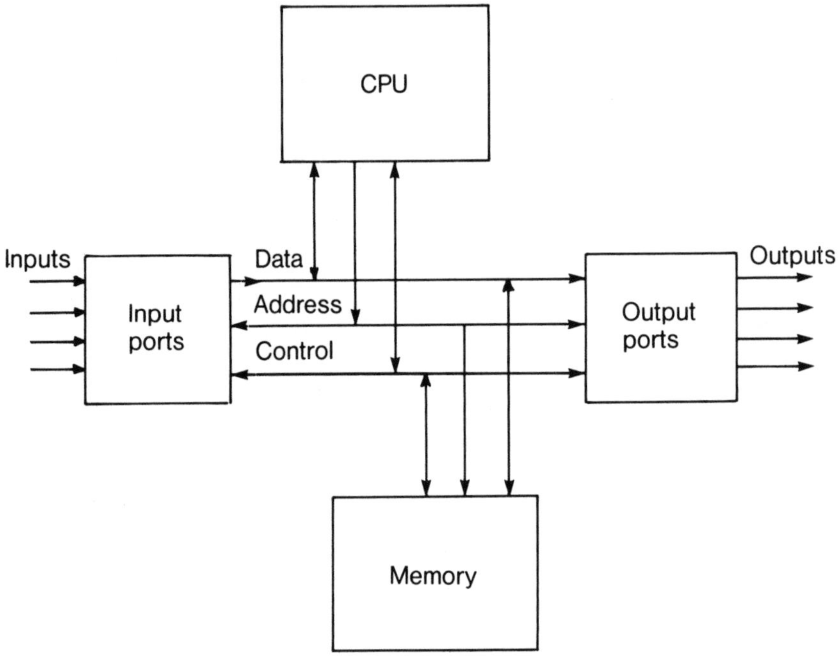

Fig. 1.3 Block diagram showing the basic components of a digital computer system.

means is provided to allow it to communicate with the outside world. This enables the computer to receive data from external equipment and to produce outputs which may be displayed or used to control the action of external devices. For most applications it is important that the user should be able to communicate with the CPU in order to select options in the program or even to load the program in from some external source. This transfer of data and commands between the CPU and the outside world is done through a series of input and output channels called 'ports'.

The sections of the computer system are linked together by three bus systems. Each bus consists of a set of interconnecting wires along which digital data may be sent. One set of wires, called the 'address' bus, is used to select a particular memory location or one of the input–output channels and cause it to be connected to the main data bus so that data can be transferred to or from the CPU. On the address bus, data always flows from the CPU to the other parts of the system. In single-chip microcomputers there may be two separate address buses, one being used to select locations in the program memory whilst the other is used for the data memory and input–output ports.

Data is transferred between the various sections of the system via the 'data' bus which is bi-directional so that data may be made to flow either to or from the CPU. The direction of data flow on this bus is governed by the CPU itself and control signals are sent to the memory, or input–output port, to indicate whether it should be sending or receiving data. Usually data is transferred in parallel along the data bus with one complete data word moved simultaneously. The microprocessor is classified according to the size of the data word that it handles within the CPU. The popular word sizes available are 4, 8 and 16 bits. Sometimes in order to reduce the number of interconnection lines, the data bus may be multiplexed so that with an 8-wire data bus a 16-bit word would be transferred in two 8-bit sections. Here, although the data bus is only 8 bits wide, the processor would still be classified as a 16-bit type.

The third bus is called the 'control' bus and carries various control and status signals between the different sections of the computer. Here some wires carry signals from the CPU whilst others pass signals back to the CPU. This bus controls the timing and general operation of the computer system.

The difference between a microcomputer and a microprocessor is that whereas the microprocessor device consists of the CPU alone, a microcomputer has some memory and input–output channels built into a single integrated circuit package. A microprocessor always needs additional support circuits to form a complete system whereas a single-chip microcomputer can operate by itself.

Instruction format

The program that tells the CPU what to do simply consists of a list of numbers stored in the memory section of the computer system. Each instruction contains an operation code or 'opcode' which defines the type of operation to be carried out. Some instructions also include an 'operand' which specifies the data that is used by the instruction. In most cases the operand specifies a particular location in memory where the data is to be found.

For the 8-bit general purpose microprocessors, the opcode is normally one 8-bit data word which allows up to 256 different instructions to be provided. The operand, if required, is made up from further one or two 8-bit data words which are held in successive memory locations after the opcode. Typical memory layouts for instructions in an 8-bit microprocessor are shown in Figure 1.4. Thus for some instructions three data words must be transferred from memory to move the instruction into the CPU. This has some disadvantages since it will slow down the operation of the computer.

The larger microprocessors with 16-bit wide data words may incorporate the opcode and operand into a single 16-bit word as shown in Figure 1.5. This allows the complete instruction to be set up with just one data transfer from memory. As with the 8-bit type processors, some instructions need a larger operand so the opcode is held in the first word and the instruction is completed by adding a further word, or words, for the operand.

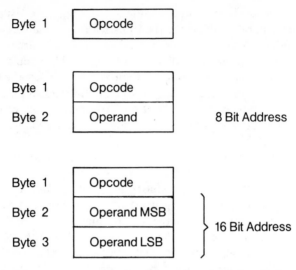

Fig. 1.4 Typical arrangements for opcode and operand data for instructions in an 8-bit microprocessor.

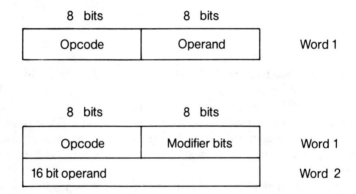

Fig. 1.5 Typical instruction formats in a 16-bit microprocessor.

The computer memory

Let us start by examining the computer memory which is similar in principle to an array of filing boxes where each holds one item which in this case is a data word. When a data word is to be transferred the memory location allocated to that particular word is selected by some addressing circuits and is connected to the processor data bus so that the data may be transferred into or out of the memory. A 'write' operation places new data into the memory and a 'read' operation is used to examine data stored in the memory.

The basic storage element or memory 'cell' usually takes the form of a

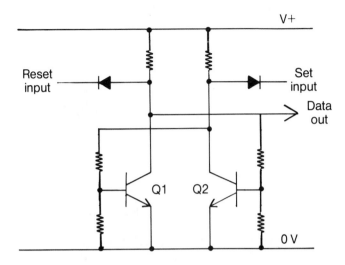

Fig. 1.6 A simple static memory cell using a flip-flop circuit.

'flip-flop' circuit in which two transistors are cross connected as shown in Figure 1.6. In this arrangement there are two stable states where one transistor is turned off and the other fully turned on. Suppose Q2 is on and Q1 is off; this will give a 'high' or '1' state at the output. If an external reset signal is applied to Q1 which causes its collector voltage to fall, this reduces the base current to Q2 and will try to turn Q2 off. As Q2 turns off, its collector voltage rises causing Q1 to turn on and reduce its collector voltage even more. The result is that the circuit rapidly flips over into its second stable state with Q2 off and Q1 fully on to give a 'low' or '0' output state. Actual memory cells are rather more complex since they contain additional circuitry to facilitate selection of the cell by the address signals.

One problem with the flip-flop style of memory cell is that it is a relatively complex circuit and takes up significant space on the silicon chip. In the early days of memory chips this limited the size of the memory to perhaps 512 or 1024 bits. In an effort to produce larger capacity memories a simpler cell structure was required and this was achieved by using the principle of charge storage. The basic principle is shown in Figure 1.7. Here a capacitor C is connected to the data bus via the switch S1 and charges or discharges to take up the logic level of the bus. Once the data level has been written as a charge in the capacitor, the switch S1 is opened and the capacitor should theoretically hold its state of charge indefinitely. To read the stored data the switch S2 is made and the data passes through to the output line.

In practice a simple capacitor-type memory cell will always have some leakage paths around the capacitor so that after a period of time the stored charge alters and the stored information becomes corrupted. This can however be overcome by 'refreshing' the charge on the capacitor at regular intervals. This is done by simply reading the state of the cell and then writing

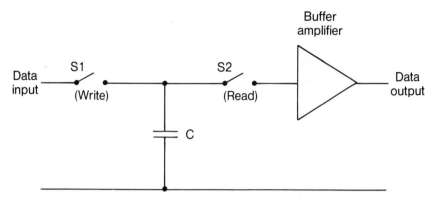

Fig. 1.7 A dynamic memory cell using charge storage in a capacitor.

the information back into the capacitor again to restore its proper data state. In a typical modern memory device of this type, the 'refresh' operation usually has to be carried out at intervals of about 2 milliseconds. The refresh process may be performed by external circuits or in some cases may be carried out automatically inside the memory chip. Because the contents of this type of memory have to be continually rewritten by the refresh action it is called a 'dynamic' memory, whilst the type using flip-flop cells is called a 'static' memory.

The memory cells are usually arranged in a pattern of rows and columns with an addressing scheme which will select one row and one column at a time. The general arrangement is as shown in Figure 1.8. The cell which is at the junction of the selected row and column is then connected to the common data bus line ready for data transfer. For a 1024 cell memory there will be 32 rows and 32 columns and these are selected by binary numbers applied at the input so that there will be a total of 10 address lines with 5 to select a row and 5 to select a column. To reduce the number of package pins, some devices multiplex the row and column inputs so that the row address is applied first and stored in an internal latch circuit, and when the column address is applied the memory location is selected.

Most memory devices have an addressing scheme which allows any individual cell to be selected at will by merely applying its address to the appropriate input lines. This type of memory is called a random access memory or RAM. In the simpler types a single cell array is used so that the memory provides a single bit of a data when a location is selected. To deal with the computer data, 8 or 16 of these memories are addressed in parallel and each device provides one bit of the data word. Some memory devices contain 4- or 8-cell arrays and will read or write a 4- or 8-bit word at a time. These types are convenient for small memories since only one package is required.

One problem which arises with both dynamic and static RAM devices is that if the power is removed from the memory the data contents are lost.

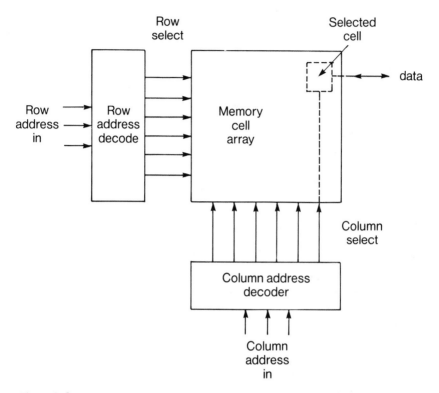

Fig. 1.8 General arrangement of row and column addressing used to select one cell from a memory array.

This type of memory is said to be 'volatile' and can present problems in a microprocessor system if the equipment is switched off, because the program held in the memory will be lost and must be loaded in again before operation can commence. This loading process would have to be done by feeding data directly to the memory from some external source since without a program the CPU will not do anything.

For small memory systems a solution to the problem of volatile data is to provide some form of automatic battery backup for the memory power supply. Now if the main memory power line fails, the backup battery automatically takes over and maintains a sufficient supply voltage to retain the data in the memory. When the main power line is restored, the program data is still available in the memory. Often only part of the memory system is maintained by the battery in order to conserve power. Any essential data needed by the CPU may also be held in the backed-up memory if desired.

Whilst battery backup systems are reasonably effective, a better alternative, certainly for the program memory, is to use some form of memory device that has the data permanently written into it. With this type of device the program data will always be available as soon as power is applied to the system.

Read-only memories

A memory with permanent data can be produced by fixing the states of the internal memory cells when the memory chip is actually made. This can often be done by programming the way in which the interconnections between cells are made in the final stages of producing the memory chip. Since the data patterns are effectively permanently wired into the memory chip, it is not possible to write new data into this type of memory. It is called a read-only memory or ROM. The actual pattern of connections is determined by a photographic mask used to produce the cell interconnections and this type of device is generally referred to as a 'mask programmed' ROM. Mask-type ROMs are often used to hold the patterns of dots needed to produce character displays on a monitor screen or the code translation table used for a keyboard encoder.

Whilst the masked ROM provides a permanent data storage device it is only really economical where a large number of identical devices are to be produced. For many applications there is a need for some form of ROM which is economical to produce in small quantities. This can be achieved by using a programmable ROM or PROM. The simplest type of PROM has a fusible wire link built into each memory cell of the device. When the PROM is initially supplied, all of the cells will be set to the same state. To program the required data into the memory each word location is selected in turn by applying the appropriate address. At this stage a large voltage pulse is applied to the input terminals for those data bits in the word that need to be changed to give the desired data pattern. The voltage pulse causes the wire link in the selected cell to fuse and break the link so that the data state of the cell is permanently altered. The main advantage of the PROM is that all of the PROMs are identical so they can be produced in vast quantities at low cost, whilst the user can program in any required data pattern which then becomes permanent.

Although the fusible link PROM is convenient it has the disadvantage that if a small change is needed in the stored data or an error is made in programming, the contents of the PROM cannot be altered and a new PROM must be programmed to replace it. For experimental work and in the development stages of producing a microprocessor system it would be helpful if the PROM could somehow be erased and reprogrammed to allow the same device to be reused for a new pattern of data.

Reprogramming of a PROM can be achieved by using a different design of PROM device which is called an erasable PROM or EPROM. The most common type of EPROM is erased by simply shining intense ultraviolet light directly on to the silicon chip. The data is stored as an electrical charge but the memory cells are so designed that the normal storage time for the charge is measured in years rather than the few milliseconds of a typical dynamic RAM. When ultraviolet light falls on the cell it causes the stored charge to be released thus erasing the stored data. To facilitate erasure the device has a quartz window built into the package to expose the silicon chip. The ultraviolet content of normal daylight is not sufficiently intense to affect the stored data but for safety many users cover the quartz window with opaque tape after the EPROM has been programmed. Programming of the data is done in a similar way to that for fusible link PROMs except that the voltage pulse used is much smaller.

Whilst the EPROM with ultraviolet erasure is very convenient there are occasions where it is useful to have a non-volatile type memory which can be erased without being removed from the circuit card. This is achieved by one of the more recent developments in the PROM field. This is the EEPROM (electrically erasable PROM) in which the erasure of the data can be performed by applying electrical signals whilst the device is still installed in the computer system.

Another useful non-volatile memory device is the EAROM (electrically alterable ROM). Whilst an ultraviolet EPROM or EEPROM can be erased, the process removes all of the data from the memory. The EAROM on the other hand operates in a similar fashion to a conventional read–write memory in that individual words can be written into the memory or read out as desired. Unlike a conventional read–write memory, however, the data pattern held in the EAROM is non-volatile and the writing process is a rather slow one.

The Central Processor

The heart of any computer is the CPU itself which is a very complex logic circuit having an internal arrangement similar to that shown in Figure 1.9. The CPU circuits can be separated roughly into two sections. One part of the CPU is concerned with the actual processing of data and normally consists of an arithmetic and logic unit (ALU) together with a selection of data registers. The registers are basically one-word memory devices built into the CPU itself and interconnected with the ALU. The remainder of the CPU is concerned with the timing and control of the microcomputer system. It is this control section which decodes the sequence of instructions forming the program and causes the instructions to be executed. This section also controls all data transfers between the CPU and the memory or the outside world.

Arithmetic and logic section
The general arrangement of the arithmetic and logic section of the CPU is shown in Figure 1.9. At the centre of this part of the CPU is a very complex logic element called the arithmetic and logic unit or ALU. Its function is to perform a variety of arithmetic and logical operations on data. Associated with this logic array is a special register called the accumulator.

There are two inputs to the ALU and one output. One of the inputs is fed

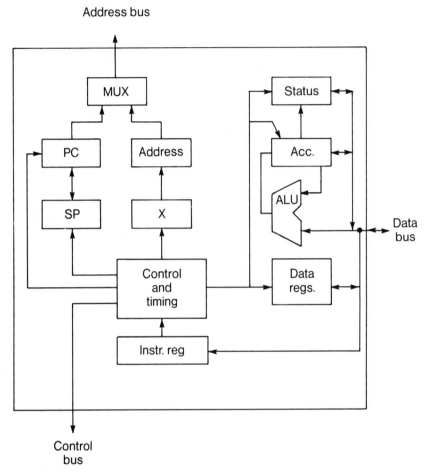

Fig. 1.9 Simplified block diagram of a typical microprocessor CPU.

with data from the accumulator and the output from the ALU is returned back into the accumulator. The second input to the ALU may be fed by data from another data register within the CPU or by data from the external memory. As an example of the operation of this section of the CPU, suppose that two data words are to be added together. The first step is to load one of the words into the accumulator. The second word is then read from memory and applied to the free input of the ALU. At this point the ALU adds the words together and their sum appears at its output and is transferred to the accumulator. The result in the accumulator may now be written to the memory or processed in some other way by further instructions to the CPU.

Some processors such as the Motorola 6809 have two separate accumulator registers and either of these may be used with the ALU by using appropriate instructions to the CPU. Some processors such as the Z80 have extra data registers which may be used to hold data temporarily within the

CPU. An important advantage of using these internal registers is that data transfers between CPU registers are generally executed faster than data transfers to or from the external memory. In the larger 16-bit processors such as the Motorola 68000, a set of eight data registers is provided and any of these may be designated to work as an accumulator as desired.

Another important register in the data processing section of the CPU is the status register. This register is used to keep a record of the current state of the calculations being carried out. Each data bit in the register may be assigned to indicate a different status condition. Thus one bit may be used to indicate that the result of the last operation was a negative number whilst another status bit would indicate if the result were zero. Sometimes status bits may be used to indicate which mode of operation the CPU is currently using. An example here might be to differentiate between simple binary arithmetic or binary-coded decimal arithmetic operations within the ALU. We shall be looking more closely at arithmetic operations in a later chapter.

The contents of the status register can be tested by using special instructions and the subsequent actions of the CPU may be modified according to the states of selected bits in the status register. This is a very important facility because it allows the computer to adapt its sequence of operations according to the results of its calculations.

The control section
The control section of the CPU contains a number of registers which can be used to control the address bus and the complex control logic needed to set up and execute the actions specified by the program instructions.

Perhaps the most important of the CPU registers is the program counter (PC). As we saw earlier, the instructions which make up the computer's program are held in the external memory and the function of the program counter register is to provide the address of the memory location that holds the opcode for the next instruction that is to be executed. This register effectively keeps track of the current position in the program list.

The data held in the PC register is switched to the address bus when a new instruction has to be fetched from memory for execution. As each instruction is executed the contents of the PC register are automatically updated to point to the address of the next instruction that is to be executed.

Although the PC is used to provide an address to fetch an instruction from memory, a different register is used for this purpose when data is being transferred between the CPU and memory. This register is called the address register. Two other registers which may be included in the control section of the CPU are the index (X) register and the stack pointer (SP) register. Both of these registers may be used to modify the contents of the PC or address registers before they appear on the actual address bus. We shall look at the action of these registers in the next chapter.

One further important register in the control section is the instruction register which is used to hold the opcode of the instruction that is being executed. This register drives the control logic of the CPU which decodes the opcode word and sets up the internal data paths and timing sequence needed to execute the instruction.

The instruction execution cycle

The timing of all operations within the CPU is governed by a master clock which might typically be running at a few megahertz. The execution of one instruction will take a number of these clock cycles and the exact timing arrangements vary from one type of processor to another.

The first step in executing any instruction is to fetch its opcode from the memory and place it into the instruction register. During this 'fetch' cycle the contents of the PC are placed on the address bus and this selects the memory location where the instruction opcode is held. The opcode data is then read from memory via the data bus and transferred into the instruction register.

The opcode word in the instruction register now passes to some decoding logic which determines the type of operation to be performed and sets up the required data pathways and the sequence of events needed to actually execute that instruction. Most instructions require further data to be read in from the memory so the next one or two clock cycles are used to carry out these data transfers. At this point the PC register is updated so that it contains the memory address for the next instruction to be executed. The current instruction is then executed and the whole cycle starts again.

The number of clock cycles needed to complete the execution of an

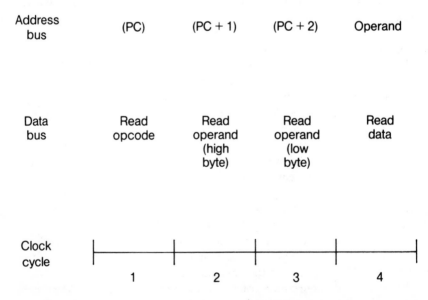

Fig. 1.10 Execution sequence for a typical data transfer instruction.

instruction will depend upon the type of instruction being performed. In a Motorola 6809 processor, for instance, most instructions take two, three or four clock cycles but a few take as many as 10 clock cycles to complete.

Figure 1.10 shows the sequence of events when an instruction to load some data from a memory location into the accumulator is executed. In this case the address for the data is stored in the two memory locations following the opcode, so two memory read cycles are needed in order to get this address into the CPU ready to make the final data transfer.

In the MC6800 series processors a two-phase clock is used and all memory data transfers occur during phase 2 whilst internal CPU operations occur during phase 1 of the clock. The entire operation actually takes up four complete clock cycles. The first fetches the opcode, then two cycles are used to load the operand and the final cycle is used for actual execution of the instruction which involves transfer of a data word from memory to the accumulator.

Chapter Two
Program Techniques

Having taken a look at the structure and basic operation of the CPU, we shall now look at the types of instruction available and some of the principles involved in program operation.

The instruction set

Each type of CPU has built into its control logic a set of instruction opcodes which it is able to recognise and execute. The actual set of instructions provided varies from one type of microprocessor device to another. In the simpler single-chip microcomputers the range of instructions provided will generally be rather limited, but despite this it is usually possible to perform any desired operation by using appropriate sequences of instructions. The 8-bit and 16-bit microprocessors are designed to provide a more general purpose set of instructions.

Examples of the increased flexibility of the larger microprocessors are the provision of a wide selection of test instructions and a variety of addressing schemes for accessing data or instructions in the memory. This can mean that an operation which might need several instructions in a simple microcomputer can be executed with a single instruction in the 8- or 16-bit CPU. The general purpose processors normally permit access to a large memory space and include facilities for interrupt operation.

The types of instruction provided generally fall into the following groups:

1 Data transfer operations
2 Data manipulation
3 Logic and arithmetic
4 Conditional operations
5 Program control

We shall now take a brief look at the functions and some applications of these different types of instruction. The logic and arithmetic instructions are examined in the next chapter.

Mnemonics

The instruction opcodes used by the CPU itself are simply binary numbers which are translated into specified actions by the CPU control logic. Thus the instruction to load the accumulator with a data word from memory might be represented by an opcode number 96 followed by one or more bytes of data which tell the CPU where the data word is located in the memory. Although the CPU understands these numerical codes they are virtually meaningless to the person who is writing the program. To overcome this difficulty the program instructions are normally written on paper using a mnemonic code. Thus the instruction to load data to the accumulator might be written

LDA 15$\emptyset$

Here the mnemonic LDA is used to represent the opcode and the operand (150) indicates the address of the memory location where the required data may be found. Some other examples of opcode mnemonics are STA (store contents of accumulator to memory), ADD (add data to accumulator) and INCA (increment number in the accumulator). Thus a short piece of program written using mnemonics might be as follows:

```
LDA       1ØØ
ADD       11Ø
STA       2ØØ
INCA
STA       21Ø
```

Each line represents one instruction for the CPU and is referred to as a 'statement'. In this case the sequence of actions performed by the CPU starts by loading the contents of memory location 100 into the accumulator. The next statement adds the contents of memory location 110 to the accumulator and then the result is stored in memory location 200. The statement INCA causes accumulator contents to be increased by one and in the final statement the new result is stored in memory location 210.

When the program has been written down as a list of mnemonic statements these have to be translated into the numbers that the CPU understands before the program can be loaded into memory and executed by the CPU. This process of conversion can be carried out manually but is more conveniently performed by using a computer. A special computer program called an 'assembler' is used to carry out this translation function. The list of mnemonic statements is referred to as an 'assembly code' program but many users call this form 'machine code'.

The mnemonic version of the program list is referred to as the 'source' code. When this source code is processed by the assembler, a set of binary numbers called the 'object' code is produced. This object code represents the data that will be held in the program memory and executed by the CPU.

The assembler may allow names to be given to the operand part of the instruction so that we could have a statement such as

LDA HEIGHT

where the name HEIGHT defines a memory location where a data variable representing height is held. At some point in the source code the assembler is told what memory address to use when it sees the name HEIGHT. This technique of naming variables can make the operation of a program much easier to understand.

Data transfer instructions

The first group of instructions governs transfers of data between the internal registers of the CPU, the memory and the input–output channels. These data transfer operations are normally called 'load' and 'store' and will transfer data in the memory to or from the accumulator or another CPU register. Other instructions may allow direct transfers of data within the CPU between its internal registers. Some processors, particularly the 16-bit types, allow data to be transferred directly between any register and the memory or another register.

Addressing modes

The instructions which tell the CPU what to do usually consist of two parts. First there is an 'opcode' which determines the type of operation required and is the minimum requirement for an instruction. For most instructions the CPU requires more information than that provided by the opcode. As an example, if we want to load some data from a memory location into the accumulator, the CPU will need to be told the address within memory where the data is to be found. This is done by adding one or more additional data words which are known as the instruction 'operand'. The operand data may represent either actual data or a memory address.

We have seen that data or instruction codes stored in the memory are accessed by applying an address code to the memory array. This selects the required set of memory cells and connects them to the CPU data bus so that data may be either written into the memory or read from it. The address signals for the memory are derived from the address bus which in turn is driven by an address register within the CPU itself. There are, however, a number of ways in which the address may be set up in this register and these are referred to as addressing modes. Simple CPUs may have just four or five basic address modes but the more sophisticated types may have a wide range of possibilities for setting up the address register. We shall now consider the operation of the more common ways of generating memory addresses which are used in typical microprocessors.

Inherent or register addressing

The simplest form of data transfer instruction is one that moves data between registers within the CPU itself. Since the memory is not involved there is no need for a memory address and the source or destination of the data is specified by the opcode itself. As an example we might have an instruction opcode called TAX which tells the CPU that it is to transfer data from the accumulator (A) to the index register (X). As the instruction opcode is decoded by the control logic in the CPU a data path is set up between the accumulator and the index register and during the execution cycle the data is transferred from one register to the other. This mode of operation is sometimes called register address mode. In some of the 16-bit CPUs, extra bits called modifiers in the opcode word may be used to specify the source and destination registers involved in the data transfer.

Immediate addressing

In the immediate mode of addressing, the operand of the instruction is the actual data that is to be used by the instruction. This means that the data to be used is in the next memory location after the opcode. In this mode the 'effective address' that is placed on the address bus for the data transfer is created by adding 1 to the contents of the program counter (PC). Note that this is done before the PC is updated to point to the address of the next instruction. This action is shown in Figure 2.1.

Address bus	(PC)	(PC + 1)
Data bus	Read opcode	Read data to accumulator
Clock cycle	1	2

Instruction cycle sequence

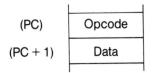

Memory data layout

Fig. 2.1 Execution sequence and memory data layout for an instruction with immediate addressing.

As an example of the operation of this mode, let us suppose that we want to load the number 5 into the accumulator. The statement for this might be written as

LDA #5

where the # sign is used to indicate that the immediate addressing mode is required. If the opcode for LDA is in memory location 100, then location 101 in memory contains the data to be loaded; so the memory contents are as follows:

```
1ØØ   96    (LDA opcode)
1Ø1   5     (data)
1Ø2   ...   (next opcode)
1Ø3   ...
```

When the opcode is decoded the immediate addressing mode is set up. The address in the program counter is incremented and copied into the address register to select memory address 101 where the data is held. This new address is called the 'effective address'. During the execution cycle the data contained in location 101 (i.e. the number 5) is read from memory and placed in the accumulator.

The immediate address mode may also be used to place data into other registers in the CPU by using appropriate instructions. Thus we might place data into the index register (X) of the CPU by using the statement

LDX #3ØØ

In many 8-bit CPU systems the index (X) and stack pointer (SP) may be 16-bit registers rather than the normal 8-bit types and here the data values used in the immediate mode will be represented by two data bytes instead of one. The statement may therefore include a data value up to 65535. The instruction operation will, however, take account of this and will break the data into two 8-bit bytes which will be stored in the two memory locations following the opcode. When the instruction is executed, the two bytes from the memory are read into the CPU in sequence to set up the data in the specified register. In the 6809 processor, which has two 8-bit accumulators, it is possible to load both accumulators with one instruction by using the LDD (load double) instruction which once again transfers the two bytes following the opcode in memory and places these in the two accumulators.

In the immediate mode the data is held in the program section of memory which on many systems will be located in a read-only memory and therefore cannot be altered. Because of this there is no immediate mode version of the STORE instruction. This mode of addressing is used for handling constant data.

Direct addressing
The main form of memory addressing used in microcomputer systems is the

'direct' address mode where the operand of the instruction specifies the actual memory address at which the data is located. Here the data read in from the operand location is used as the 'effective address' that is placed on the address bus for the data transfer operation.

As an example we might have the instruction

LDA 1ØØ

which tells the CPU that it has to read data from memory location 100 and place it into the accumulator register.

When the instruction is executed the program counter contents are first transferred to the address bus to allow the opcode to be read in. The address register is then incremented to read in the operand and this data is then placed into the address register to provide the address for the data transfer from the memory to the accumulator. This action is shown in Figure 2.2.

Address bus	(PC)	(PC + 1)	Address
Data bus	Read opcode	Read address	Read data to accumulator
Clock cycle	1	2	3

Instruction cycle sequence

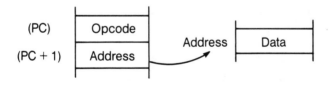

Memory layout

Fig. 2.2 Execution sequence and data layout for a directly addressed instruction.

In some processors, such as the 16-bit types, the address may form part of the instruction word rather than being a separate data word. In this case the upper 8 bits of the instruction word contain the opcode and the lower 8 bits form the direct memory address for the instruction.

Most 8-bit processors have a 16-bit address bus to provide addressing for a useful size of memory. An 8-bit address would allow only 256 bytes of memory to be accessed. A variation of direct addressing called 'extended' addressing is generally employed in which the two bytes in memory following the opcode are used to build the 16-bit address operand as follows:

LDA opcode
memory address high byte
memory address low byte

When this instruction is executed the two bytes of the operand are read into a temporary holding register within the CPU and then transferred into the address register to provide the memory address during the actual data transfer.

In a 16-bit computer system a similar extended direct addressing scheme may be used since these CPUs often have a 24- or 32-bit address bus system. In this case a 24-bit address may be generated by using 8 bits within the instruction word and a further 16 bits in the following operand word. For a 32-bit address, two memory words following the instruction word would be used to build up the effective address.

In an 8-bit microprocessor the simple one byte direct address mode is sometimes referred to as zero page addressing. The concept here is that the 64 kbytes of memory that can be addressed by the 16-bit address bus is divided into 256 byte segments called 'pages'. The upper 8 bits of the 16-bit address can now be looked upon as a page number which ranges from 0 to 255. For the first 256 bytes in the memory the page number is 0 and this is referred to as the zero page area. For this page only the lower 8 bits are significant so the simplified 8-bit direct address mode may be used.

Some processors such as the 6809 have an extra register within the CPU which is called the page register. This page register is set at 0 when the processor is started up and it provides the upper 8 bits of the address when the 8-bit direct addressing mode is used. Thus, at the start, the CPU operates 8-bit direct addressing as a page zero addressing mode. By setting the page register contents it is possible to specify any page in the entire memory map as the page used for 8-bit direct addressing.

The paged memory scheme is useful because a simple direct addressed instruction with an 8-bit operand needs only one address cycle and executes faster than an instruction using the full extended addressing mode. Thus if most of the instructions can be arranged to use the direct page address mode the program execution speed can be improved.

Indexed addressing
A very useful form of memory addressing which is provided with all general purpose microprocessors, and sometimes in more limited form in the single-chip computers, is called indexed addressing. This makes use of the index register in the CPU.

In its simplest form the indexed addressing scheme produces the 'effective address' that is output to memory by adding the contents of the index register to the address specified by the instruction operand. The action as the instruction is executed is shown in Figure 2.3.

With direct addressing the address used is fixed by the program

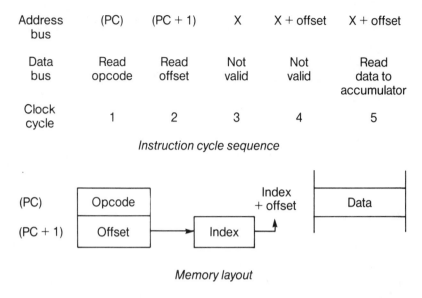

Address bus	(PC)	(PC + 1)	X	X + offset	X + offset
Data bus	Read opcode	Read offset	Not valid	Not valid	Read data to accumulator
Clock cycle	1	2	3	4	5

Instruction cycle sequence

Memory layout

Fig. 2.3 Execution sequence and data layout for an instruction with indexed addressing.

statement. By using the combination address produced by adding the contents of the index register it becomes possible to alter the actual address used for data transfer as the program is being executed. This is done by simply changing the data stored in the index register. One of the commonest applications of this 'indexed' addressing mode is in dealing with tables of data stored in the memory.

Indirect addressing

A rather more complex and very powerful mode of addressing is known as 'indirect' addressing. In the normal direct addressing mode the memory address is specified by the operand itself. In the indirect addressing mode the operand specifies a memory address at which the actual address to be used by the instruction is stored. When this type of instruction is executed the operand sets up a memory address and the contents are read into a temporary register in the CPU. This register is then used to provide the effective address for the instruction being executed. This action is shown in Figure 2.4.

As an example, we could have an instruction to load the accumulator which has an operand value of 200. In immediate addressing, the data itself will have the value 200. In direct addressing the CPU will transfer the data from location 200 in memory. In the indirect address mode the CPU will read the contents of location 200 and use them as the address from which the data is read. Thus if location 200 contained 120, the data in location 120 would be loaded into the accumulator.

Address bus	(PC)	(PC + 1)	Address 1	Address 2
Data bus	Read opcode	Read address 1	Read address 2	Read data
Clock cycle	1	2	3	4

Instruction cycle sequence

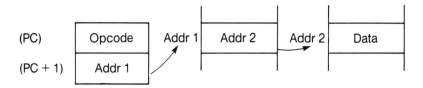

Fig. 2.4 Execution sequence and data layout for an indirectly addressed instruction.

A useful feature here is that the address at which the data is to be found can be altered whilst the program is running, whereas with direct addressing the address is fixed by the original program instructions. This can be useful where the value of a result is used to determine which item of data is to be used for the next calculation. It is in some ways similar to indexed addressing in that the effective address can readily be altered during the program.

Indirect addressing can also be combined with indexed addressing to give a very powerful addressing scheme known as indexed indirect or indirect indexed. There is an important difference between these two combination modes.

In the indexed indirect mode the indexing is applied to the instruction operand to find a new address at which the data address is held. Thus we can work through a table of indirect addresses. In the indirect indexed mode the indexing is applied to the address specified by the indirect operand. In this case, the indirect address merely specifies the starting address of a table in memory and the index value indicates how far through the table the data is located.

Data manipulation

A second group of instructions is used to manipulate the data within a memory location or register. Typical operations here might be to shift the bit pattern in the register one position to the right or left.

Suppose we shift the data pattern to the right. When the bit pattern in a register is shifted one place to the right this will cause the right-hand bit to spill out of the register and this bit would normally be lost. To avoid this the state of the bit which is spilled out is saved as a 'carry' flag bit in the status register. At the left-hand end of the register the vacant space left by the shift operation is filled with a '0'. This action is shown in Figure 2.5. This type of operation is usually called a logical shift right and might have the mnemonic LSR.

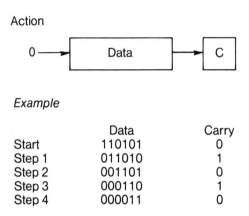

Action

Example

	Data	Carry
Start	110101	0
Step 1	011010	1
Step 2	001101	0
Step 3	000110	1
Step 4	000011	0

Fig. 2.5 Data manipulation using a logical shift right instruction.

The left shift action operates in a similar way with the bit spilled from the left end of the register passing into the 'carry' status bit and the right end being filled with a '0' as shown in Figure 2.6.

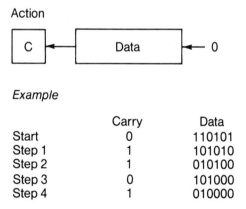

Action

Example

	Carry	Data
Start	0	110101
Step 1	1	101010
Step 2	1	010100
Step 3	0	101000
Step 4	1	010000

Fig. 2.6 Data manipulation by a shift left instruction.

Another type of shift action is called an arithmetic shift. When an arithmetic shift is made to the right (ASR) the data pattern moves as before but the way in which the left end bit is handled is changed. Instead of setting this bit to '0' the ASR instruction simply copies the original state of the bit. If the left end bit is '0' the action becomes exactly the same as that of an LSR instruction. When the left end bit is '1', however, the data pattern fills with '1's from the left end as successive shift operations are carried out. The action of this arithmetic shift right is shown in Figure 2.7. The bit spilled from the right end goes into the carry status bit as before. The arithmetic shift left (ASL) is identical to the logical shift left (LSL) and in many cases the instruction is given the mnemonic ASL rather than LSL.

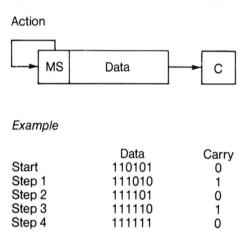

Action

Example

	Data	Carry
Start	110101	0
Step 1	111010	1
Step 2	111101	0
Step 3	111110	1
Step 4	111111	0

Fig. 2.7 Action produced by an arithmetic shift right instruction.

Shifting the data pattern to the right or left has an interesting effect on the numerical value of the data in the register. Shifting the data pattern one position to the right effectively divides the numerical value of each data bit in the pattern by two as shown in Figure 2.8. Thus a right shift can

Data	Numeric value
1 1 0 1 0 0	52
0 1 1 0 1 0	26
0 0 1 1 0 1	13
0 0 0 1 1 0	6

Fig. 2.8 Numerical effect of shifting binary data to the right.

conveniently be used as a simple method of halving the value of a data word.

Shifting the data pattern to the left doubles the value of each bit and effectively multiplies the data value by two as shown in Figure 2.9. It is important to remember that any bits spilled out of the register must be taken into account when using a shift to halve or double a data value.

Data   Numeric value

| 0 | 0 | 0 | 1 | 0 | 1 | 5

| 0 | 0 | 1 | 0 | 1 | 0 | 10

| 0 | 1 | 0 | 1 | 0 | 0 | 20

| 1 | 0 | 1 | 0 | 0 | 0 | 40

Fig. 2.9 Numerical effect of shifting binary data to the left.

Another data manipulation is 'rotation'. In a rotate operation the shift to the right or left is made as before but the existing state of the 'carry' bit is moved into the vacant bit position at the end of the register before the bit spilled from the other end of the register is moved into the 'carry' status bit. This is shown in Figure 2.10. The effect of successive rotate operations is to shift the data through the carry bit and then back into the register again. Thus with an 8-bit word a series of nine successive rotation steps will return the data word to its original position.

This type of operation is often used for examining the individual bits of a word by shifting them one at a time into the 'carry' bit and then testing the state of the 'carry' bit. If a simple shift operation is used for this the original data word is lost after it has passed out of the register whereas with a rotate operation the original word is retained and may be restored to its original state in the accumulator or other register.

Conditional instructions

One of the key features of a digital computer is its ability to modify the action of a program according to the results obtained from calculations being made. This is achieved by the use of conditional instructions where the

Rotate right action

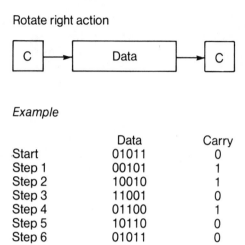

Example

	Data	Carry
Start	01011	0
Step 1	00101	1
Step 2	10010	1
Step 3	11001	0
Step 4	01100	1
Step 5	10110	0
Step 6	01011	0

Rotate left action

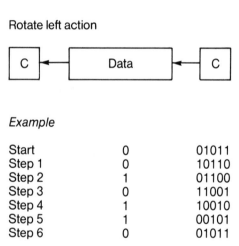

Example

Start	0	01011
Step 1	0	10110
Step 2	1	01100
Step 3	0	11001
Step 4	1	10010
Step 5	1	00101
Step 6	0	01011

Fig. 2.10 The action of rotate instructions.

action of the instruction depends upon the state of one or more of the bits in the CPU status register. The three common forms of conditional instruction are the SKIP, BRANCH and JUMP operations.

The simplest form of conditional instruction is the SKIP operation. The test condition to which this responds is specified as part of the instruction opcode. As an example, let us consider the action of a simple SKIP instruction which responds to the state of the Z (zero) status bit.

We will assume that the instruction is called SKIPZ. When this instruction is executed a check is made on the state of the Z bit in the status register. If the Z bit is 0, indicating that the result of the last instruction is not zero, the program simply goes on to execute the next instruction after

SKIPZ in the normal way. When the Z bit is 1, however, the program execution skips over the instruction following SKIPZ and goes to the next instruction in the sequence. Thus the SKIP instruction allows us either to execute or skip the next instruction according to the state of the specified status bit.

As an example, we may have a situation where a zero value for a variable is not permissible. In this case a SKIPNZ (skip when not zero) instruction is used to see if a zero result has been produced. If the result is zero the next instruction could simply increment the accumulator to give a non-zero result. When the result is already non-zero this increment instruction is skipped over. This is shown in Figure 2.11.

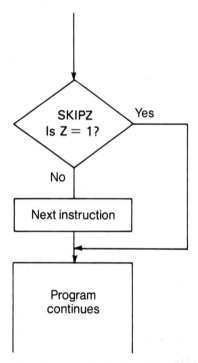

Fig. 2.11 Program execution sequence when using a SKIP instruction.

Jump and branch

The simple skip-type instruction is rather limited since it will only allow the program to skip over one instruction. Two rather more powerful conditional instructions are BRANCH and JUMP which allow program execution to be switched directly to a different point in the program sequence.

The action of a jump instruction is shown in Figure 2.12. As in the case of a skip instruction the test condition is specified by the instruction opcode. Thus JMPZ might be used to indicate that the instruction will respond to

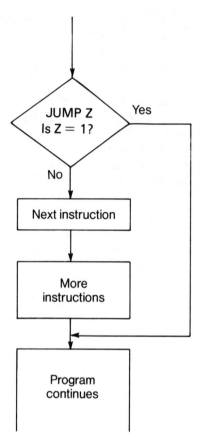

Fig. 2.12 Program action produced by a conditional JUMP instruction.

the state of the Z (zero) bit in the status register.

When the test fails (i.e. Z bit = 0) the program execution continues in the normal way with the instruction that follows JMPZ. When the test condition is met (Z bit = 1) the program execution jumps to a new instruction at a memory address specified by the operand of the jump instruction. In this case the operand address is transferred into the program counter of the CPU so that it becomes the address of the next instruction that is to be executed.

Thus if the jump instruction were

JMPZ 5ØØ

the next instruction executed after the JMPZ would be the one whose opcode is held at memory location 500. The jump instruction may use a number of different addressing modes in the same way as data transfer instructions. The usual modes provided are direct, indexed and indirect, or combinations of these.

The main difference between a branch and a jump instruction is the way in which the address of the point to which execution is to switch is specified. Unlike the jump instruction, a branch instruction uses a special form of addressing which is called 'relative addressing'. Here the effective address from which the next instruction opcode will be read is produced by adding the operand of the branch instruction to the contents of the program counter register. The operand of the branch instruction is generally referred to as its 'offset'.

Thus if we have an instruction such as

BEQ 1Ø

this would cause the program counter to be advanced by 10 when the zero bit is set at 1. Thus the program execution moves forward by 10 memory locations from the point that it would normally have used. An important point to remember here is that the program counter will already have been updated to point to the next instruction after the branch instruction when the offset is added. Therefore all calculations of where the branch will go to must be made relative to this next instruction rather than the branch instruction itself. If the operand of the branch instruction is negative this means that program execution will branch back to some point in the program before the branch instruction itself.

In an 8-bit processor the offset of a branch instruction is normally represented by just one byte of data which allows values from −128 to +127 so this will limit the span over which a branch can be made. When a larger shift in execution point is required a jump instruction is needed since this allows any address within the available range to be specified. Some processors such as the 6809 do not have conditional jump instructions but this is readily dealt with by using a combination of a conditional branch and a direct jump. Here the conditional instruction is set to detect the opposite of the required condition and simply skips the program over the following jump instruction. When the required condition occurs the jump instruction is executed and the program operation transfers to a new point in the memory as required.

Some processors provide two versions of the branch instruction. One of these gives a normal branch with its range limited to −128 to +127, whilst the alternative is a long branch instruction which has a 16-bit offset allowing it to span the entire memory range.

Loop operations

Sometimes in a program a short sequence of instructions may need to be repeated several times in succession. An example of this might be where a series of data values in successive memory locations are to be processed in sequence using exactly the same series of operations for each data value.

The simplest approach to this problem would be to write the set of instructions the required number of times with different data addresses for each set of instructions so that the appropriate data values are used. These repeated instructions will, however, take up memory space and if the operation is to be repeated many times this becomes very wasteful of the available memory. Since the actual sequence of instructions is identical for each repetition it would be convenient if we could have just one set of

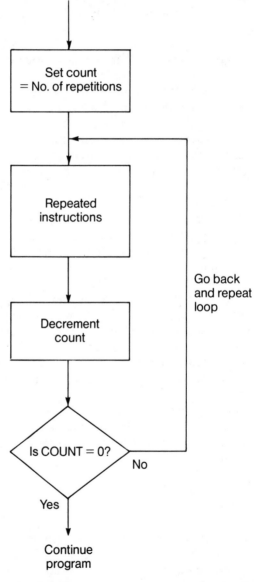

Fig. 2.13 Use of a loop to repeat a sequence of instructions.

instructions stored in the memory and arrange that when the CPU reaches the end of the sequence it branches back to the start and goes through the same set of instructions again. The program execution sequence might be as shown in Figure 2.13. This type of program operation is called a 'loop'. Here the branch instruction at the end of the loop sends the program execution back to the start of the sequence which is the instruction with the label LOOP written alongside it.

Suppose we want the loop to be executed eight times. This could be done as shown in Figure 2.13. The first step is to set a variable, which we shall call COUNT, equal to 8 before the start of the loop. This is followed by the set of instructions that is to be repeated. At the end of the set of repeated instructions the value of COUNT is decremented by 1 and then its value is tested by the BNE (branch if not equal to zero) statement to see if it has reached 0. If the value of COUNT is greater than 0, the program is branched back to the first of the repeated instructions which is labelled with the name LOOP and the instruction sequence is repeated. When the eighth pass through the loop has been completed the value of COUNT will have reached zero and the test will fail. At this point the program does not branch back but goes on to execute the next section of the program which follows the branch instruction.

One useful application of a loop operation is in storing or processing a table of numbers. Let us suppose that we wish to calculate a series of numbers and then store them in successive locations in the memory as a table.

We can start by specifying the start address of the table as say STBLE. Before starting the loop the index (X) register is set at 0. The loop might then be as shown in Figure 2.14. After the data has been calculated it is stored using indexed addressing and a basic address equal to STBLE. On the first pass through the loop when X = 0 the data will be placed in location STBLE. The X register is then incremented and the loop repeats. Since X is now 1 the second data item is stored in location STBLE+1. On each pass, X increases and data is stored in successive memory locations. A further test in the loop will check to see if the value of X has reached the total number of items to be placed in the table and when this is reached the loop ends and the table of values is stored in memory.

Subroutines

In all but the simplest of programs there are likely to be sequences of instructions which are repeated at several points within the program. These could of course be written into the program in the normal way but each new sequence takes up a section of the program memory. As an example, we might consider the routine used to read a single character from a keyboard into the computer memory. This might be used thousands of times during

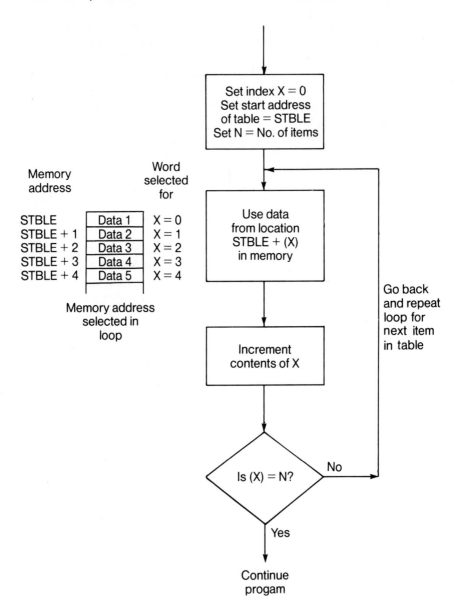

Fig. 2.14 Use of a loop combined with indexed addressing to access successive items in a data table.

the execution of the program and is best dealt with by using a technique known as a 'subroutine'.

The subroutine approach involves storing the set of instructions that are to be repeated in a separate part of the memory from the main program. When the instruction sequence is to be executed a special JSR (Jump to Subroutine) or CALL instruction is inserted into the main program sequence. This instruction has as its operand the address of the first instruction in the subroutine sequence. When the JSR is executed the processing of the main program is temporarily halted and the CPU starts to execute the subroutine instructions, as shown in Figure 2.15. At the end of the subroutine sequence another special instruction is included. This is RTS (ReTurn from Subroutine), or RET on some CPUs, and its function is to indicate the end of the subroutine sequence and to cause the execution of instructions to return to the main program. In fact execution of the main program will resume at the instruction immediately following the JSR instruction.

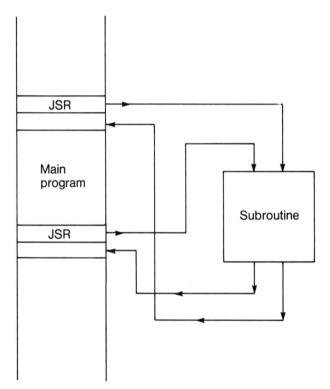

Fig. 2.15 Basic flow of program execution when executing a subroutine.

In order to return to the correct position in the main program sequence the CPU needs to remember its current main program instruction address before branching off to the subroutine. In simple one-chip computers this is done by having an extra register in which contents of the program counter can be saved. At the end of the subroutine the saved address is restored to the program counter and the processor goes on to execute the next instruction in its main program sequence.

Whilst a simple PC SAVE register can cope with one subroutine, if another subroutine were called whilst the first subroutine is executing then the original main program address would be overwritten. At the end of the new subroutine the first subroutine would resume but when it completed, the CPU would have no return link and the program would crash. One solution to this is to have more SAVE registers arranged in the form of a 'stack'. This can be envisaged as a stack of boxes. As each new subroutine is called the contents of the PC are put in a box which is placed on top of the pile. When the current subroutine ends the box at the top of the pile (the last one placed on the pile) is removed and its contents restored to the PC. The next box down now becomes the top one and will be used the next time the PC has to be restored.

When a data word is added to the stack the operation is called a 'PUSH' and when a word is removed from the top it is 'PULLed' or 'POPped'. The important point to note is that when data is taken from the stack it is always the last piece of data that was pushed on to the stack so the device is effectively a 'last in first out' memory.

When a subroutine is called the program counter word is pushed on to the stack before the jump is made to the subroutine. Once this return address has been saved on the stack, the operand of the JSR instruction is loaded into the program counter so that the next instruction to be executed is the first instruction of the subroutine. When RTS is executed at the end of the subroutine it causes the return address to be pulled from the stack and placed in the program counter so that the main program execution recommences with the instruction following JSR.

The main advantage of using a subroutine system is that the set of instructions comprising the subroutine is stored only once in memory although the sequence may be executed many hundreds of times during the course of the program. The subroutine can be called from many different points in the program as required. In general purpose processors subroutines can be 'nested' which means that a new subroutine can be called by an instruction in a subroutine. Here the subroutine that is executing will be suspended until the new subroutine is complete.

Stack operation
We have seen that the stack is used by the CPU to hold return addresses when it is executing a series of subroutines. It is also possible to use the stack to store data. This can be particularly useful where an intermediate result needs to be held temporarily and the CPU does not have any spare registers available for this purpose.

An advantage of the stack system is that no memory address operand is required so the instruction executes more rapidly than a normal data transfer instruction. It is important to remember the sequence of data held on the stack to ensure that the desired data will be transferred by the PUSH or PULL operation. One disadvantage of a stack-orientated system is that access to data on the stack is purely sequential so that if the data item is located some way down the stack, all other items above it have to be removed before the desired item can be accessed.

In small dedicated microprocessors the stack will often consist of perhaps five or six registers connected together with some control logic to form a stack-oriented memory. The stack is used as a small temporary store for holding one or two data items or addresses whilst some other operation is carried out in the accumulator.

The general purpose microprocessors use a different approach for the implementation of a 'stack'. Instead of using special registers for the stack they use the main computer memory itself. A register within the CPU called the 'stack pointer' register is used to hold the address of the memory location which is currently acting as the top of the stack. A PUSH operation to the stack causes data to be written into the top of stack location in the memory. After the data transfer the address held in the stack pointer is decremented so that the new top of stack is one location lower in the memory. Successive PUSH operations will cause the stack to build downwards in the memory.

When a data item is pulled from the stack the stack pointer is automatically incremented by one so that it points to the last item that was pushed to the stack. The data transfer is then made and the location from which the data was read becomes the new top of stack in the memory. The action of incrementing and decrementing the stack pointer has the same overall effect as moving the data position up or down in a real stack. Most of the widely available microprocessors build their stacks downwards through memory.

It is possible to access data that is not at the top of the stack by manipulating the contents of the stack pointer which tells the CPU where the current top of the stack is in the actual memory. Incrementing and decrementing the stack pointer in this way does not alter the data held in the stack. An important point to remember when manipulating a stack in this way is that when this is done within a subroutine the stack pointer must be restored to its original state so that it points to the return address before the end of the subroutine is reached.

By storing the contents of the stack register and loading a new address into it, a number of different stacks can be created in memory and operation can be switched from one to another by simply calling up the appropriate stack pointer value from memory.

Subroutine data transfers
Many subroutines that are likely to be used in a program will involve data transfers between the main program and the subroutine and we shall now consider the various approaches which may be adopted for these data transfers.

Where a single data word is to be transferred this can readily be achieved by placing the data into a register such as the accumulator just before the end of the subroutine so that it is available for use by the main program when the latter is resumed. In a keyboard input routine the data from the keyboard is placed in the accumulator and when the main program resumes this data may be stored or processed as desired.

Transferring data to a subroutine can be carried out in the same way. Thus a byte of data to be printed may be placed in the accumulator prior to the subroutine call and is then output to the printer by the subroutine. If the subroutine performs some processing function which produces a result then a data word is input to the subroutine by placing it in the accumulator and the processed result is placed in the accumulator by the subroutine for later use by the main program.

If two or three bytes of data are to be transferred it is possible in many microprocessors to use some of the other internal registers of the CPU for data transfer. Thus data may be stored in the index registers or in any general purpose registers. One register which may not be used for this purpose is the stack pointer since this is required for the subroutine return address. Sometimes it may not be practical to use index registers for data transfer since these may already be in use for indexed addressing so alternative methods may be required for transfer of several bytes of data to or from a subroutine,

Where several variables are to be transferred to a subroutine this is possible by simply using the same variable addresses within the subroutine as those used by the main program. In some cases the subroutine is used to process different main program variables at various points in the program. Thus for example a multiplication routine might be used on a whole range of variables at different points in the program.

In a simple multiplication routine there will be two input variables known as the multiplicand and the multiplier plus an output variable known as the product. We can now allocate three variable locations in memory to these data items and all addressing within the subroutine will refer to these variable addresses. Now, before calling the subroutine, the main program must transfer the data for the numbers to be multiplied into a pair of dedicated memory locations. The subroutine is then called and generates a product. On resumption of the main program this product data must be transferred from the dedicated locations to an appropriate variable location in the data area of the main program memory.

Using fixed locations for the subroutine data has the disadvantage that the subroutine may need to be altered to suit different applications where the available memory is located at a different point in the memory map. It would be useful to have a data area for subroutine variables which is readily adapted for any system memory layout without having to alter the subroutine memory address information. This can be achieved by using the stack for data transfers between the main program and the subroutine.

In the stack transfer approach the variables required by the subroutine are pushed to the stack prior to the subroutine call. On entry to the subroutine itself we now have the stack set up with the return address at the top and the variables immediately below this. The stack pointer may now be incremented or decremented as required to place the input data at the top of the stack, at which point the data may be pulled from the stack to the accumulator or other registers as required. Results produced by the subroutine may also be pushed to the stack into positions below that occupied by the return address. Some care is needed here to ensure that any existing data in the stack at that point is no longer required by the subroutine or main program. Finally at the end of the subroutine the stack pointer must be manipulated to place the return address back at the top of the stack ready for the return to the main program. When the main program has resumed operation the results data can be located and pulled from the stack for further use in the main program sequence.

The advantage of using the stack in this way is that the subroutine no longer imposes restraints on the location of data that is to be transferred and the only constraint on the main program is that the subroutine start address must be correctly located. It now becomes possible to write a completely relocatable subroutine which may be incorporated with any main program sequence, provided that the subroutine instructions are loaded at the appropriate location in the memory map as specified by the JSR or CALL instructions in the main program.

Chapter Three
Arithmetic and Logic Operations

As we have already seen, the function of the ALU section of the CPU is to carry out Boolean logic and arithmetic operations. Where two data items are required, as in the case of an addition of two numbers, then one of the numbers will be held in the accumulator whilst the other is called up from memory. The result of the operation is returned to the accumulator from which it may be transferred back into memory if desired. We shall now look at some aspects of these arithmetic and logic functions and we shall start with the logical operations.

Logical operations

All currently available microprocessors feature some Boolean logic instructions. The functions generally provided are AND, OR, EXCLU-SIVE OR and NOT or COMPLEMENT. For these functions, the individual bits of the word or words used by the instruction are processed independently. Let us examine the action of these logic operations and see how they may be used in programs.

The 'NOT' function
In the NOT function the states of all of the data bits in the word being processed are inverted so that a '1' becomes a '0' and vice versa. In many processor instruction sets this function is called COMPLEMENT. The action of the COMPLEMENT or NOT operation is shown in Figure 3.1.

The NOT function is often used in the smaller microcomputers to provide a subtraction facility since some of these devices provide addition only in the instruction set.

The 'AND' function
The results obtained by applying the AND function to two data bits are shown in Figure 3.2. When both bits are at the '1' level the result is a '1' whilst for all other combinations the result is '0'. Thus a '1' result occurs only when both the bit in word A and the corresponding bit in word B are at '1'.

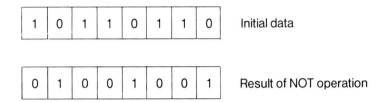

| 1 | 0 | 1 | 1 | 0 | 1 | 1 | 0 | Initial data |

| 0 | 1 | 0 | 0 | 1 | 0 | 0 | 1 | Result of NOT operation |

Fig. 3.1 The action of a NOT or COMPLEMENT operation on a data word.

Bit A	Bit B	Result A AND B
0	0	0
0	1	0
1	0	0
1	1	1

Fig. 3.2 Results of carrying out an AND operation on a pair of data bits.

The most common use for the AND operation is that of masking off parts of a data word. As an example, in the data code for text from a keyboard the codes for the numbers 0 to 9 have actual numerical values from 48 to 58. This is the actual value of the number with 48 added to it. To convert from this letter-code into actual binary numbers we simply have to chop off the upper four bits of the number which effectively removes 48 from the data value. This can be done by using the data pattern 00001111 as a mask. If an AND operation is now carried out between this mask pattern and the keyboard code, a number from 0 to 9 will be left as shown in Figure 3.3. Wherever there is a '0' in the mask word the data bit will become a '0' in the output data irrespective of the state of the data bit in the word that is being masked.

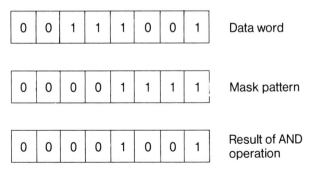

| 0 | 0 | 1 | 1 | 1 | 0 | 0 | 1 | Data word |

| 0 | 0 | 0 | 0 | 1 | 1 | 1 | 1 | Mask pattern |

| 0 | 0 | 0 | 0 | 1 | 0 | 0 | 1 | Result of AND operation |

Fig. 3.3 Use of the AND operation to mask off part of a data word.

Where the mask bit is a '1' the data state of the bit in the word being masked is unaffected. Thus in this case the upper four bits are set at '0' and the lower four bits remain unaltered. The AND function may be used to reset specific bits of a data word by using a mask pattern which has the selected bits set at '0' and all other data bits set at '1'.

The 'OR' function
In the OR operation when either or both of the data bits being ORed is at '1', the resultant bit will also be '1'. The possible results of ORing two data bits together are shown in Figure 3.4.

Bit A	Bit B	Result A OR B
0	0	0
0	1	1
1	0	1
1	1	1

Fig. 3.4 Results of an OR operation on a pair of data bits.

The OR function is primarily used for setting individual bits in a word to the '1' state without altering the remaining bits in the word. This is done by using a mask pattern with all bits set at '0' except for the bit that is to be set at '1'. The OR function can also be used to add a fixed pattern into a data word. Thus to convert from the binary numbers from 0 to 9 to the equivalent text code for those numbers we need to use a mask with the pattern 00110000. When the data word is ORed with the mask pattern the result is that bits 4

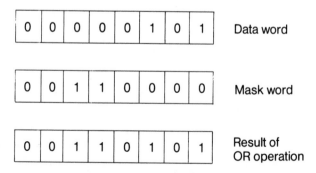

Fig. 3.5 Use of an OR operation to set extra bits in a data word.

and 5 are set to the '1' state to give the desired character code as shown in Figure 3.5.

The 'EXCLUSIVE OR' (XOR) function

In the OR function it will be noted that the result is a '1' when either or both data bits are at '1'. In the EXCLUSIVE OR function the result is '0' when both bits are at '1' or both are at '0'. When either one or other of the bits is at '1' the result becomes '1'. This is shown in Figure 3.6

Bit A	Bit B	Result A XOR B
0	0	0
0	1	1
1	0	1
1	1	0

Fig. 3.6 Results of XOR operation on a pair of data bits.

This function is particularly useful in comparing two data patterns for a match. If the two data words are identical the result will have all of its bits set at '0'. Any pair of bits that do not match will be indicated by a '1' at the corresponding bit position in the result. This is shown in Figure 3.7.

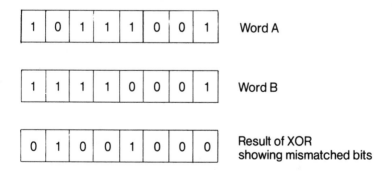

| 1 | 0 | 1 | 1 | 1 | 0 | 0 | 1 | Word A |

| 1 | 1 | 1 | 1 | 0 | 0 | 0 | 1 | Word B |

| 0 | 1 | 0 | 0 | 1 | 0 | 0 | 0 | Result of XOR showing mismatched bits |

Fig. 3.7 Use of XOR instruction to detect a data pattern mismatch.

Another useful result with EXCLUSIVE OR is that where the data bit in the mask word is a '0' the original state of the data bit is reproduced in the output. Where the masking bit is a '1' the corresponding bit in the original data word is complemented. Thus EXCLUSIVE OR can be used to provide a selective complementing action by using a mask pattern with '1's at the bit positions where data is to be inverted and '0's in all other positions as shown in Figure 3.8.

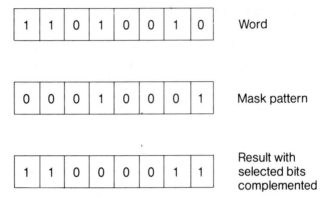

| 1 | 1 | 0 | 1 | 0 | 0 | 1 | 0 | Word |

| 0 | 0 | 0 | 1 | 0 | 0 | 0 | 1 | Mask pattern |

| 1 | 1 | 0 | 0 | 0 | 0 | 1 | 1 | Result with selected bits complemented |

Fig. 3.8 Use of XOR to selectively complement bits in a data word.

Addition and subtraction

The two primary arithmetic operations provided by the ALU of a microprocessor are the addition and subtraction of two binary numbers. Some simpler devices do not provide a separate instruction for subtraction

A	B	Carry in	Sum	Carry
0	0	0	0	0
0	1	0	1	0
1	0	0	1	0
1	1	0	0	1
0	0	1	1	0
0	1	1	0	1
1	0	1	0	1
1	1	1	1	1

Fig. 3.9 Addition of a pair of binary bits and the effect of including a carry from a previous operation.

but this operation can be achieved by simply making the number to be subtracted negative and then adding the two numbers to obtain the required result.

The results of adding two bits together are shown in the first four rows of Figure 3.9. When both bits are at '1' the numerical result is 2 so a 1 is carried over to the next higher bit position and added in to the sum at that bit position. The lower four results in the table show the effect of adding in a carry from the next lower bit calculation. There can of course also be a carry at the most significant bit position and this effectively spills out from the top end of the accumulator. Any carry bit produced in this way is held in the carry flag bit of the status register. A carry produced by some previous instruction may need to be taken into account in the addition. Some processors have two different ADD instructions, one of which ignores any existing carry whilst the other takes any carry produced from a previous instruction and adds it in at the least significant end of the new calculation.

The process of addition simply involves loading the first number (the addend) to the accumulator. An ADD instruction then specifies the number to be added (the augend) and the result which appears in the accumulator may then be stored as the sum. A typical program sequence might be:

```
LDA    ADDEND
ADD    AUGEND
STA    SUM
```

Subtraction follows basically the same format and in most processors special SUB instructions are included for this operation. If the processor does not have a subtract instruction the same result can be achieved by negating the number to be subtracted and then adding it to the first number. Negation is achieved by complementing the number and then incrementing it by one.

Negative numbers
The simple pure binary word assumes a positive integer number which, for an 8-bit word, ranges from 0 to 255. In the real world we need to be able to deal with negative quantities, so we need some method of representing negative numbers.

If we consider the numbers from 0 to 16 as shown in Figure 3.10, and take into account only the lower four data bits, then the data for 16 becomes the same as that for 0. Now the value 15 is one less than 16, so we could equally well call this number −1 and go on to use the data for 14 to represent −2 and so on. It will be noted that using this scheme the numbers −1 to −8 all have a '1' bit at the most significant position. We can use this left hand bit as a sign marker so that when it is '0' the positive numbers 0 to 7 are produced, and when it is '1' the word represents a negative number having a value from −1 to −8. Using this scheme we now have a number range which runs from −8 through to +7. This form of representation is called 'complementary

Number	Binary	Complement Binary
0	0000	0
1	0001	1
2	0010	2
3	0011	3
4	0100	4
5	0101	5
6	0110	6
7	0111	7
8	1000	−8
9	1001	−7
10	1010	−6
11	1011	−5
12	1100	−4
13	1101	−3
14	1110	−2
15	1111	−1
16(or 0)	0000	0

Fig. 3.10 Representation of negative numbers in a binary data system.

binary'. In an 8-bit processor this scheme will give a number range from −128 to +127.

To convert a number from positive to negative we simply complement the data bits and increment the result by 1. Thus if we take the number +5 (0101) the complement is 1010 and adding one gives 1011 which as we see from Figure 3.10 is equivalent to −5. This process is called 'negation' and many microprocessors have a special instruction to perform this function. The arithmetic operations in a microprocessor automatically work using this complemented binary notation and will give the correct results whether the numbers are positive or negative.

Sometimes a subtraction can produce a result which is outside the range of numbers that can be represented by the data word and this could lead to errors in subsequent calculations. When a number overflow of this type occurs an 'overflow' flag bit in the status register is set at '1'. If this is checked after the calculation step, appropriate steps can be taken to deal with the overrange number to maintain correct results.

Handling larger numbers

In an 8-bit processor system the range of numbers that can be represented by a single word is from 0 to 255. If the numbers are treated as signed numbers then the range becomes −128 to +127. Such a small number range will limit the usefulness of the processor so we need to consider ways of representing larger numbers. The simplest approach is to use double or triple precision formats where each number is represented by a combination of two or three data words. Thus a double precision number consists of two successive words in memory and represents a 16-bit data item with a numerical range from 0 to 65535, or alternatively −32768 to +32767. This range of values will often suffice for most applications but, if need be, three words may be combined to form a triple precision number with a range from 0 to about 4 million.

The process of handling multiple precision numbers is quite straight-forward. Suppose we wish to add together two 16-bit numbers. First the two lower 8-bit words are added together and the result is stored. Next the upper pair of 8-bit words are added, taking into account any carry produced by the first addition, and this result is stored to complete the 16-bit result. As an example the program might be as follows:

```
LDA    LSBYTE1
ADD    LSBYTE2
STA    RESLTLS
LDA    MSBYTE1
ADC    MSBYTE2
STA    RESLTMS
```

Some processors, such as the MC6809, have two accumulators which makes the handling of 16-bit numbers quite straightforward, producing the following program steps:

```
LDD    NUM1
ADDD   NUM2
STD    RESLT
```

Here the load and store operations transfer the data between two successive memory locations and the A and B accumulators respectively, and the double length addition instruction, ADDD, automatically carries out a complete 16-bit add operation including any carry between the two 8-bit bytes.

The time taken for this double length operation is slightly shorter than for the scheme using 8-bit additions because the computer has fewer instructions to read and interpret, although the actual data transfer and addition process is the same.

Binary coded decimal

The basic operation of arithmetic in a microprocessor uses simple binary arithmetic and binary number data. In the real world we are normally used to handling numbers using the decimal format in which each digit may have ten different values and each digit represents a scale of ten (decimal) weighted number (i.e. units, tens, hundreds, etc.).

It is, of course, possible to input data in the binary format as a sequence of 1 or 0 digits and to output the results in the same way. In a control system this might be perfectly acceptable since the input and output devices may be made to work with binary data and there may be no need for keyboard data input or a display for the output. When a human operator is required to either input the data or interpret the output data then the system tends to be impractical since the majority of human operators will be unable to cope with binary numbers having a large number of bits.

Conversion of numbers from binary to decimal or decimal to binary can be relatively complex. A simpler solution is to use the binary coded decimal or BCD system of numbering. In this system each digit of the decimal number is represented by a 4-bit binary number. These 4-bit binary numbers are then assembled together to form the binary coded decimal value as shown in Figure 3.11.

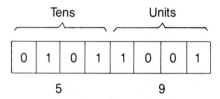

Fig. 3.11 Data format for binary coded decimal (BCD) numbers.

Generation of the BCD form of a number is fairly straightforward since all that is required is a series of switches each with ten positions where each position produces a unique 4-bit binary code ranging from 0000 (0) to 1001 (9). The switch positions are labelled with the decimal equivalent. Once the switches have been set to the desired decimal number the 4-bit binary code for each decimal digit is read as a separate data word into the computer.

In a keyboard system each key when pressed is arranged to output the appropriate 4-bit binary code. As successive keys are pressed the 4-bit data words are pushed into successive memory locations and when the complete number has been entered the series of 4-bit words can be processed as required.

In BCD addition, a carry is produced if the sum of two BCD digits is greater than 9 and the result is reduced by subtracting 10 to bring the BCD digit into its proper 0 to 9 range. The carry from one decade of the BCD number is then added in when the next more significant digits are added. Some CPUs have special instructions for performing addition and subtraction on numbers in BCD format.

To save memory space BCD numbers are often packed with two BCD digits in an 8-bit word or four BCD digits in a 16-bit word.

Multiplication and division

Although some of the more advanced processors such as the 6809, 68000 and Z8000 have instructions for executing simple integer multiplication, it is likely that for most systems the multiplication operation will be carried out by a software routine. We shall take a look at the principles and techniques involved in such routines.

The process of multiplication is effectively one of successive addition. If we wanted to multiply 12 by 7 this could be achieved by setting the accumulator to 0 and then adding the number 12 to the contents of the accumulator a total of seven times. Whilst this approach is quite practical for small multiplier values it becomes unwieldy and very slow when the multiplier is large. Thus, if the number being multiplied (the multiplicand) were 12 and the multiplier were say 2500 then we would need to make 2500 successive additions in order to get to the product.

```
        5 6 7
        1 2 3
       ─────────
        1 7 0 1     Partial product
      1 1 3 4       Partial product
      5 6 7         Partial product
      ─────────
      6 9 7 4 1     Product
      ─────────
```

Fig. 3.12 Multiplication process using decimal numbers.

Consider what happens when we carry out a multiplication using decimal numbers as shown in Figure 3.12. Here a separate multiplication is made for each digit of the multiplier and a set of partial products is produced. The multiplicand is first multiplied by the units digit of the multiplier to give the first intermediate result. Next the tens digit is used as a multiplier to give a further intermediate result and so on. At the end the partial products are summed to give the final product. Note that for each successive digit of the multiplier the partial product is moved one digit position to the left.

Binary multiplication can be carried out on paper in a similar fashion, as shown in Figure 3.13. Here the process is greatly simplified since the digits of the multiplier can only have the values 0 or 1, so the partial product is either the multiplicand or zero and, as in the case of the decimal version, it is added in at positions progressively shifted one place to the left. Finally the partial products are added as before to give the complete product.

```
      10110      (22)
        101      (5)
      ───────
      10110    ⎫
      00000    ⎬  Partial products
      10110    ⎭
      ───────
     1101110     (110)
```

Fig. 3.13 Multiplication process using binary numbers.

In the computer, the product is built up by examining the multiplier one bit at a time starting from the least significant and adding in the appropriate partial product. Since it is more convenient to add the multiplicand to the accumulator by a simple ADD instruction, the running total in the accumulator is shifted right by one position between each addition. This has

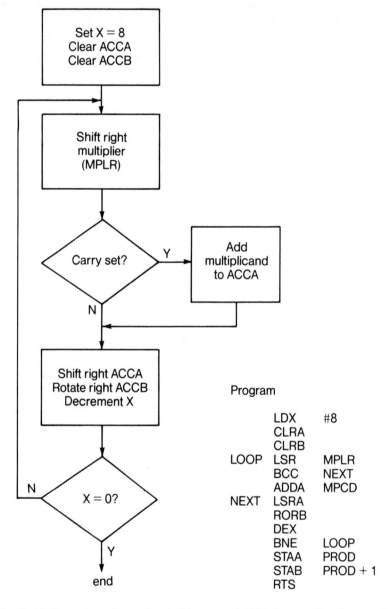

Fig. 3.14 Flow chart for a simple binary multiplication routine for positive integer numbers.

the same effect as shifting the multiplicand one bit to the left before adding it to the running total.

The basic flow chart for the multiplication process is shown in Figure 3.14. At the start, the accumulator and the register being used as an extension to the accumulator are both set to zero. A count variable is then set up and stored either in a register or in a memory location. This count is set at the number of bits in the multiplier. Thus if we are carrying out a multiplication of 8-bit numbers this count variable is set at 8.

The multiplication process proper is carried out in a loop since the operation for each partial product is identical. The multiplier is shifted right by one bit to place the least significant bit into the carry position. Carry status is tested and if there is a carry the multiplicand is added to the accumulator. If there is no carry the addition step is skipped. The next operation is to shift the contents of the accumulator and extension to the right by one bit position. Note that a rotate instruction is used to shift the contents of the extension register. This ensures that any bit carried out of the lower end of the accumulator is transferred into the most significant position in the extension. The loop count is then decremented and tested for a zero status. If the result is not zero the loop is repeated. When the loop has been executed the required number of times the product will be stored in the accumulator and the extension register and may be transferred to a suitable pair of locations in memory.

The process of dividing two integer numbers is more complex than that for multiplication but is basically a series of successive subtraction operations. Each time the divisor is successfully subtracted from the dividend a '1' bit is placed into the quotient. In this case the dividend (the number being divided) is held in the upper part of a double length register. After each subtraction step the dividend and quotient are shifted one bit to the left ready for the next step. An important point in the division routine is that it must first check for a possible 'divide by zero' condition by testing the divisor. If the divisor is zero the division routine is skipped and the quotient is set to the highest number available in the number format that is being used.

The simple multiplication and division routines assume that the numbers being multiplied or divided are positive. If both positive and negative numbers are to be handled the signs must be taken into account. The sign of the result can be directly predicted since if both numbers have the same polarity the result is always positive whilst numbers of opposite sign always give a negative result. Having determined the required sign this may be stored in memory. Any negative numbers are then negated to make them positive and the calculation is carried out. Finally the sign of the result is changed to the required polarity by negating the result if appropriate.

Because of the repeated operations in the loop, the multiplication and division of numbers is a much slower operation than addition or subtraction.

Some microprocessors include a special instruction to carry out the multiplication of two integer numbers. The CPU carries out the same process as that described above but it is done within the CPU and will execute much faster than the software routine using successive additions. Some of the more sophisticated 16-bit microprocessors also incorporate an instruction for dividing one integer number by another but it will be found that for most microprocessors this operation has to be carried out by a software routine.

Dealing with fractions

So far we have considered the basic arithmetic operations using integer numbers but in real life calculations it is likely that fractional quantities will be involved.

We can treat an 8-bit binary number as a fraction by assigning the value 0.5 to the most significant bit, 0.25 to the next lower bit and so on, with each bit having half the value of the one to its left in the normal way. This fraction data word may be combined with an 8-bit integer data word to form a fixed point number as shown in Figure 3.15. Here the lower word provides fractional values in binary in much the same way as we would use decimal fractions in conventional decimal arithmetic. As far as the computer is concerned the entire number appears to be an integer but its value in terms of the program is simply scaled down by a factor of 256 so that the least significant bit of the double word has an effective value of 1/256.

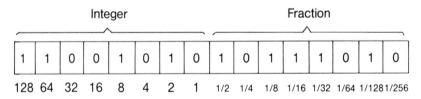

Fig. 3.15 Data layout for fixed point binary numbers.

Binary coded decimal can be treated in a similar way so that some of the BCD digits at the right-hand end of the number are considered to be decimal places instead of integer numbers.

Floating point numbers

So far we have seen that the basic arithmetic operations of addition, subtraction, multiplication and division can be carried out fairly readily with a microcomputer by using simple sequences of instructions. Larger numbers than those permitted by the basic word length of the CPU can be handled by using double or treble precision arithmetic where each number is represented by two or three data words.

Whilst the use of integer numbers may be adequate for many tasks, we shall find that in real world problems, such as those encountered in control systems, it becomes a requirement that the CPU be able to handle fractional quantities and perhaps be able to handle a range of numerical values which is very much larger than that provided by double or triple precision arithmetic.

Fractions can be handled by using a fixed point scheme as we have just seen but the range of numbers that can be handled is limited by the number of bits used to represent a data value. Often we may be able to accept a data resolution of say 16 bits, but need to handle both very large and very small quantities at the same time. This can be achieved by using a floating point arithmetic scheme.

In floating point arithmetic each numeric variable is represented by two components. One of these is known as the fraction or mantissa and will have a fractional value between 0 and 1. The second component is called the exponent and represents the power of two by which the fraction must be multiplied to give the actual value of the variable. Thus the number 6 might be represented by a fractional value of 0.75 with an exponent value of 3. In this case the value 0.75 is multiplied by 2 raised to the power 3 which is 8 and the final result is 8×0.75 which is 6.

In a simple floating point system, using an 8-bit word for the fraction and a second 8-bit word for the exponent, the number range will extend from 2^{-127}, which is a very tiny fractional quantity, to 2^{+128} which is an enormous number. Although the range of the numbers that can be represented is very wide, the actual precision to which any number can be represented is governed by the number of bits in the fractional part. Thus, with an 8-bit fraction the precision is limited to $1/256$ of the full scale value or about 0.5%. If the fraction is represented by a 16-bit value, then the precision rises to 1 part in about 65000 which is roughly 0.002% and is normally adequate for practical applications of microcomputers. Figure 3.16 shows the typical format for such a system. The fraction may of course be a signed number with the sign located in the most significant bit.

In many cases a fraction with 12 bits and a 4-bit exponent would probably be adequate. This might seem attractive since it could be fitted into a single

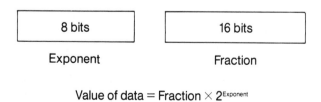

8 bits	16 bits
Exponent	Fraction

Value of data = Fraction $\times$ 2^{Exponent}

Fig. 3.16 Data format used for floating point binary numbers.

16-bit data word, but in practice it would be difficult to implement so it is usual to employ the 8-bit exponent and 16-bit fraction, although this may provide a much wider number range and higher precision than is actually needed for a particular task.

It is important to note that it is not possible to have a value of zero for a variable in the floating point number scheme. Making the fraction equal to zero will usually cause problems in the normalisation process that is carried out after each arithmetic operation. The usual solution is to set the value to the smallest that the system can use. This number will be virtually zero anyway.

It would be perfectly feasible to have a floating point system in which the fraction was represented as a binary number but the exponent was based on a power of 10 rather than a power of 2. This scheme however presents some problems in calculating new exponent values when the fractional result exceeds 1, and is not particularly practical.

The binary coded decimal format can be used in floating point form. In this case the fraction is represented as a decimal fraction and stored in BCD form as a series of 4-bit binary segments each representing one decimal digit of the fraction. Here the exponent may represent the power of 10 by which the fraction has to be multiplied to give the actual value. Thus a fraction of 0.75 and an exponent of 3 would represent 0.75×1000 which is 750. In a BCD scheme of this type a 4-bit exponent would permit a range of numbers from 10^{-7} to 10^{+7} which is probably adequate for most applications. Once again the fraction determines the precision with which numbers may be represented and here a 24-bit BCD number would provide six significant places in the resultant decimal numbers. An additional bit or word might be needed to provide a sign indicator. The BCD format is particularly useful where data is to be input from a keyboard or where a display in decimal form is required for use by the operators of the system. Computer systems using the BASIC language generally use the BCD format with floating point numbers for their internal arithmetic operations.

Floating point arithmetic
The process of carrying out arithmetic operations on floating point numbers becomes rather more complex than for a similar operation on integers. As a result floating point arithmetic tends to be very slow when carried out purely by software routines.

For addition and subtraction, the first step is to scale the numbers until the exponents are the same. This is done by shifting the fraction part of the smaller number to the right. Each time the fraction is shifted to the right its value is scaled down by a factor of two and this is compensated for by adding one to the exponent value. Once the exponents are equal, the two fractions can be added or subtracted in the normal way. The exponent of the result will be the same as for the numbers being added or subtracted. Figure 3.17 shows the basic sequence of operations.

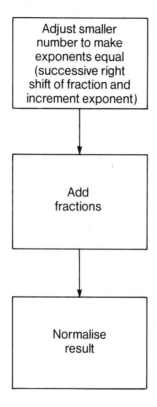

Fig. 3.17 Sequence of operations for addition or subtraction of floating point binary numbers.

For multiplication, the exponents of the two numbers are added together to give the exponent for the result. The fractional parts are then multiplied in the normal way, as shown in Figure 3.18. Division involves subtracting the exponent of the divisor from that of the dividend to give the quotient, and then the fractions are divided in the normal way to produce the fraction part of the quotient. It is important to include a test for a divide by zero condition. If this occurs the floating point number should be set to its highest possible value.

Normalisation
In a floating point system the result of a calculation will often give a result in which the fraction part becomes greater than unity, particularly when multiplication is involved. Since this result is beyond the permissible range of the fraction part of the number, some action must be taken to restore this result to the normal floating point format.

The fraction can be restored to an acceptable value by simply dividing it by two which is achieved by shifting the fraction one bit to the right. The result however now has a value which is half its correct value. This situation

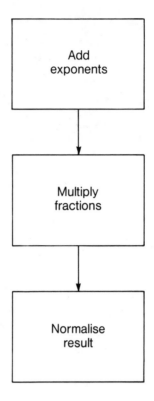

Fig. 3.18 Sequence of operations for multiplying two floating point binary numbers.

can be corrected by simply increasing the value of the exponent by 1 which has the effect of multiplying the floating point value by a factor of two. This process of correcting the overflow condition in the fractional part of the number is called 'normalisation' and is usually applied after every calculation is carried out. Generally the fraction is shifted until its value lies between 0.5 and 1.

Normalisation is important when the result of a calculation gives a fraction which is less than 0.5 since this would result in a loss of precision in the calculations. In this case the fraction is repeatedly multiplied by two and the exponent decremented until the fraction becomes greater than 0.5.

Trigonometric functions

In many applications the calculations required may involve trigonometric functions such as SIN(x) or COS(x). One method of generating such functions is to use a mathematical series and to evaluate this for the desired value of x. As an example the series for SIN(x) would be:

$$SIN(x) = x - \frac{x^3}{3!} + \frac{x^5}{5!} - \frac{x^7}{7!} + \dots$$

where x is the angle in radians.

This series goes on to infinity, but for practical purposes we need evaluate only the first three or four terms to obtain acceptable values for $SIN(x)$. The addition of further terms will provide increased precision but there is little point in calculating the function to any better precision than the arithmetic being used will handle. For a system using an 8-bit word, the first two terms will probably produce acceptable values for the function. Other common trigonometric functions such as $COS(x)$ and $TAN(x)$ may also be calculated using the series form. Functions such as $SEC(x)$, $COSEC(x)$ and $COTAN(x)$ may be evaluated in a similar fashion by using the appropriate mathematical series.

Since the results from functions such as $SIN(x)$ or $COS(x)$ are fractional values, the arithmetic scheme used will generally need to be in floating point form. Because the evaluation process involves a series of multiplication and division operations, it will be relatively slow. This slowness of computation may be acceptable in a computer system which is merely solving equations with no particular time restraints, but in a practical control or instrumentation application the calculation times involved may not be acceptable and an alternative approach is needed.

Using a look-up table

If we consider a function such as $SIN(x)$, its value follows a cyclical pattern which repeats every 360 degrees (2π radians). In a practical system it is often acceptable to use discrete angular values at, say, 1 degree intervals for the x parameter. In this case there would be just 360 possible values for $SIN(x)$ and these could be held in the computer memory in the form of a table. Now if the value of x is used as an index for the table address we can automatically call up the corresponding value for $SIN(x)$. This process eliminates the multiplication and division steps of a series evaluation and can give a very rapidly calculated $SIN(x)$ function.

Thus we might use a sequence of instructions as follows:

```
LDX   ANGLE
LDA   X,SINTAB
```

where SINTAB is the address of the start of the table of values of $SIN(x)$.

Here the values in the table are assumed to be a single data word. In an 8-bit system it is likely that a two-byte word might be needed to provide acceptable precision. Here we have to move twice as far down the table because the words are stored in pairs. This may be achieved by doubling the value of ANGLE, which can be done by left shifting it by one bit position before loading it into the X register as follows:

```
ASL    ANGLE
LDX    ANGLE
LDAA   SINTAB,X
LDAB   SINTAB+1,X
```

In a symmetrical function such as SIN(x) or COS(x) it will be noted that the actual numerical value of the function follows the same pattern over the second half of each cycle (180–360 degrees) except that the numbers are negative. Also we find that the set of values from 0 to 90 degrees is the same as that from 90 to 180 degrees, except that the sequence is reversed. Thus we need only store the set of values from 0 to 90 and the remaining values can be derived by simply applying some simple tests and either reversing the sign or altering the index sequence.

In a practical scheme where floating point numbers are used, each value in the table might consist of three bytes of data. These could be stored in consecutive locations in memory but this tends to make the indexing more complex since the index value will need to be three times the value of ANGLE. An alternative scheme, which allows simple indexing, is to arrange the data as three separate tables with one containing exponent values and the others containing the higher and lower bytes of the fraction respectively. Now the data is loaded by simply specifying the start address of the table for the part of the number being loaded.

Another approach which would require less memory is to store the SIN values as two-byte integer numbers. When the number is read in it can readily be converted to a fractional component with the exponent value set at 0. The normalisation process may then be applied to produce the desired floating point number format. This approach is likely to be more suitable where a ready-made SIN or COS function ROM is being employed.

In a practical system the table of sine values would not normally be held in the main memory since this would mean that the values would have to be loaded as part of the program every time the system was switched on. A more practical approach is to have the sine or cosine data permanently written in a ROM which may be located at the required position in the computer memory map. There are available special ROM devices which contain such trigonometrical function data. These generally have the data in the form of a simple 12- or 14-bit binary number, so some form of scaling or format conversion will usually be required to change the data into a form that is compatible with the arithmetic scheme being used in the computer system.

Other functions

In some applications it is likely that we may wish to calculate square or cube roots or logarithmic functions. As with the trigonometric functions, these may be evaluated by using an appropriate mathematical series with its associated slowness in operation. If the range of possible values for the variable is limited and discrete steps are permissible, it is possible to use the table look-up approach. An important difference, however, is that most of these other functions will not have the convenient cyclic nature of the trigonometric ones so that the range of the variable must be limited in order to conserve memory space.

Differentiation

In control applications and for some calculations on data measurements, we need to find the rate of change of a signal with time. Thus we may be able to measure the velocity of a shaft fairly readily but need to calculate the acceleration which is the rate of change of shaft velocity. This involves the use of differentiation.

The differential of a function with respect to time dF/dt is a measure of the slope of the graph of that function plotted against time. This is shown in Figure 3.19. If we consider the two readings F_n and F_{n-1} and join them with a line, the slope of the line is given by the difference between the two readings divided by the time interval between them. The true differential assumes that this time interval is infinitely small.

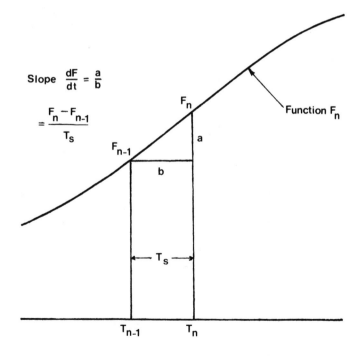

$$\text{Slope } \frac{dF}{dt} = \frac{a}{b}$$

$$= \frac{F_n - F_{n-1}}{T_s}$$

F_n

Function F_n

F_{n-1}

a

b

T_s

T_{n-1} T_n

Fig. 3.19 Principles of implementing differentiation by using the difference between successive sample values.

In a computer, differentiation can be achieved by operating upon the differences between the latest reading of a value and the previous reading. Thus the rate of change of a function is:

$$\frac{\mathrm{d}F}{\mathrm{d}t} = \frac{F_n - F_{n-1}}{T_n - T_{n-1}} = \frac{F_n - F_{n-1}}{T_s}$$

where F_n is the latest sample of the signal F and F_{n-1} is the previous sample, whilst T_s is the time between samples. This calculation is however only approximate and depends upon making a sensible choice for the time interval between samples T_s.

Integration
The second function regularly used in control system equations is that of integration which is effectively the opposite of differentiation. Integration is a process of summation of a number of small increments and the integral can be represented by the area under the function curve on a graph. This is shown in Figure 3.20.

If the total area under the curve is divided into a large number of vertical strips of equal width, we can calculate the area of each strip and then add these to give the total area. If we assume that the piece of the curve between two successive sample points can be represented by a straight line then the area of each strip is approximately given by the height of the strip multiplied by its width, and the total area under the curve is obtained by adding up the areas of individual strips.

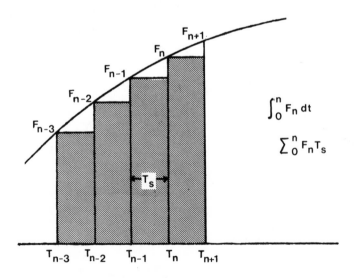

$$\int_0^n F_n \, dt$$

$$\sum_0^n F_n T_s$$

Fig. 3.20 Principles of integration using the sum of the areas of columns formed by successive sample ordinates.

If the function is sampled at regular time intervals, T_s, to give a set of N values from F_0 to F_n the integrated value becomes:

$$X_n = \int_o^n Fdt = \Sigma_o^n F_n T_s$$
$$= X_{n-1} + F_n T_s$$

Here the height, F_n, of each strip is taken as the measured value of F at time T_n. If the sampling time T_s is made small then the result will approximate to true integration of the input signal. Here, X_n is the current value for the integral term and X_{n-1} is the previous calculated value for X. Note that X_{n-1} is set equal to zero when calculating the first value for the integral term.

In practice the simple calculation of the sample amplitude multiplied by the time increment is not quite correct since it does not take into account the small triangular area at the top of the ordinate rectangle. A small correction can be added to take this into account so that the new equation becomes:

$$X_n = \int_o^n F \; dt = X_{n-1} + \frac{(F_n + F_{n-1}) \; T_s}{2}$$

Here the value used for the sample is the mean of two successive samples.

Hardware arithmetic devices

Although in most applications the software routines for arithmetic operations are perfectly adequate, there are cases where the speed of such calculations is too slow. Examples are in high-speed controllers and in operations such as fourier or spectrum analysis where large numbers of multiplications need to be carried out.

Although one possible solution is to use a faster CPU in the processor system, this will usually only provide up to twice the calculation speed. An alternative solution is to carry out the slower calculations in an external arithmetic hardware unit. As an example, a fast multiplier can be produced by literally using a large array of adder elements so that all of the partial products are calculated and added together in one operation. By using such a device the multiplication can be carried out in perhaps one computer instruction cycle. The speed of calculation is now limited by the time taken to set up and output the numbers to the arithmetic device and to read the result back into the computer.

Other types of hardware arithmetic device are, in fact, fast dedicated microprocessors, generally using high-speed bipolar logic devices, which can calculate at perhaps ten times the speed of the main processor device. Once again data has to be output to the external unit and results input from it, and this will often be the limiting factor in the amount of speed gained by using such a device.

Chapter Four
Parallel Input-Output

As we saw in Chapter 1, one of the essential requirements of any practical microcomputer system is the ability to transfer data between the CPU and the outside world. This is achieved by using special input–output (I/O) channels which are referred to as 'ports'. The simplest and most rapid form of I/O data transfer moves all of the bits of the data word simultaneously on a set of parallel wires in much the same way as data is transferred over the main computer data bus. We shall now examine some of the techniques used in providing this form of data transfer which is known as 'parallel' input–output.

Use of dedicated CPU registers

In single-chip microcomputer devices the input and output interfaces are often implemented by using additional registers within the CPU which are dedicated to input or output functions. A typical I/O scheme using dedicated registers might be organised as shown in Figure 4.1.

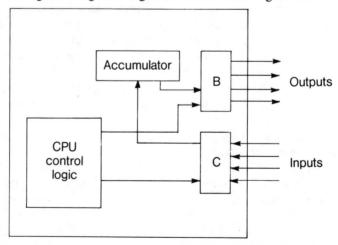

Fig. 4.1 Input – output scheme using dedicated registers in the CPU.

In this arrangement register B provides data output. The logic states of the individual bits in this register are brought out via driver circuits to separate pins on the device package. When a data word is to be output from the CPU the first step is to load the data word into the accumulator from the memory. A data transfer instruction is then used to copy the data from the accumulator into register B. Once the data has been placed in register B the required bit pattern will automatically be presented on the output data lines.

Register C acts as a dedicated input channel. Here the data pattern on the input data lines is fed to the inputs of register C and the operation of the register is arranged so that its bit pattern continually follows the data states of the input lines. When data is to be input to the CPU a data transfer instruction is used to copy the current data in register C into the accumulator. Once the data word is in the accumulator it may be stored in memory or processed in any other desired fashion.

In both of these cases the transfer of data between the input or output lines and the CPU is controlled directly by special data transfer instructions and the signal lines are permanently allocated to their input or output roles. Single-chip microprocessors usually have a selection of these dedicated input or output lines available to suit a variety of different applications.

Input-output to external registers

The general purpose microprocessors do not have dedicated I/O registers built into the CPU itself. This means that the I/O registers have to be added externally and the data must be transferred between the accumulator and the I/O registers via the CPU data bus. The instruction set of the processor may include special instructions, such as IN or OUT, for this purpose.

Under normal operating conditions the data bus carries data between the CPU and the memory, and data transfers are performed by using LOAD and STORE instructions. When a data transfer is to be made between the CPU and an I/O register, an extra control bus signal (M/IO) is used which selects the I/O register instead of the memory for connection to the data bus. Special I/O data transfer instructions such as IN or OUT may be included in the CPU instruction set and these will automatically set the required state on the M/IO control line.

A simple IN or OUT opcode allows access to only one I/O channel. This facility can be expanded by adding an address operand to the IN or OUT instruction. The operand produces an address output when an input or output data transfer is made. The I/O address is generally output on the same address bus lines as the memory address. By decoding the I/O address, one particular I/O register may be selected from a group of input and output channels. The decoded address is then gated with the M/IO control line so that the I/O register will respond only to an I/O data transfer. If this type of I/O addressing is used the memory address must also be gated with the

M/IO line so that the memory responds only to memory data transfer instructions. This scheme is used in the Z80 processor where the lower 8 address bus lines may be used to select one of 256 different I/O channels when an IN or OUT instruction is used. The general arrangement of such an input – output scheme is shown in Figure 4.2.

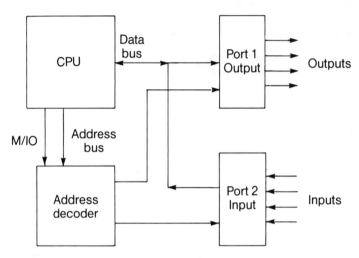

Fig. 4.2 Input – output scheme using external registers addressed via the CPU address bus and IN or OUT instructions.

Memory-mapped I/O

Some microprocessors, such as the Motorola 6800 series have neither dedicated internal I/O registers nor special IN or OUT instructions. This type of processor treats all data transfers via the data bus as read or write operations to the memory. We can still use the data bus to carry data to and from external I/O registers by simply treating the I/O registers as if they were locations in the main computer memory.

The signals on the data bus are multiplexed and may include some data which is merely being transferred inside the CPU itself. Any input or output device must therefore be connected to the data bus only when the appropriate data for transfer is present on the bus. In the case of memory data transfers, the individual memory location is selected by data on the address bus of the CPU. The connection of the memory to the data bus and the timing of the data transfer are governed by clock and control signals generated by the CPU itself.

A memory address may be allocated to each input or output channel and data may be transferred by simply using the same STORE or LOAD instruction that would be used for data transfers between CPU and memory. The addresses used for I/O channels cannot now be used by the memory since this would introduce a conflict of signals on the data bus. Because the I/O channels now occupy part of the memory address map this type of I/O scheme is usually referred to as 'memory-mapped I/O'.

The general layout of a memory-mapped output port is shown in Figure 4.3. The data is first placed on the data bus and then is transferred into the output data register. The timing pulse which initiates this data transfer is generated by clock and control signals from the CPU, gated with a selection signal from an address decoder which selects the particular output register to which the data is transferred. The output from the register may then pass through output buffer stages to provide a parallel digital output.

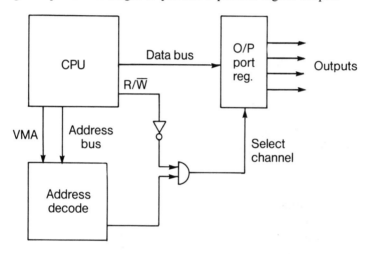

Fig. 4.3 Memory-mapped output port accessed by using a STORE instruction.

Once data has been written to the output register it will be held until the selected memory location is again written to by the CPU. It is important to include the read/write control line in the clock decoding so that the output register will not respond if the CPU selects the memory address for a read operation.

An input port can consist simply of a set of gates that feed data into the data bus as shown in Figure 4.4. In this case tri-state gates must be used. This type of gate can output the normal '0' and '1' states but has, in addition, a third operating state where its output is effectively open circuit. When in this disabled 'tri-state' mode, the gate will not conflict with any other circuit that is driving the same data bus line. When data is to be read in, the gate is enabled by a signal from its address decoder circuit and switches to its normal mode of operation so that it places data signals on to the data bus wires. The function of the address decoder is to detect a particular address code on the address bus and will also include gating with control and clock pulses so that the input gate is enabled only when the data bus is ready to accept data from that particular input. When the LOAD instruction is

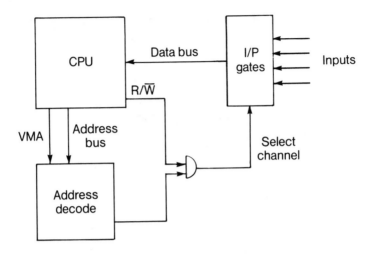

Fig. 4.4 Memory-mapped input port accessed by using a LOAD instruction.

executed, data is transferred from the input gate via the data bus to the CPU accumulator or perhaps to one of the other registers within the CPU.

Handshake signals

So far we have output ports which will present a particular word of data on the output signal lines whenever commanded to do so by the computer. This is perfectly satisfactory if the external device that is to receive the data is always ready to accept new data. Unfortunately this is not always the case.

Consider the situation where the external device is a printer. When data is sent to it the printer will select one particular text character and print it out on a sheet of paper. This printing action takes some time and whilst it is in progress the printer cannot cope with a new set of character data. If the computer is told to send a series of character codes one after another it will take only a very short time to set up new data and output it. This gives a conflict of timing between the computer and the printer with the result that because the printer is not ready it will ignore the new data being output by the computer.

If we know how long the printer takes to print a symbol it is possible to write the computer program so that it waits for an appropriate time period before trying to output the data code for the next symbol to be printed. This is not a very good scheme since, if the printer is changed for another machine, the timing of the computer program may have to be changed and this involves writing a new version of the program. What we need is some scheme by which the external device can tell the computer that it is ready to accept some new data. This is achieved by adding an extra pair of lines to the input–output interface. The signals on these new lines are called the 'handshake' signals.

Firstly, we can have a line carrying an output signal from the computer to indicate that new data is now available at the output. The second line is an input from the external device which will indicate that it is now ready to accept new data. The arrangement is as shown in Figure 4.5.

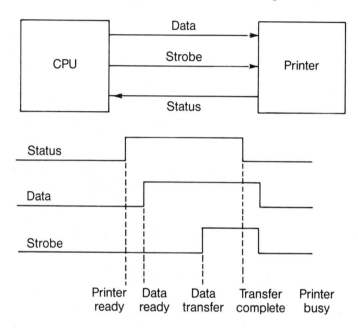

Fig. 4.5 The strobe and status handshake lines and their relative timing on a data port.

When the computer has some data ready to output to the printer it will first of all check the state of the input handshake signal. This input signal is often called the 'status' input. If the printer indicates that it is not yet ready, by sending a '0' on this line, the computer waits and regularly rechecks the status input. When the printer is ready it puts a '1' on its status line. When the computer detects the '1' indicating that the printer is ready, the next data word is sent via the output port to the printer. At the same time the computer outputs a '1' on its handshake line. The output handshake line is sometimes called a 'strobe' output and may be used by the printer to clock the data off the parallel data lines ready for printing. When it has accepted the new data the printer sets its status line to '0' to indicate that it is busy printing a symbol. When the '0' is detected on the printer status line the computer sets its strobe output line back to '0' to indicate that the data is no longer new and the whole handshake process is ready to begin again. This process of handshaking between the computer and the external unit is repeated for each data byte that is transferred through the data port.

When the port is used to input data to the computer the roles of the handshake lines are reversed. Now the output handshake line acts as a status signal to indicate that the computer is ready to accept new data, and the input line becomes a strobe signal and tells the CPU that new data is ready to be read in through the port.

Bidirectional data ports

So far we have looked at input–output ports where the external connections are permanently set as either an input or an output. In a single-chip microcomputer, where the number of available connection pins is usually limited, this inflexible approach can be a disadvantage. If the standard device has, say, 8 inputs and 8 outputs, we shall often find that practical applications may require, say, 12 inputs and 4 outputs or perhaps 6 inputs and 10 outputs. To cater for such variations a number of different types of processor device would have to be produced. A more flexible scheme would be to arrange that the input–output pins could be made to operate as either an input or an output at will. This type of data port is called a 'bidirectional' port.

A bidirectional data port has separate registers for data input and output and these are selected as required by a read/write control line which selects the appropriate register for connection to the data bus. To prevent problems on the input–output data lines the output line drivers are disabled when not in use.

With a simple bidirectional port, all of the data lines of the port are set to transfer data in the same direction. A more flexible scheme is to arrange that individual lines of the port may be set independently as either input or output lines. This can be done by including an additional register in the data port to control the direction of data flow. Each bit in this data direction register controls the function of one data line in the port. Normally all of the lines will be set as inputs by placing '0's in all bits of the data direction register. When a line is required to be an output, the corresponding bit in the data direction register is set at '1' to change the internal connections and the direction of data flow for that data line.

In single-chip microcomputers a simpler form of bidirectional port is often used. This is called a quasi-bidirectional port and uses circuitry similar to that shown in Figure 4.6. Here, only one of the data lines is shown. The output register has transistor outputs with open collector circuits which are capable of drawing current from a load when in the low state. An external resistor connected to the positive power rail provides the load to enable the line to be used as an output. The output wire also feeds a tri-state gate which may be connected to the CPU data bus. Now if an input signal is applied to the output terminal and this gate is enabled, the data may be read into the CPU system. The input signal must also be produced by an open collector

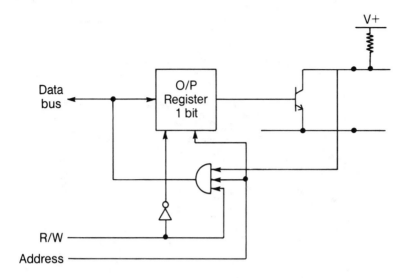

Fig. 4.6 Principle used in a quasi-bidirectional I/O port.

transistor circuit. Thus the input can pull the line down to the '0' state or can switch off and allow the pull up resistor to bring the logic level up to the '1' state.

With this type of input–output interface, if data is written to the port from the CPU then the data line effectively becomes an output line. If the output register is set at '0' the line is held at '0' irrespective of any input signal that may be applied. If however the output register is set to the '1' state and an input is applied to the data line then an input signal can control the line state and a LOAD command will cause the external data to be read into the CPU. The action can therefore be determined by the way in which the CPU is programmed rather than by altering the hardware wiring of the port.

Programmable I/O ports

Instead of having dedicated input or output circuits to provide data ports, it is more usual for the available devices to be organised as flexible interfaces where the input–output lines may be set up as either inputs or outputs as required by issuing instructions from the CPU itself.

These programmable bidirectional data ports have an arrangement similar to that shown in Figure 4.7. Here, just four lines are shown but typical devices usually provide 8 or more data lines for use as inputs or outputs. Registers are provided for holding output data and for receiving input data. Each bit circuit in these registers may be enabled to act as either an input or an output as required. When set up as an output the register will provide an active drive to the output line which drives the line voltage to the '1' or '0' level and no pull up resistor is needed. When the register is disabled,

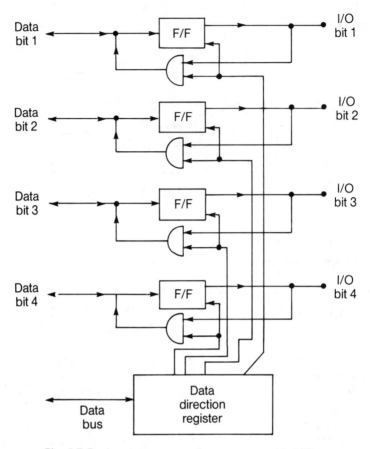

Fig. 4.7 Basic arrangement of a programmable I/O port.

the output stage goes into a 'tri-state' or open circuit mode so that it will not conflict with any input signal that might be applied to the line. The direction of data flow on each input–output line is governed by a control register called the data direction register. In this register, if a bit is set at '0' then the corresponding data line is enabled as an input, whilst if the bit is set at '1' the data line operates as an output.

The data registers are enabled by one or more select lines and these are driven by a signal derived from the CPU address bus when data is to be transferred. If data is written to the data port it will be transferred into the output register, but only those lines which are selected as outputs by the data direction register will be enabled. When data is read in from the port the states of all of the lines are read in. To avoid conflicts, however, only those lines selected as inputs should have input signals applied. If this were not done the output stage of the port would try to drive current into the input signal source and this could result in one or both of the circuits being destroyed.

Apart from the data direction register, the interface device will usually contain some form of control register which may also act as a status register. If separate control and status registers are used they may share the same select address, since the control register will be a write-only type whilst the status will be read-only, so the appropriate register is automatically selected when a read or write operation is performed.

The 6821 PIA

To see how a programmable input–output interface operates, let us consider the Motorola MC6821 PIA (Peripheral Interface Adapter) which is a typical device of this type. The 6821 provides two complete bidirectional 8-bit wide parallel data ports in a single 40-pin integrated circuit package. Each port contains input and output data registers, a data direction register and a control register as shown in Figure 4.8.

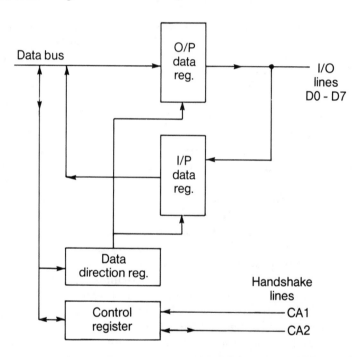

Fig. 4.8 Internal arrangement of a 6821 Programmable Interface Adapter.

When the 6821 is connected into the microprocessor system it appears to the CPU as four memory locations, two for each port. One memory location is used for the data register whilst the other selects the control register. The control register governs the mode of operation of the port and its contents can also be read into the CPU to indicate the status of the port. The data direction register does not have its own address but shares the same address as the data register and is selected by setting bit 2 of the control register to '0'. To select the I/O data register, bit 2 of the control register is set at '1'.

Each port of the 6821 has eight data lines and two handshake control lines. All of these are set up as inputs when the system is switched on. To set the direction of data flow on the I/O lines the data direction register must be selected. Each bit in this register corresponds to one data line and by setting the bit to '1' the associated data line becomes an output. As an example, suppose we wish to set up the port with lines D0 to D3 set as inputs and lines D4 to D7 as outputs. The setting up instructions would be:

```
CLRA
STAA    CREG     select direction register
LDAA    #$FØ     select I/O lines
STAA    DREG     write to direction register
LDAA    #4
STAA    CREG     select data register
```

Here the first step is to set the control register, CREG, to zero thus selecting the data direction register for data transfers via the bus. The pattern of input and output lines is then set up in the accumulator and written into the data direction register. This sets up the inputs and outputs of the device. Finally, bit 2 of the control register is set to '1' so that the input–output data registers are selected for data transfers. To input or output data, an LDAA or STAA instruction is used with the address operand set to the address of the data register in the port.

Other data bits in the control register determine the way in which the control lines on the port will respond to input signals. These control lines are used to handle handshake signals to and from the outside world. Both control lines are initially set up as inputs but the CA2 line (CB2 on the second port) may be set as an output by setting bit 5 of the control register to '1'. The way in which CA2 operates is governed by control register bits 3 and 4, and the action of the input line CA1 (or CB1) is governed by bits 0 and 1. Bits 6 and 7 in the control register are used as flag bits and are set to '1' when a level change or a pulse occurs on a handshake input line. By reading the control register and testing the states of these bits it is possible to determine when a handshake input occurred. The flag bits are automatically reset to '0' when the data register of the port is read by the CPU.

The 6821 has three chip select lines which may be used to select part of the memory address to which it will respond. There are two register select lines which are normally connected to the two least significant address bits so that the four registers appear in four consecutive memory addresses. There is also an enable line which in a 6800-based system is usually connected to phase 2 of the CPU clock. As an example, Figure 4.9 shows a very simple address decoding scheme using only the CS and RS inputs of the 6821. The RS inputs are driven by address lines A0 and A1 and select one of four consecutive addresses. The VMA (Valid Memory Address) control line

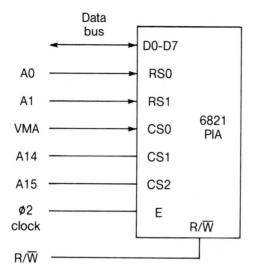

Fig. 4.9 Interfacing the 6821 PIA to a 6800 based CPU system.

from the CPU is used to drive CS0, and the two upper address lines, A14 and A15, drive the other two CS inputs. The CS2 input is inverted so a '0' is needed here together with '1' states on CS0 and CS1 to select the 6821.

Address

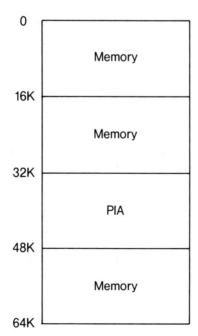

Fig. 4.10 Address map produced by the simple addressing scheme shown in Figure 4.9.

Because the address is only partly decoded the chip will respond to all of the address codes from 32768 to 49151, as shown in the memory map of Figure 4.10. When setting up the memory address selection circuits, or the selection for any other peripheral circuit, these addresses allocated to the 6821 must not be used otherwise two circuits may try to write to the data bus at the same time with the possibility of damage to one or both of the circuit devices.

I/O signal levels

Most of the input and output lines from microprocessors or their associated input–output port devices are designed to interface to Transistor Transistor Logic (TTL). In TTL systems the '0' state is represented by a voltage level between 0 V and +0.5 V whilst the '1' level has a voltage range of perhaps +3 V to +5 V. To drive a single TTL logic input the circuit must be able to sink a current of 1mA in the '0' state without exceeding the +0.5 V output level.

Generally microprocessors will drive just one TTL load but some input–output port devices may be capable of driving more logic circuits. If the output line is required to provide more current, to drive perhaps a relay or a lamp, then an extra output driver circuit must be used which presents one TTL load to the microcomputer system but may produce large amounts of current or power to actuate the relay or other device.

Some single-chip microcomputers have specially designed output circuits which will drive light-emitting diodes or vacuum fluorescent displays. For a light-emitting diode, the output is usually an open collector transistor circuit and the transistor is designed to be able to draw some 10 to 20 mA through its load which will be a light-emitting diode with perhaps a current-limiting resistor in series. The vacuum fluorescent tubes are designed to work with relatively high voltages (10–20 V) so in this case the output transistor is designed to be capable of handling the higher voltages that will be present, whereas the internal circuits of the processor chip will be designed for operation on perhaps +5 V only.

Inputs are usually designed to be TTL compatible and here it is important that if high voltages may be generated by the external circuits then some form of overvoltage protection must be provided at the inputs to prevent damage to the microcomputer chip. Most microprocessors will incorporate some form of protection against static charges but this is not intended to provide protection against excessive signal input voltages.

The Centronics interface

The most popular parallel output interface scheme for use with printers is the one introduced by Centronics for their printer units and this has been adopted by most other printer manufacturers. This interface may also be used on other output peripheral units such as plotters.

Pin	Signal	Direction
1	STROBE	OUT
2	DATA 1	OUT
3	DATA 2	OUT
4	DATA 3	OUT
5	DATA 4	OUT
6	DATA 5	OUT
7	DATA 6	OUT
8	DATA 7	OUT
9	DATA 8	OUT
10	ACK NLG	IN
11	BUSY	IN
19-30	GROUND	–

Note: Pins 12 – 18 and 31 – 36 may be used for control or status lines on some peripheral devices.

Fig. 4.11 Signal connections for a Centronics parallel printer port.

The Centronics interface signals and connections are shown in Figure 4.11. The connector used is a 36-pin Amphenol type 57-30360, or equivalent, which has side contacts rather than pins for the connections. Eight lines are allocated for parallel data and there are two handshake lines. The strobe line is an input to the printer and is used to indicate that data is ready on the data lines. The status line is used to indicate whether the printer has accepted the data or not. The usual mode of operation is that after the computer has sent one byte of data it waits for the ACKNLG signal from the printer before sending the next byte of data.

Centronics interface cables are usually made up using flat ribbon cable and the ground return wires for the data signals are on pins 19 to 30. These lie between the data lines in the flat cable so that they provide some degree of shielding and prevent crosstalk between adjacent data wires in the cable. The data lines and their associated grounds may also be used for twisted pair cable connections if desired.

Most systems use only the signals on pins 1 to 10 which provide a minimal interface scheme. The printer may use pins 11 to 18 and 31 to 36 to carry various command and status signals and the printer manual should be consulted for details of these signals. To avoid possible conflicts the computer output cable may not connect these pins in any way.

The STROBE and ACKNLG signals use inverse logic so they are

normally held in the '1' state. When data has been placed on the lines the STROBE signal is pulsed to the low state for at least 0.5 microseconds. This pulse is used to clock the data into the printer's data register. When the printer has accepted the data it will switch the ACKNLG line from its normal '1' state to '0' for a period of about 5 μs to acknowledge receipt of the data. This ACKNLG pulse also indicates that the printer is ready to accept new data.

All signal levels on this interface are normally compatible with TTL having a '0' level of less than +0.5 V and a '1' level greater than +3 V.

IEEE 488 instrument bus

So far we have looked at I/O ports where individual signal lines may be programmed as inputs or outputs. In typical instrumentation and control activities we are likely to want to interface a number of different instruments to the microcomputer system and with conventional data ports we should need separate I/O channels for each instrument. This can become a cumbersome arrangement with large numbers of connectors and cables tied into the computer unit. Hewlett Packard, who produce a wide range of laboratory instruments, solved this problem by devising a general purpose bus system to which a number of instruments could be attached and which would allow the computer and the instruments to communicate with one another over a common cable system. This scheme was initially introduced as the HP Instrument Bus but has since been adopted as an industry standard under the general title IEEE 488 General Purpose Instrument Bus or GPIB. Many modern laboratory instruments are now fitted with facilities for connection to this type of bus and most popular microcomputer systems can be provided with an interface for the IEEE 488 bus system.

Listeners and talkers
The basic arrangement of a system using the IEEE 488 bus is shown in Figure 4.12. The bus itself consists of eight data lines and eight control lines which we shall look at in more detail in a moment. Each device connected to

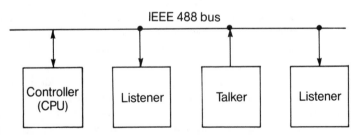

Fig. 4.12 The basic arrangement of the IEEE 488 General Purpose Instrument Bus.

the bus may take up one of three basic roles which are called listener, talker and controller. It is also possible to have a device which although physically connected to the bus system is electrically disabled.

A device when set up as a 'talker' will place data on the bus for transmission to other devices connected to the bus system. To avoid conflicts only one device may act as a talker at any time. When a device acts as a 'listener' it may accept data from the bus. There may be several 'listeners' active on the bus at any time so that a 'talker' may transfer data through the bus to a number of other 'listener' devices.

The operation of the instrument bus system is governed by one device which acts as the 'controller' and there may be only one controller on the system at any time. The controller itself may act as either a 'talker' or as a 'listener' as required. It is possible for the controller to transfer the control function to another device on the bus. In systems where a microcomputer is employed to govern the activities of an instrumentation system, the computer is normally set up to act as the bus controller. Other instruments connected to the bus may, of course, use dedicated microprocessors internally but will usually be configured simply as listeners or talkers as far as the bus is concerned.

The bus system

The IEEE 488 bus system consists of sixteen signal lines plus a number of ground return lines. Eight lines are used as a bidirectional data bus and it is along these lines that data is transferred and that commands are sent to the various devices on the bus. Unlike the bus system in a microprocessor there is no separate address bus. Individual devices connected to the bus are addressed by sending address information over the main data bus itself.

The remaining eight signal lines are used to control the operation of the bus system. Of these, five are used for bus management whilst the other three are used for handshake signals which control the flow of data.

The connector used is of a similar type to that used on a Centronics interface but has only 24 contacts. The pin functions are shown in Figure 4.13.

The management bus

The five bus management signals are ATN, EOI, SRQ, REN and IFC. We shall now examine the action of each of these.

The ATN (Attention) signal is used by the controller to signal to other devices on the bus that it is about to transmit a command on the data bus. This signal is also used in conjunction with the EOI signal to carry out a poll of the status of devices connected to the bus.

The EOI (End Or Identify) signal also has two functions. By itself it is used by a device acting as a 'talker' to signal the end of a block of data. When used together with the ATN signal, however, it causes a parallel poll of the status of the devices on the bus to be initiated. In response to this ATN +

Pin	Signal	Description
1	DIO 1	Data 1
2	DIO 2	Data 2
3	DIO 3	Data 3
4	DIO 4	Data 4
5	EOI	End or identify
6	DAV	Data available
7	NRFD	Not ready for data
8	NDAC	Not data accepted
9	IFC	Interface clear
10	SRQ	Service request
11	ATN	Attention
12	Screen	Ground and screen
13	DIO 5	Data 5
14	DIO 6	Data 6
15	DIO 7	Data 7
16	DIO 8	Data 8
17	REN	Remote enable
18	GND	Logic ground
19	GND	Logic ground
20	GND	Logic ground
21	GND	Logic ground
22	GND	Logic ground
23	GND	Logic ground
24	GND	Logic ground

Fig. 4.13 Connections and signals used on the IEEE 488 bus system.

EOI signal, each device on the bus will return a status bit which indicates whether the device needs service. These individual bits are combined together to form a status word so that eight different devices on the bus can be checked simultaneously. This facility may not be implemented on some instruments but it can provide a fast check on the state of the devices on the bus.

The SRQ (Service Request) signal is generated and placed on the SRQ line by any device which requires servicing by the controller. This is used when a device has data ready for transfer or needs data from the bus. In response to the SRQ signal the controller must be programmed to poll the devices on the bus to see which one requires attention and then to provide the required data transfer operation.

The REN (Remote Enable) line is used by the controller to switch a selected device so that its operation can be controlled from the bus rather than from its own local control panel. This allows such possibilities as switching the range on a multimeter via the bus.

The IFC (Interface Clear) signal is really a form of 'panic button' and when it is activated all devices on the bus are reset to some pre-arranged condition.

The handshake signals

To control the transfer of data, three handshake signals NRFD, NDAC and DAV are used.

The NRFD (Not Ready For Data) is used by listener devices as a form of busy signal to the controller. Data will not be placed on the bus until all of the listeners have set their NRFD outputs to 'false'. The line is wired OR, so that any one device can effectively hold the NRFD line 'true' until it is ready to accept data from the bus.

The DAV (Data Available) line is used by a talker to indicate that it has placed data on the bus ready for listeners to accept it. This line will not become true until after the NRFD line has become false.

The NDAC (Not Data Accepted) signal is used by a listener to indicate that it is in the process of dealing with data that has been presented on the bus. This line ensures that the data will remain on the bus until all of the listeners have accepted it. It might be thought that this function could be handled by using the NRFD control line but the use of a separate control signal caters for those devices which may have accepted data from the bus but have to process it in some way before new data can be handled.

Command mode operation

When the controller places the ATN line in the true state this indicates that it is about to place command codes on the data bus. These codes are used to control the operation of devices on the bus and select the mode and types of data transfer that will take place.

Each device connected to the bus may be assigned a unique 5-bit binary address in the range 0 to 30. This is normally done in the remote instrument by pre-set switches. It is important to ensure that no two devices have the same address. The actual address codes sent by the controller have hexadecimal values in the range 20 to 7E since bits 5 and 6 of the command are used to indicate whether the device is to talk or listen, or if the address is a secondary address.

When the controller wishes to set devices up as listeners it asserts the ATN status line and then outputs a sequence of binary numbers corresponding to the addresses of the devices to be activated. If the remote unit is to act as a listener, address bits 5 and 6 are set to 1 and 0 respectively. If the selected device is to act as a talker, bits 5 and 6 of the code would be set at 0 and 1, as shown in Figure 4.14. If bits 5 and 6 are both at 1 the address bits are treated as a secondary address. There is no rigid format for secondary address codes and individual manufacturers may use these addresses in different ways, so the appropriate equipment manual must be consulted for details.

When bits 5 and 6 are both set at 0 this indicates that the data being sent is a command. Some of the commands used and their corresponding hexadecimal codes are shown in Figure 4.15. When bit 4 of the command code is set at 1 (i.e. the first hexadecimal digit = 1) the command is a universal one to which all of the devices on the bus will respond

Bit 7	Bit 0	
0000CCCC		Addressed command
0001CCCC		Universal command
001AAAAA		Address to listen
010AAAAA		Address to talk
011AAAAA		Secondary address

A = address bit
C = command bit

Fig. 4.14 Format of the control commands sent along the GPIB when the controller sets ATN to true.

immediately. The other commands are preceded by a string of device addresses and will only affect those devices listed in the address string.

The listen address 31 (hex code 3F) is used as an UNLISTEN command and tells all devices on the bus to stop acting as listeners. Similarly, the talk address 32 (hex code 5F) acts as an UNTALK command which tells the device currently set as a talker to stop acting as a talker. Two other command codes are hex 60 and hex 70 which disable and enable the parallel poll facility.

When all of the devices on the bus have accepted the command code or address data, the ATN signal reverts to false and any signals placed on the bus are then treated as data and will be accepted by all devices that have been set up as listeners.

The SPE command starts a serial poll operation, whilst SPD is used to terminate the polling action. SDC returns an addressed device to its factory set condition, whilst DCL does this to all devices on the bus simultaneously.

0	0	0	1	0	1	0	0	Device clear (DCL)
0	0	0	0	1	0	0	0	Group execute trigger (GET)
0	0	0	0	0	0	0	1	Go to local (GTL)
0	0	0	1	0	0	0	1	Local lockout (LLO)
0	0	0	0	0	1	0	1	Parallel poll configure (PPC)
0	1	1	1	0	0	0	0	Parallel poll disable (PPD)
0	1	1	0	0	0	0	0	Parallel poll enable (PPE)
0	0	0	1	0	1	0	1	Parallel poll unconfigure (PPU)
0	0	0	1	1	0	0	1	Serial poll disable (SPD)
0	0	0	1	1	0	0	0	Serial poll enable (SPE)
0	0	0	0	0	1	0	0	Select device clear (SDC)

Fig. 4.15 Some of the command codes used on the IEEE 488 bus system.

LLO disables the front panel controls of a selected device, whilst GTL returns a device to local control. The GET command allows a series of devices to be told to take a reading simultaneously.

Typical bus operation

Let us suppose that the computer has the device address 1 and that device number 5 has some data ready to be transferred. The sequence of commands and bus signals would be as shown in Figure 4.16. Here the handshake signals are not shown but the handshake operation will occur for every byte of data or command that is passed over the bus.

Data bus	Management bus
—	SRQ (from device 5)
SPE	ATN + SRQ
Talk address 5	ATN + SRQ
UNLISTEN	ATN + SRQ
MLA	ATN + SRQ
Status byte 5	SRQ
SPD	ATN + SRQ
Talk address 5	ATN + SRQ
UNLISTEN	ATN + SRQ
MLA	ATN + SRQ
Data byte	SRQ
Data byte	SRQ
—	EOI

Fig. 4.16 Typical command and data sequence on an IEEE 488 bus system.

The first step is that device 5 will pull down the SRQ bus line to signal that it needs attention. In response the computer sets ATN to 'true'. This tells all devices on the bus that commands are now being sent. The computer then sends the SPE (Serial Poll Enable) command followed by a command to address device 5 as a talker. This will in fact be the hexadecimal data word $45. The next command is an UNLISTEN, which turns off all listeners, followed by MLA (My Listen Address) which sets the controller (the computer in this case) into the listen mode. The ATN signal is then made false and device 5 sends a single status byte to the computer. The computer then sets ATN again and sends the SPD (Serial Poll Disable) command to terminate the serial polling sequence.

At this point the computer can examine the status byte to see what action is required. In this case the device wants to send some data, so the computer sets ATN to 'true' and once again addresses device 5 to act as a talker. The UNLISTEN command and MLA are sent to turn off the other listeners and set the computer as a listener. ATN is then set to 'false' so that device 5 can send a number of bytes of data followed by a carriage return code, or alternatively by an EOI signal on the management bus. The data transmitted over the bus is accepted by the computer and may then be processed as desired.

When data is to be accepted by more than one device the listen addresses of all of the devices concerned are sent one after another before ATN is set 'false' and the talker places the string of data bytes on the bus.

Data coding

Although the IEEE 488 interface specification does not actually lay down any standard for the coding of data, it is usual to adopt ASCII character codes. This is the convention used in the original HP instrument bus system upon which the IEEE 488 standard is based.

Data is sent in the normal left to right sequence so the decimal number 832 would be transmitted as three hexadecimal character codes in sequence as follows:

38 ('8'), 33 ('3'), 32 ('2')

and this might be followed by a carriage return code (hex 13). There may also be a line feed code (hex 10) sent as well, instead of using the EOI management line to indicate the end of message.

Because the data coding uses the ASCII code the messages transmitted over the bus may include text information. Thus information regarding the measurement units (e.g. millivolts or degrees Celsius) may be sent from one instrument to another. This is important since devices on the bus may include printers or plotters which need this information in order to annotate tables of results or graphs. Some instruments may also require alphanumeric messages as commands for setting up their operating modes or conditions.

The handbook of the piece of equipment connected to the bus will need to be consulted to discover the format of commands that have to be sent to the instrument. The format of the data returned by the instrument will also be given in its handbook and the computer will need to be programmed to handle the data in that format.

Signal levels and connections

The IEEE 488 bus uses voltage signals which are the inverse of the normal TTL-type signal levels and all of the data and control lines use a wired OR configuration.

A voltage level of 0 V is used to indicate a 'true' logic state and a voltage level of +5 V indicates a 'false' logic condition. When a device has its output in the 'false' state it is effectively disconnected from the bus and has no effect on any other device output. When the bus is pulled low to indicate a 'true' state, any number of devices may place a 'true' signal on a line with no conflict. To maintain switching speed the output circuits will usually have

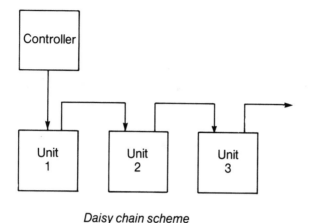

Daisy chain scheme

Star bus scheme

Fig. 4.17 Daisy chain and star configurations for the connection of instruments to the GPIB.

some form of 'pull up' resistor, and the number of devices actually connected to the bus at any one time will usually be limited to 15 although 30 different devices may be addressed. In most systems the effective address of a device will change according to whether it is acting as a listener or as a talker.

Because the output drive capability of the signal lines is limited, the length of cable that can be used between devices is also limited. Generally the length of cable to any device will be limited to about 20 metres divided by the number of devices connected. Typical interconnection cables are likely to be of the order of two metres in length.

The system may be configured in two different ways. The most popular is the 'daisy chain' scheme shown in Figure 4.17. Here the main bus loops through each device on the system. The alternative arrangement is a 'star' connection in which the connectors for the cables to all of the remote devices are stacked at the controller device and then run out to each individual unit on the bus. Most IEEE 488 connectors are designed to facilitate this stacking by having a socket mounted piggy-back on the plug at the end of the device cable. The plugs for the other devices are then stacked on top of one another but this can produce a rather unwieldy arrangement.

For data transmission over longer distances than the normal cable length limitation it is possible to use 'repeater' devices but these tend to be rather expensive and are not often used.

Applications for parallel I/O ports

In general the parallel port scheme is obviously well suited for communications with other devices which have data in parallel format. A hardware multiplier for instance might be driven by two 8-bit output ports which feed the multiplier with the two numbers it is to multiply whilst the output of the multiplier is fed back into the computer via an 8-bit input port. Digital shaft encoders usually have a parallel coded output which indicates the amount of shaft rotation relative to some reference position. A point to watch with these devices is that most of them use special cyclic codes intended to reduce errors and these will need to be converted into pure binary number form once they are in the computer.

Parallel ports can readily be used to decode a simple keypad using a scheme similar to that shown in Figure 4.18. Here one port provides output lines to each of the columns of the keyboard switch matrix. If these lines are set to '1' in turn, easily achieved by shifting a single bit through the data word that is being output, then the columns are selected in sequence. The output from the row lines of the keyboard can now be read in as each column is selected. If a switch in the column is made its row output will be at '1'. By examining the bit pattern received from the row lines the particular switch or key that has been activated can be determined. If two keys in one column are pressed they will set different bits in the row word and can therefore be identified. As each switch is identified as being pressed, its corresponding character code may be pushed to a data stack. In a conventional text input keyboard scheme, the key codes are entered until the code for carriage return is detected when the stack is processed and the data transferred into memory or the command that it represents is obeyed. If the keys are to represent perhaps specific actions to be carried out by the computer system then the detection of the key press can be made to call an appropriate subroutine to perform the function allocated to that key.

Parallel ports can also be used to drive displays of various kinds. An indicator lamp can of course be controlled by a single output line so an eight-

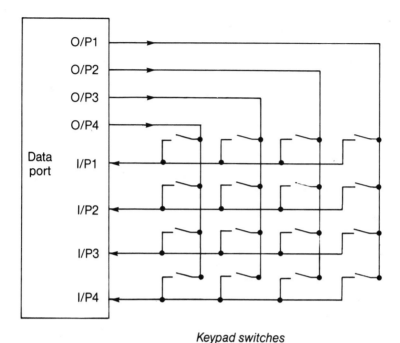

Keypad switches

Fig. 4.18 Simple scheme for interfacing a keyboard to the CPU bus using a parallel programmable port.

way port can control up to eight separate lamps. An OR mask is used to turn on an individual lamp with a '1' set in the mask at the bit corresponding to the lamp being controlled and all other bits of the mask word set at '0'. To turn off the lamp an AND mask is used with the lamp bit set at '0' and all other bits at '1'. Solenoids and relays may be driven in a similar way. Usually some form of driver circuit will be needed to drive the lamp or solenoid since the port output is generally limited to driving one or two TTL logic loads.

Seven-segment displays can also be driven by parallel ports with one set of lines providing the segment pattern and another set used to select the particular digit of the display that is activated. In practice it is usually more convenient to use say an 8-bit port to output two BCD digit codes and use external logic to actually drive the display device.

Chapter Five
Serial Input-Output

So far we have looked at input–output ports where all of the data bits are transferred across the port simultaneously with a separate signal wire for each data bit. Although the operation of such data ports is easy to understand and program, one of the disadvantages of the parallel data transfer scheme is that it requires a relatively large number of interconnecting wires. If we consider a simple 8-bit parallel data port there will be eight data wires, a common ground line and one or two wires for handshake signals.

If the data is to be transmitted over a long cable it is best to use a separate ground return wire for each data line to reduce the possibility of crosstalk between adjacent data lines in the cable. Cables with multiple cores suitable for such a system become expensive and bulky. The capacitance and inductance of a long cable can also present problems so that special line drivers and receivers may be needed for each signal line which increases the cost of the system.

In some applications the number of input–output connections that can be used may be governed by space limitations or the need to have a thin flexible cable linking the computer to its peripheral device. Where part of the data path involves the use of a radio transmission link, a separate channel would be required for each data bit. Any alternative transmission scheme which uses fewer interconnections will obviously be more attractive for use in these situations.

Serial input-output

As an alternative to the simultaneous parallel data transfer we can arrange to transmit the data along a single wire by sending the individual data bits one after another along the same wire. The signal transmitted along the wire is a sequence of pulses, each representing the state of one data bit, as shown in Figure 5.1. This scheme is called serial data transmission and it requires only one data wire, and a common ground return wire.

A serial data output signal can readily be produced by using a shift

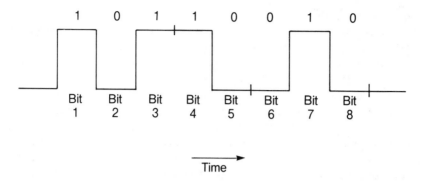

Fig. 5.1 Simple serial data signal format with bits following one another in sequence.

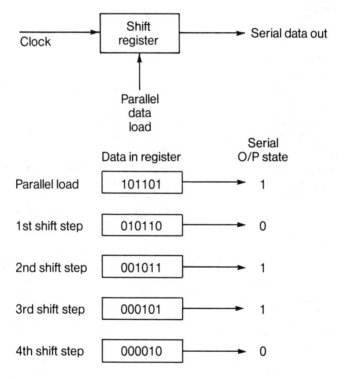

Fig. 5.2 Use of a shift register to convert data from the parallel format into a serial data stream.

register as shown in Figure 5.2. Here the state of the right-hand (least significant) bit of the register is used to drive the input–output line through an output driver stage. The data to be transmitted is loaded in parallel into the shift register. At this point the state of the LS bit appears on the output line. The shift register is then switched to its shift operation mode and, after a fixed time period, the data is shifted to the right to bring the state of the next bit on to the output line. This shift process continues at fixed time intervals and as each bit reaches the right-hand end of the register it produces a corresponding '1' or '0' state on the output line. The length of each bit period in the transmitted data is governed by the timing of the clock pulses applied to the shift register.

Serial data input can be handled by a similar shifting technique. In this case the input data signal is fed into the left-hand end of the shift register. When the first data bit is presented on the input line, a clock pulse is applied to the register and the data is transferred into the left-hand (most significant) bit position of the register. As successive data bits arrive at the input further clock pulses are applied and the data pattern moves to the right through the register. After the last bit of the word has been shifted into the MS bit of the register the complete word will be held in the shift register. At this point the complete word may be transferred in parallel to CPU.

Data synchronisation

If the received data is to be decoded correctly it is important that the clock pulses are applied to the shift register when the successive data bit states are presented on the input line. This presents a problem because the receiving system does not know when a data bit is due to arrive, since this is governed by a clock at the remote end of the line. One obvious solution to this problem is to use another wire to carry the timing clock signals so that the receiving shift register can be kept in step with the data. For optimum results the clock signal would be arranged so that its transitions occurred half-way through each bit period of the data signal. This ensures that the input data state is stable when the clock pulse shifts the data pattern through the register. This arrangement requires a three-wire link cable with one wire for data, a second for the clock pulses, and a common return. A serial input–output scheme of this type can readily be implemented in a microcomputer system by using just three lines of a parallel input–output port. For a two-way serial communications link, two further wires will be needed for the return data and clock signals as shown in Figure 5.3.

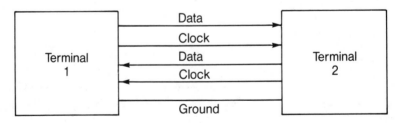

Fig. 5.3 Basic arrangement of a two-way serial data link with separate wires for the data and clock signals.

Some early types of microprocessor, such as the National INS8060 (SC/MP), used a simple serial output scheme along these lines. Here the data was loaded into the accumulator and the carry bit was connected to the output line as a serial data output. A clock pulse derived from the processor clock was then fed out on a separate line. When data was to be transmitted, the byte in the accumulator was shifted eight times to the right and a stream of eight clock pulses was sent along the associated clock line. Assuming that another similar processor were used at the other end of the line, this remote CPU would detect the clock pulses and for each one would shift the data right into the accumulator. After the eighth pulse the transmitted data would be stacked in the accumulator of the receiving CPU and might then be processed or stored as required.

Synchronisation of the operation of the circuits at each end of the data link is very important in any serial data transfer system since, if the data at the remote end is not shifted in sympathy with the transmitted data, the numerical value of the information will be in error. Although the transmission of separate clock and data signals works quite well, it would be better if the data and clock signals could be combined in some way so that the entire signal could be sent over one pair of wires. This is in fact possible and there are two basic techniques which may be employed. These differ in the method used to ensure proper synchronisation between the sending and receiving systems.

If we consider the serial input operation, it is important that the clock pulses which insert the data bit into the shift register, or accumulator, must be synchronised with the incoming bit data and should occur when the input data is stable. The timing circuits of the devices at each end of the line, however, will usually have independent clocks so some form of synchronising signal needs to be sent as well as the data.

Asynchronous serial transmission

The simplest and oldest of the serial data schemes is known as asynchronous transmission and works by sending marker signals at the beginning and end of each data word. This scheme was originally developed for use in teleprinter systems where the data was initially input via a typewriter-style keyboard. The typing rates of different operators can differ widely. As a result the character codes may be sent at irregular intervals as the operator pauses between words or searches for a particular letter on the keyboard. The transmission system was therefore designed to handle irregular timing of the data and uses a synchronisation system which deals with each data word as a separate message or packet of information. The basic system of coding used is shown in Figure 5.4 and this method of transmission is called 'asynchronous'.

When no data is being transmitted the signal line is held at the '1' level. In

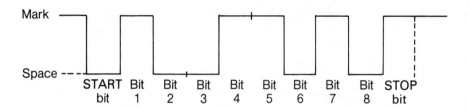

Fig. 5.4 The format of an asynchronous serial signal.

data transmission terminology the '1' state is generally referred to as a 'mark' whilst the '0' state is called a 'space'. By using a mark level rather than space for the resting condition it is possible to detect a failure in the transmission link which would produce a continuous space condition on the line. When a data word is to be transmitted the data signal changes to the 'space' level for one time period. This forms a 'START' pulse which tells the remote unit that a data word is about to be transmitted. The following seven or eight time periods are used to transmit the states of the individual data bits one after another starting with the least significant bit. At the end of the transmission the signal is restored to the 'mark' level for at least one time period to form a 'STOP' bit. The function of this STOP bit is to act as a separator between successive data words when the signals are being transmitted in a continuous stream. After the STOP bit has been sent the signal remains at the mark level until a new word is transmitted. Thus, after each word the receiving end unit will always be waiting for a new START bit to indicate the start of a new data word.

The time period allocated to each data bit is made constant and determines the rate at which data words can be transmitted. For proper operation of the system the timing of the circuits at each end of the data link must be kept in step. Whilst this could be done by sending a timing clock signal on a separate wire, it is usual to have just the data signal and to carry out synchronisation between the two systems at each data word. The receiving clock can be brought into step with the transmitting clock when the leading edge of the START pulse is detected. For proper decoding this receive clock must remain in step for the next 8 to 10 time periods.

To allow the maximum latitude in the receive clock frequency, the timing is arranged so that the first receive clock pulse occurs roughly half-way through the time period of the START pulse. Now successive clock pulses will occur half-way through each bit period where the data state for the bit is stable. If the receive clock is not exactly synchronised the later clock pulses will occur earlier or later than the centre of the bit period. If there are 8 data bits and we allow the clock position to drift by a quarter of a bit period on the 8th bit position, then the clock frequency must be within $\pm 0.25/8$ (or approximately $\pm 3\%$) of the data clock frequency. This can be achieved by using a well designed free-running oscillator, but for most systems a quartz crystal controlled oscillator is used. The drift between the two clocks is not cumulative with time since the receive clock is pulled into step at the start of each new data word.

In most systems a frequency division scheme similar to that shown in Figure 5.5 is used to synchronise the receive clock. Typically the clock oscillator runs at 16 times the actual bit rate and is fed to a divide-by-16

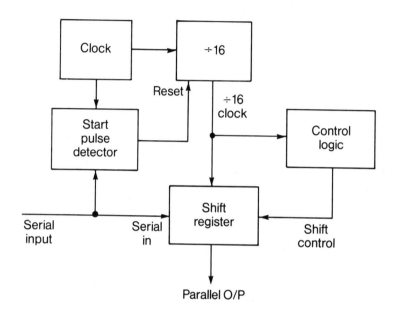

Fig. 5.5 Use of a 16-bit frequency divider to provide a synchronised clock for the serial-to-parallel conversion register.

counter whose output produces the actual clock used to input and shift the data. To detect the START pulse the incoming data is shifted through a short shift register using the fast clock, and the states of two adjacent stages are gated to detect the 1 to 0 transition at the leading edge of the START pulse. When this edge is detected the divide-by-16 counter is reset thus pulling the actual decoding clock into step with the data. The shift clock used to decode the incoming data is generated at the 8th count of the counter so that it always occurs roughly at the middle of each bit period of the incoming data. In some systems the counter is held in a reset state until the START pulse is detected. After the START pulse a complete word decoding sequence is executed and then the counter returns to the reset waiting state ready for the next data word.

Handshake signals

As in the parallel data interface it is usual to provide some handshake signals between the devices at the two ends of the transmission link. Four signals are commonly used for this purpose.

The transmitting device generates an output signal called RTS (Request To Send) when it has some data ready for transmission whilst the device at the receiving end will send back a status signal CTS (Clear To Send) to indicate that it is ready to accept data.

The unit acting as the data terminal, which is generally the computer, generates a further output signal called DTR (Data Terminal Ready) to indicate that it is operational and an input signal called DSR (Data Set Ready) indicates that the remote unit is also ready.

If the handshake signals are not connected the link will not normally work but this can be overcome by linking RTS to CTS and DTR to DSR locally at each end of the line.

Baud rate

The speed of data transmission along any serial communications link is governed by the length of the time period allocated to each data bit in the serial stream. This is usually expressed in a unit called the baud. In a binary data link the baud rate becomes simply the number of data bits sent per second. This measurement is based upon the time period of a data bit during the transmission of a message and not the overall rate at which data is sent.

Remember that on an asynchronous link there will be intervals between successive data words where no information is conveyed at all and, of course, the valid data represents only part of the complete bit pattern. The usual range of data rates found in practice includes 120, 300, 600, 1200, 2400, 4800 and 9600 baud, but some systems go as high as 19200 baud or more, especially when the synchronous mode of transmission is used. The most common rates used on data terminals are 300, 1200 and 4800 baud.

The UART

Although it is possible to program a microprocessor to produce and decode the signals for an asynchronous serial data link using two lines of a parallel data port for input and output, there are available a number of devices specially designed to perform this task. The general name for these devices is Universal Asynchronous Receiver Transmitter or UART.

A typical UART has an internal arrangement similar to that shown in Figure 5.6. There are shift registers for generating the serial output from a parallel input and for converting the received serial data into parallel form. Most of these devices use a buffered data system in which an extra register is included in the transmit and receive sections. When a data word is to be set it first goes to the buffer register. If the transmit register is empty, the word is

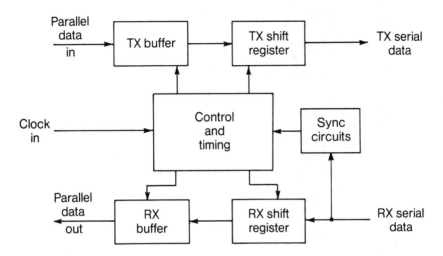

Fig. 5.6 Simplified block diagram for a Universal Asynchronous Receiver Transmitter (UART).

loaded into it and the conversion to serial starts. Whilst the word is being sent a new data word can be loaded into the buffer. A similar buffering action is used for received data.

The UART also includes the clock generation and control logic to produce the serial data format with START and STOP pulses, and to handle the synchronisation and decoding of the received data. Most UARTs are programmable so that they can handle various coding formats with numbers of data bits ranging from five to eight. Some UARTs, such as the Intersil IM6402 are general purpose devices with separate sets of pins for the parallel input and output data. Most microprocessor device families include some form of UART chip specifically designed for use with the microprocessor. Examples of these are the 6850 which matches the 6800 series CPUs, and the 8550 which is designed to work with the 8080 and 8085 type processors.

The 6850 ACIA

As an example of the microprocessor-compatible devices let us take a look at the MC6850 ACIA (Asynchronous Communications Interface Adapter). The internal organisation of this device is shown in simplified form in Figure 5.7. Four of the internal registers can be directly accessed by the computer. These are the transmit and receive buffer registers and the status and control registers. Unlike the 6821 parallel port, the ACIA has separate status and control registers since the functions of the bits in these two registers are different.

The addressable registers are selected by a single register select RS control

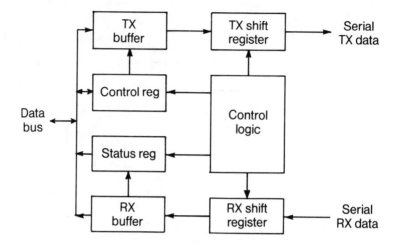

Fig. 5.7 Simplified block diagram of the 6850 Asynchronous Communications Interface Adapter (ACIA).

line. When this is set at '1' either the transmit or receive buffer register is connected to the data bus. Selection between these registers is governed by the state of the read/write control signal from the CPU. When this control line is set to write the transmit buffer register is selected, whilst a read state selects the receive buffer register. If the RS line is set at '0' the control and status registers are selected, with control connected to the bus by a write operation and the status register activated by a read command.

Figure 5.8 shows the allocation of the bits in the control register. Bits 0 and 1 allow the clock operation to be set up. The options are either to use the input clock directly or to use a divide-by-16 or a divide-by-64 option on the clock. When both of these bits are set at '1' a master reset operation is performed. This chip does not have an input signal pin for the reset operation so at the start of any program it is essential that the 6850 is initialised by sending a master reset command to the control register.

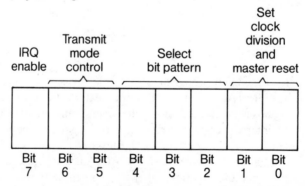

Fig. 5.8 Allocation of bits and their functions in the control register of a 6850 ACIA.

Control bits 2, 3 and 4 of the control register allow eight different options for the serial data format to be selected. These allow the possibility of seven or eight data bits with either one or two STOP bits, and the operation of the parity bit may also be defined. Bits 5 and 6 control the operation of the RTS output signal and the IRQ output in the transmit mode. Finally bit 7 controls the IRQ output in the receive mode.

The status register provides a set of flag bits which indicate the current condition of the ACIA as shown in Figure 5.9. Bit 0 indicates that a data word has been received and is ready for transfer to the CPU. Bit 1 indicates that the transmitter section is ready to accept a new data word for transmission. Bits 2 and 3 indicate fault conditions on the DCD and CTS control inputs. Bit 4 indicates a framing error where the data has been incorrectly decoded, whilst bit 5 indicates that a new word has been received

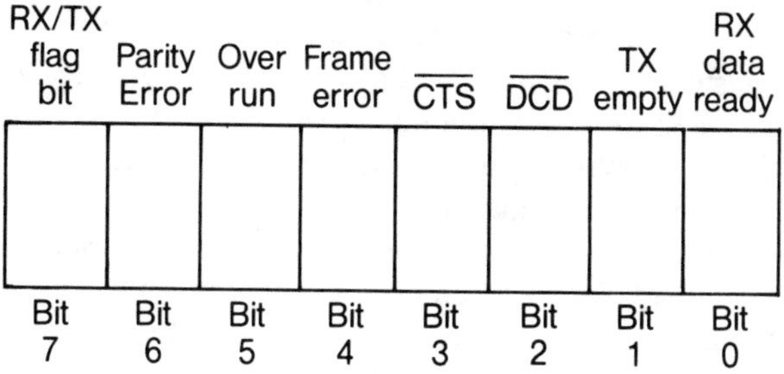

RX/TX flag bit	Parity Error	Over run	Frame error	$\overline{CTS}$	$\overline{DCD}$	TX empty	RX data ready
Bit 7	Bit 6	Bit 5	Bit 4	Bit 3	Bit 2	Bit 1	Bit 0

Fig. 5.9 The status register of the 6850 ACIA.

before the last one was read out of the buffer so that a data word has been lost. Bit 6 indicates a parity error in the received data and bit 7 is used to indicate the state of the IRQ output line.

Once the 6850 has been initialised and the control register set to select the desired operating mode, the transmission of a byte of data is quite straightforward and might use the following sequence of instructions:

```
LOOP    LDAB    CSREG
        LSRB
        LSRB
        BCC     LOOP
        STAA    DREG
        RTS
```

Here the instructions are written as a subroutine and it is assumed that the data word to be transmitted has already been loaded into the A accumulator just before the subroutine is called. The status is read into the B accumulator and then right-shifted twice to place the transmitter status bit into the carry flag, which is then tested, and the program loops until the transmitter is ready to accept a new word. Finally the data is written into the transmit buffer register and this will clear the transmit status bit to show that the buffer is full. The 6850 will automatically produce the required serial output.

In the receive mode, when a data word has been received, the flag bit in the status register is set and the data may be read in from the receive buffer register. The routine for a 6800 CPU will be similar to the following:

```
LOOP   LDAB   CSREG
       LSRB
       BCC    LOOP
       LDAA   DREG
       RTS
```

Here, only one right shift is used to bring the receive status bit into the carry position for testing, and the program loops until the receive flag is set to indicate that a data word has been received. When the receive flag is set, the word is read in from the data register and this automatically clears the receive flag bit. An important point to note here is that if the current data in the receive register is not read before the next data word is received then the new word may be lost since it will not be transferred to the receive buffer. When the subroutine returns to the main program, the received data word will be held in the A accumulator.

In both receive and transmit routines other tests may be included to check or set up the state of the communications link control lines such as RTS, CTS, DCD and so on. For other processors, or different serial interface devices, the program procedures will follow similar lines.

Interfacing the 6850

As far as the microprocessor is concerned, the 6850 appears as a consecutive pair of locations in the memory map. Eight data lines are brought out from the 6850 and these connect directly to the CPU data bus. These are tri-state lines which are activated only when the 6850 is selected by its address inputs. Three chip select lines, CS0, CS1 and CS2, are provided to allow partial address decoding for selecting the chip. CS2 requires a '0' input and the other two CS lines must be at '1' to select the chip. The RS line is normally driven by the least significant address line A0. There is also an enable input which will usually be driven by phase 2 of the CPU clock. Setting up an address decoding scheme follows the same general principles as are used for the 6821 PIA. Figure 5.10 shows a simple address coding arrangement which places the 6850 at addresses 16384 and 16385. The device will however respond to other addresses in the next 16 kilobytes of the memory.

The transmit and receive clock signals used for encoding and decoding the serial data are fed in on separate pins. These may be generated by a special clock generator circuit or they may be derived by simply dividing the frequency of the CPU clock using an external counter chain. It is important that the data rates selected by the transmit and receive clocks on the 6850 match up with the data rates produced by the device at the other end of the serial data lines.

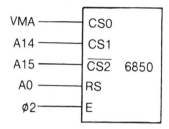

Fig. 5.10 Simple addressing scheme for interfacing a 6850 ACIA to a 6800 CPU system.

Line drivers and modems

If conventional TTL logic devices are used to provide the serial output signal to the transmission line then the distance over which the signals can be reliably transmitted will be limited to perhaps a few metres. If longer lines are used the logic signal at the receiving end is likely to be so badly distorted that errors will be produced in the received data.

To transmit signals over a longer distance, special line driver devices are normally used. Many systems use the 1488 line driver at the transmitting end and the 1489 line receiver at the receiving end of the line. This type of system is generally capable of sending data successfully over distances of perhaps a few tens of metres. For longer distances a more powerful line driver circuit may be used and it then becomes possible to transmit data over perhaps a kilometre or more. By using special coaxial cables this type of link may be extended even further but the cost of the cables becomes very high.

For long distance communication it is convenient to use an ordinary telephone line which is generally a twisted pair cable. The telephone circuits are primarily designed to carry audio frequency signals and will usually distort the sharp-edged square pulses used in data transmission. As a result the data signals become difficult to read at the receiving end and errors result.

One solution to this problem is to convert the digital signal into audio frequency tones which the telephone line can handle. Thus the '1' level might be represented by a 2400 hertz tone and the '0' level by a 1200 hertz tone. For reliable operation we might allow a minimum of three cycles of audio tone in a bit period. Thus a '0' bit might consist of three cycles of 1200 hertz tone and a '1' bit would be represented by six cycles of 2400 hertz tone as shown in Figure 5.11. This limits the transmission rate to perhaps 300 bits per second.

The conversion from data signals to audio tones is carried out by a 'modulator'. When the audio tone signal is received at the far end of the line it is fed to a 'demodulator' circuit which converts the tones back into digital logic level signals again. Since most data links are two-way circuits there will in fact be a modulator and a demodulator at each end of the link and two transmission line paths would be used as shown in Figure 5.12. The

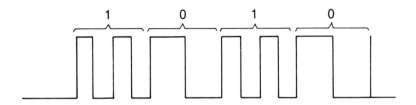

Fig. 5.11 Modulated tone signals used to transmit serial data over long distance via the normal telephone network.

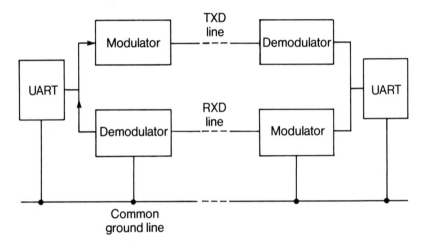

Fig. 5.12 Typical serial link using modems at each end of the line.

combined unit at each end of the link is called a 'modem' and the audio tones used to convey the data are usually called the carrier signal.

A link using modems and a telephone line can be used to transmit data over thousands of kilometres. The signals may also be sent via radio links which may include links through space satellites.

The RS232 interface

Although it would be perfectly permissible to adopt any convenient interconnection scheme for a serial data channel used in a dedicated system, there is in fact a standard for the interconnections for serial data transmission. This is generally known as the RS232C interface and was originally laid down by the EIA in the United States. The equivalent international standard is ISO V24 which is generally compatible with the RS232C version.

The RS232C standard lays down the signal levels, the signal functions and the connector details. A 25-way D-type connector is used at each end of the link and the basic signal connections are as shown in Figure 5.13. In a

Pin	Signal	Description	IN/OUT
1	GND	Screen + power ground	–
2	TXD	Transmitted data	OUT
3	RXD	Received data	IN
4	RTS	Request to send	OUT
5	CTS	Clear to send	IN
6	DSR	Data set ready	IN
7	GND	Signal ground	–
8	DCD	Data carrier detect	IN
20	DTR	Data terminal ready	OUT

Fig. 5.13 Pin connections and signals used on an RS232C serial transmission link.

practical system it is common to find that only a few of the signals are actually used.

The connections given here are for a unit which is configured as DTE (Data Terminal Equipment) and in most systems this will be the computer itself, and the fixed connector on the unit will be a socket. The unit at the far end of the line is usually configured as DCE (Data Communications Equipment) and is fitted with a fixed plug. In a DCE unit the functions of pins 2 and 3 are transposed so that data is sent on pin 3 and received on pin 2. The functions of some of the control signals will also be changed. One problem here is that some pieces of equipment that are to be connected to the computer may be configured as DTE units and in order to achieve correct operation some cross connections will have to be made in the interconnection cable. When interfacing any unit with a serial interface to the computer it is important to check the user's manual to ensure that the correct signals are linked together through the interface.

The signal levels used by the RS232C interface are not the normal logic levels but generally use +12 V for 'mark' and −12 V for 'space'. Some equipment will operate successfully with signal levels as low as +3 V and −3 V. The translation between logic level signals and the required line signals can be carried out by using interface chips such as the 1488 for TTL to RS232 and the 1489 for RS232 to TTL.

The data is sent along the TXD line and received on the RXD line. The RTS (Ready To Send) and CTS (Clear To Send) lines may be used to provide a simple handshake facility. The DTR (Data Terminal Ready) and DSR (Data Set Ready) may also be used in the handshake process if desired. DCD (Data Carrier Detect) is normally used only when the data communications equipment is a modem since the DCD line checks that a tone is being received and indicates that the line from the modem to the remote terminal is actually working.

In many systems only the TXD, RXD and signal ground are used. At each end of the line the RTS and CTS pins are linked together and the DSR and DTR pins may also be linked so that the DTE and DCE units are both permanently ready to send or receive data.

Although the RS232C interface is perhaps the most commonly used serial interface scheme there are alternative schemes which provide better performance without the need to use modems. Two of these are known as RS422 and RS423 and the main difference between them and the RS232 is the way in which the data signals are handled. In the RS232 system the data signal is measured relative to a common ground line and for proper operation the received signal needs to change by at least 1.5 V when switching between the 0 and 1 levels. If the cables run through an electrically noisy area the signal line will usually pick up some noise in the form of spikes and perhaps low frequency components from mains power cables. As the line becomes longer the differential between the 1 and 0 levels is reduced and eventually the noise may introduce false logic states at the receiver end.

One solution to the noise problem is to use a pair of wires to carry the data signal in each direction. The two wires are balanced electrically relative to the ground level and driven in anti-phase so that when one wire is at the $+12$ V level the other is at -12 V and vice-versa. The data signal is represented by the difference in voltage between the signal levels on the two wires. Any noise picked up on the line relative to ground potential will affect both signal wires equally and is effectively cancelled out. At the receiving end the data wires feed the inputs of a differential amplifier whose output responds only to the difference between its two inputs. As a result the amplifier responds to the desired data signal but rejects the interference which is common to both inputs.

In both the RS422 and RS423 schemes a differential signal on a pair of data wires is used for both the RXD and TXD signal link. The differential between the wires needed to switch from one state to the other is typically about 100 mV minimum. In the RS423 scheme the signal levels on the wires are balanced relative to the ground potential. In the RS422 scheme only the differential between the two wires is of importance so that both wires may be biased above ground level if desired.

One advantage of the differential signal scheme is that signals can be sent over much longer distances, typically some 2000 metres, before noise and signal distortion become important. Another advantage is that much higher data rates may be used than would be possible with a single ended transmission system. Typically the RS423 system allows data rates up to 100 kilobits per second whilst the RS422 is even better with rates up to 1 million bits per second.

The hardware difference between the transmission schemes is primarily in the line drivers and receivers used at each end of the transmission line. The actual UART used may be identical to that in an RS232 scheme but with a faster clock signal. The line itself usually consists of a screened, twisted pair cable or alternatively two twisted pairs with a common outer screen if both the RXD and TXD are to be in one cable. The handshake lines may be the same as for an RS232 system and since these are usually relatively low frequency signals they may be fed via a normal screened multicore cable.

Usually, separate signal paths are provided for the TXD and RXD signals so that data can be sent in both directions at the same time. This is known as a 'full duplex' system. It is possible however to operate with just one signal path so that the TXD and RXD share the same pair of wires. Now transmission is possible only in one direction at a time and this mode is called 'half duplex'. In this type of system the RTS and CTS handshake signals are used to control which unit is allowed to transmit at any time and hence govern the direction of data flow.

In some systems, where the microcomputer or terminal devices operate on a network or serial bus scheme, a half duplex arrangement may be used and the system is organised in a similar fashion to the IEEE 488 bus where only one device may transmit at any time but all other devices may receive data. Unlike the IEEE 488 scheme there is no management bus so the operation of the system is governed by control codes sent as part of the data signal. The line drivers in such systems use either tri-state logic or a wired-OR output to avoid contention between two devices which try to drive the line simultaneously.

Synchronous operation

One of the disadvantages of the asynchronous mode of transmission is that for each data word transmitted there are two or three bit time periods occupied by the START and STOP bits which convey no useful data. Thus, even with transmissions where there are no gaps between successive words, only about 70% of the available time is used to convey data. This situation can be improved by using an alternative scheme for synchronising the operation of the circuits at each end of the transmission path.

If the data can be sent as a continuous block of perhaps 256 data bytes at a constant bit rate, we can carry out the synchronisation function at the start of the block rather than for each individual data word. There are two actions required. Firstly the receiving clock needs to be synchronised to the same frequency and phase as the incoming data. The second requirement is that the receiver must know where the first byte of data starts. Once these two synchronisation steps have been performed the receiver will be able to decode the entire block. Here it is assumed that either the receiver clock generator is sufficiently stable to remain in step for the entire block or that it is resynchronised by comparison with data transitions as the block is received.

The initial sychronisation of the receiving clock may be achieved by sending one or two bytes of a synchronisation pattern at the start of the block. This pattern normally consists of alternate 1 and 0 bits, from which the clock timing can be derived. In some cases this synchronisation pattern may be sent throughout the idling period between blocks.

Following the clock synchronisation words, a frame identification word is sent. This consists of a unique code which the receiver is designed to detect. When this frame code is detected the main process of decoding can start since the frame code will define the starting point of the first data word that follows the frame code. The receiver now counts off groups of 8 bits and treats these as data bytes, converting them into parallel form for transfer to the CPU or other data device.

Assuming a 256-word data block we have now used only three data words to synchronise the entire block so that the effective data content rises to some 95% of the available transmission time. If the block is made longer, say 512 bytes, then this data transmission efficiency improves further.

The internal organisation of the synchronous data transmission devices is similar to that of the asynchronous versions except that the arrangement for synchronising the clock and the decoding process are different. In many cases the serial transmission interface device may be designed to handle either mode of transmission by simply selecting the mode using a command or control code.

Data link control

In a synchronous data link the data format of each block of data sent along the line is governed by a set of rules known as a 'data link control protocol'. This in fact forms part of a more general data communications standard which, in the ISO/ECMA version, is divided into seven levels as follows:

(1) Physical layer
(2) Data link control
(3) Network control
(4) End to end transport control
(5) Session control
(6) Presentation control
(7) Application control

Most systems will only be compatible over a few of these levels working up from level 1. The physical link level is in fact the line hardware scheme such as RS232C. The data link level covers synchronisation, data format, error checks and control of the link between two terminal units. The third level governs the control of a network system containing more than two terminals. Usually these three levels are the only ones that will concern us in a simple microcomputer system. If the system is linked via a telephone network then level 4 may become important. Levels 5, 6 and 7 may come into play when the microprocessor system is linked to a large mainframe machine and will govern the dialogue needed to communicate with the mainframe system, any coding or encryption schemes that may be required and any system commands that may need to be used to operate the mainframe system correctly. In such cases the communications protocol used by the microcomputer must match that used by the mainframe system.

Data link control (DLC) protocol schemes can generally be divided into two basic types. In early forms of synchronous transmission the data format was based on a sequence of character codes using either the ASCII, EBCDIC or some other similar code. In these schemes, of which IBM's Bi-Sync system is typical, the control of the link is governed by control codes inserted in the character data stream and this type of link control is called a character-oriented protocol or COP. The message block usually starts with two SYN control codes which provide clock and frame synchronisation. This is followed by a header record containing control and address information. The header data starts with an SOH (Start Of Header) control code and ends with an EOH (End Of Header) code. Next comes the data record section which starts with an STX (Start of Text) code and ends with an ETX (End of Text) code. The data itself will usually be in the form of text symbols since the whole system is designed to handle character codes rather than binary data words. Finally there will be an error check word or words.

Most current data link protocol schemes use a bit-oriented protocol (BOP) and examples of these are SDLC (Synchronous Data Link Control), ADCCP (Advanced Data Communications Control Protocol) and HDLC (High level Data Link Control).

In bit-oriented protocols the message block is divided up into a series of 'fields'. At the start is a 'FLAG' word which provides the framing synchronisation. Following this flag word are three or four bytes of data which form the header field and provide address and control information for the data link system. The next field is the data itself and this may be of any length up to perhaps 500 or even 1000 bits as defined by the header field. The data field is followed by an error check field consisting of one or two bytes of data and the message block concludes with another flag code. The general arrangement might be as shown in Figure 5.14. An advantage of the

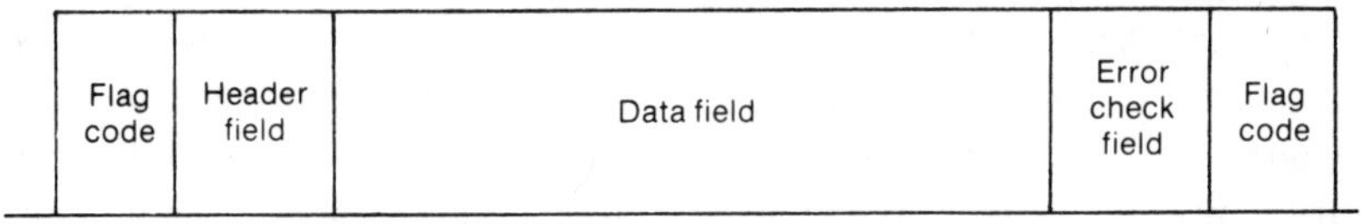

Flag code	Header field	Data field	Error check field	Flag code

Fig. 5.14 Typical layout of a data block in synchronous data transmission.

bit-oriented protocol is that within this general format the data may be text character codes, binary numbers, floating point numbers or even individual bit patterns if desired. If the microprocessor system is to be linked with a minicomputer or another microcomputer system then the data link protocol and data layout must be chosen to be compatible with the remote computer.

USRT and USART devices

As in the case of asynchronous serial operation it is convenient to use dedicated integrated circuits to perform the transmit and receive logic functions. Such devices are called USRTs (Universal Synchronous Receiver Transmitters). In many cases the dedicated chip can handle both types of serial communication and is called a USART (Universal Synchronous and Asynchronous Transmitter Receiver).

The Motorola 6852 provides a synchronous transmit and receive capability for character-oriented protocols such as Bi-Sync whilst the 6854 can handle bit-oriented protocols such as SDLC and HDLC. The Intel 8255 handles both asynchronous and COP type synchronous modes whilst the 8273 may be used for SDLC and HDLC protocols. The Zilog Z80-SIO device is more sophisticated with both asynchronous and synchronous modes of operation including HDLC and SDLC type protocols. These devices are all rather more complex than the 6850 ACIA but the principles involved in inter-facing them to the CPU and programming them follow generally similar lines.

Error detection

One problem which can occur in a serial data link is that one or more bits may be incorrectly received giving an error in the received data. This may occur due to a timing error or may be due to signal distortion along the transmission line. It is desirable, therefore, that some means of detecting the presence of such errors should be incorporated into the data transmission system. This may be achieved by adding one or more extra data bits to the message.

A simple error detection scheme involves adding one extra data bit which is called a 'parity' bit. This extra bit does not convey any actual data but merely provides a check on the validity of the actual data bits of the word being sent. We can arrange that the state of the parity bit is chosen so that the total number of bits set at '1' in the data transmitted, including the parity bit, is always an odd number. Thus if two of the bits in the actual data word are '1's the parity bit would also be set at '1' to give a total of three '1' bits which is an odd number. If three data bits in the data word were set at '1' then the parity bit would be set at '0' so that the total number of '1' bits remains odd. At the receiving end the number of bits set at '1' in the received data stream is checked and if the result is an odd number then the data is probably correct. If the result is even this indicates that the data is incorrect and some action needs to be taken to deal with this condition.

One shortcoming of the simple single bit parity check system is that if two bits in the received data are in error their effects on the parity check may cancel out so that the error check actually indicates that the data is correct. In most situations the single parity check is perfectly adequate to detect occasional reception errors. The presence of an error is usually dealt with by requesting that the data word or perhaps a complete sequence of words be repeated until error-free reception of the data message is achieved.

By using more parity check bits it becomes possible not only to detect the presence of data errors in a message but also to correct them. This is done by carrying out a series of cross checks on the data and the various parity check bits to detect which individual data bit in the received word is in error. The state of the bit is then inverted to correct the received information.

Uses of serial transmission

In general the most likely form of serial transmission to be useful in instrumentation and control tasks is the asynchronous mode. Synchronous transmission, although more efficient, requires that the data be transmitted in blocks of perhaps 256, or more, bytes at a time, and for most instrument and control applications it is likely that only a few bytes will need to be sent at a time. A possible application might be if the remote device is acting as an independent data logger and the requirement is to download a large collection of data from the remote unit to a central control computer. Here the synchronous serial mode would be useful.

The serial asynchronous mode is generally used by computer terminal devices for communication with the CPU, so if a terminal is used a serial port will be needed. This mode is also useful if data is to be sent long distances over simple telephone-type circuits. Serial transmission may also be a useful mode of communication when several devices each containing a microprocessor system need to be linked together and where very high data transfer rates may not be required.

Chapter Six
Counting and Timing Operations

A frequent requirement in instrumentation measurements and in control systems is that of counting. This function is readily provided in a microprocessor since there is normally an instruction which will allow the contents of a register or memory location to be incremented or decremented by one.

Counting objects

Let us suppose that we have a production line and that we wish to count boxes passing along a conveyor belt. We will assume that a batch of 12 boxes must be counted and then the program is required to do something else. As an example, it might then stop the line and wait for an operator to press a button to indicate that the boxes had been loaded into a van and a new batch could be accepted.

The first requirement is that of detecting the boxes as they pass some point on the line. This can be achieved by using a light beam which is directed across the path of the boxes to fall on a photocell unit as shown in Figure 6.1. Each time a box passes the sensing point the light beam is

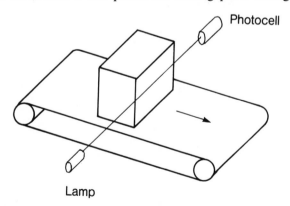

Photocell

Lamp

Fig. 6.1 Basic photocell and lamp system for detecting the passage of boxes along a production line.

blanked off and the photocell unit produces an output pulse. Suppose that the photocell voltage is normally at a '1' level and falls to '0' as a box passes.

The signal from the photocell can be input to the microprocessor via one line of a parallel data port and we shall assume that bit 0 is used. Assume also that the address assigned to the input line is represented in the program by a variable name CELL. We will assume that the microprocessor is a Motorola 6800 in this case, although the principles involved are applicable to other processors except that different instruction names may be used. The box-counting program becomes:

```
         CLR    COUNT    Set count to 0
LOOP1    LDAA   CELL     Check cell
         ANDA   #1       Mask other bits
         BNE    LOOP1    Cell lit?
         INC    COUNT    Box detected
         LDAA   COUNT
         CMPA   #12
         BEQ    NEXT     Batch complete?
         BRA    LOOP1    More to come
NEXT     ...             Continue prog.
```

In the program the first step is to set the batch count to 0 and this can be stored in memory as the variable COUNT. The next step is to check the photocell for a '1' output which will indicate that the first box has not yet arrived. This is done by reading the data port which has the address variable name CELL. To check the state of the data we can AND the accumulator with 1 to select the least significant bit and then test for a non-zero result (cell lit) using BNE. If the cell is lit the program loops back (to LOOP1) and repeats the test.

When the box passes the cell the input falls to '0' so the test fails. The program now moves on to the next instruction which increments the value of COUNT to indicate that a box has been detected. We now have to check to see if the batch is complete and this is done by loading COUNT into the accumulator and comparing it with 12. If COUNT has not yet reached 12 the program loops back to LOOP1 to check for the arrival of the next box. When the count is 12 the program continues with the next section of instructions.

There is a problem with this simple routine. When the computer detects the arrival of a box it increments the count and then goes back to check the cell again. Unless the box is an extremely narrow one the cell will still be dark so the program assumes that a box has arrived and will count the same box again. Since the computer only takes a few microseconds to do the test, it will probably count the first box as an entire batch which is not very satisfactory.

The solution to this problem is to add a further test loop which checks to see if the current box has passed the cell before checking for the arrival of a new box. So the program now becomes:

```
          CLR    COUNT   Set count = Ø
LOOP1     LDAA   CELL    Check cell
          ANDA   #1
          BNE    LOOP1   Cell lit?
          INC    COUNT   Box found
          LDAA   COUNT
          CMPA   #12     Batch done?
          BEQ    NEXT    Yes
LOOP2     LDAA   CELL    Check cell
          ANDA   #1
          BEQ    LOOP2   Cell dark?
          BRA    LOOP1   Gap found
NEXT      ...            Continue prog.
```

Here LOOP1 checks the cell and loops back when it is lit. When the box blocks the light and brings the cell output to 0, the count is incremented because we have detected a box. The current count is compared with 12 to see if the batch is complete. If there are more boxes to come (i.e. COUNT is less than 12) then LOOP2 is started. This time the loop repeats whilst the cell is dark. When the box has passed, the light beam again falls on the cell to give a '1' state and the program branches back to LOOP1 to check for the next box. Here we are detecting the space between boxes. If this were not done the computer would count the same box several times since it is almost certain that the computer will have completed its program loop before the box on the line has completely passed the cell. The program continues executing the two loops, detecting and counting each box as it passes, until 12 boxes have been detected. At this point COUNT reaches 12 and the program branches out of LOOP1 to its next section.

This program will now successfully check the batch of boxes as required. We can however improve things by setting the count to 12 at the start and decrementing it each time a box is detected as follows:

```
          LDAA   #12
          STAA   COUNT
LOOP1     LDAA   CELL
          ANDA   #1
          BNE    LOOP1
          DEC    COUNT
          BEQ    NEXT
LOOP2     LDAA   CELL
          ANDA   #1
          BEQ    LOOP2
          BRA    LOOP1
NEXT      ...
```

Here when a box is detected the value of COUNT is decremented and a test is made to see if it has reached zero. When COUNT=0 the 12 boxes have been detected and the program branches to the next section. If COUNT is not zero LOOP2 is executed to check for the gap between boxes, and on detecting the gap the program goes back to LOOP1 to check for the next box. When the 12 boxes have been detected the value of COUNT reaches zero and a branch is made to the instruction labelled NEXT at the start of the next section of the program.

Using a microswitch

A rather simpler device which is often used for sensing an event is the microswitch. If a switch were used to sense the passage of the boxes on our production line, the basic program would be similar to that for the photocell scheme except that the switch would probably make when the box passes, so the data input is a '1' when the box is present and a '0' in the gaps between. This is easily accommodated by changing the branch tests in LOOP1 and LOOP2.

There is however an added complication when a switch is used as a sensor. Virtually all switches exhibit contact bounce when they make or break. The effect is that instead of the data simply switching from '0' to '1', or vice versa, it oscillates between the two for a short period after the making or breaking of the contact as shown in Figure 6.2. This, of course is not noticed when a switch is used to turn on a lamp but because the microprocessor is very fast in operation it will detect the oscillations of the data and will give a false count.

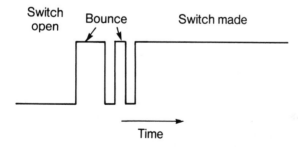

Fig. 6.2 Type of waveform produced by a switch which has contact bounce.

There are two basic approaches to 'debouncing' a switch signal. One is to use a monostable or 'one shot' device which when triggered produces an output pulse for a pre-set time period. If we arrange that the pulse is perhaps 2 to 3 milliseconds in duration, the bouncing action of the switch will have stopped by the time the pulse ends. If the output of the monostable is now used to feed the microprocessor system only one data pulse will be detected when the switch operates. A typical circuit might use the 74121 monostable device as shown in Figure 6.3.

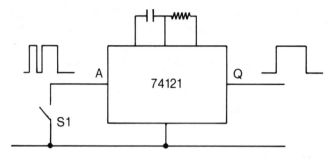

Fig. 6.3 Basic arrangement of a switch debouncer using a 74121 monostable device.

As an alternative to using an external monostable circuit we can perform the debouncing operation by means of the computer program. All that is needed is a delay of some 2 to 3 milliseconds after the first pulse is detected and before the computer goes back to check for a new input. So we get the following sequence of program instructions:

```
LOOP1    LDAA    SWITCH
         ANDA    #1
         BNE     EVENT
         BRA     LOOP1
EVENT    INC     ECNT
         LDAA    #250
DELAY    NOP
         DECA
         BEQ     LOOP2
         BRA     DELAY
LOOP2    ...
```

Here the first loop tests for the switch being closed (SWITCH = '1') and on detecting the first make of the contact goes to EVENT where the event count (ECNT) is updated. The accumulator is then set at 250 and the delay loop is entered. On each pass through this loop the accumulator is decremented and when it eventually reaches zero the program jumps out and continues with LOOP2 which might check for the switch opening again. The instructions within the delay loop are arranged here to have an execution time of 12 clock cycles or 12 microseconds with a 1 megahertz CPU clock. The branch instructions take 4 cycles each whilst the DECA and NOP take 2 cycles each. There are 200 passes so the loop introduces a time delay of some 2.4 milliseconds before the processor goes on to make any further checks on the state of the switch. The length of the delay can be adjusted by simply adding more instructions which do nothing useful apart from taking up execution time. The NOP is a convenient instruction for this purpose. Another possibility is BRA #0 which branches to what would have been the next instruction anyway but takes up 4 microseconds to do it.

Generating time delays

As we have just seen, a time delay can fairly readily be generated by the CPU itself. The basic timing clock which is driving the computer system is generally produced by a crystal-controlled oscillator and is therefore likely to be constant and, with a suitable choice of crystal, may be quite accurate.

A time delay is produced by simply setting the CPU into a counting loop which repeats for some pre-set number of times. Each pass through the loop will take the same number of instruction cycles and this forms one 'tick' of the time delay clock. After the required number of passes through the loop the program jumps out and continues with its next operation. The usual method of implementing such a time delay scheme is to set a number into the accumulator and then repeatedly decrement it until the result reaches zero. The program sequence becomes as follows:

```
          LDA     COUNT
LOOP      DECA
          BNE     LOOP
          ...     process event
```

Here if the value of COUNT is set at 100, the computer will execute the DECA and BNE instructions 100 times before going on with the next part of the program. For a 6800 processor running from a 1 MHz clock, the DECA instruction takes 2 μs and the BNE takes 4 μs, so each pass through the loop takes 6 μs and the total delay time is 600 μs for this loop.

For longer time delays, the time of cycling through the loop needs to be padded out. This may be done by including one or more NOP (No Operation) instructions which merely use up instruction cycles without altering the state of the CPU. Thus if we add one NOP instruction into our simple timing loop the total execution time increases to 8 μs per pass and a 100 pass delay represents 800 μs.

For much longer delays, two timing loops may be nested as follows:

```
          LDA     #TIME1
          STA     COUNT1
LOOP1     LDA     #TIME2
          STA     COUNT2
LOOP2     DEC     COUNT2
          BNE     LOOP2
          DEC     COUNT1
          BNE     LOOP1
```

Here it is important in working out the total time delay to remember that the time for the instructions which load the count for timing loop 2 must be included when working out the time delay for each pass through loop 1.

Where the computer is carrying out some repetitive series of operations which are required to take place perhaps once per second it would be possible to calculate the execution time of the active part of the program and then add a delay loop to make the total time of each repetition equal to 1 second. This process can become rather complicated, however, if the active part of the program includes alternate branching paths since all of these would have to be adjusted so that the total execution time is equal whichever path the program takes.

Generating pulses and waves

Now that we can produce delays in the computer it becomes possible to generate variable length pulses or square waves using the computer. The output is produced by simply setting or resetting the state of a line on an output port.

Thus to produce a pulse we might use a small subroutine as follows:

```
PULSE   LDAA   #1
        STAA   PORT      Set O/P = '1'
        LDX    LENGTH
DELAY   NOP
        DEX
        BEQ    PEND
        BRA    DELAY
PEND    CLRA
        STAA   PORT      Set O/P = '∅'
        RTS
```

Here the X register is used for the delay counter which will allow counts up to 65535, and the variable LENGTH will determine the time period of the pulse. Each time the subroutine is called, a pulse will be generated on bit 0 of the output port.

A square wave of variable mark-to-space ratio may be generated in a similar fashion by using two time delay loops as follows:

```
GMRK   LDX    MARK
       LDAA   #1
       STAA   PORT
DLY1   DEX
       BEQ    GSPC
       BRA    DLY1
GSPC   LDX    SPACE
       CLRA
       STAA   PORT
DLY2   DEX
       BEQ    GMRK
       BRA    DLY2
```

Here MARK and SPACE are count values to give the desired on and off time periods for the square wave and the ouput is sent to bit 0 on the I/O channel labelled PORT.

The square wave may be switched on and off by inserting a further test after the space delay loop (DLY2) and this test would check the state of a switch which might be fed in on an input line of the port. When the switch is 'on' the square wave routine executes, but if the switch is 'off' the CPU can simply recycle and continually test the switch state.

Using an external clock

A much more reliable method of producing accurate timing for repetitive program operations is to use an external clock generator. This clock may be generated from the CPU clock by using an external counter chain to divide down the frequency of the CPU clock to give the desired clock frequency.

The external clock signal may be fed in on one line of a parallel port in the same way as was used for the photocell sensor earlier, but a better method is to use one of the control inputs to the port. Suppose that the port device is a 6821, then we might use the CA1 input and set it up to detect low to high transitions in the input signal. The program for detecting the clock input becomes:

```
        LDAA   #6        Set up CA1 mode
        STAA   CREG
LOOP    LDAA   CREG      Read port status
        ASLA             Test CA1 flag bit
        BCC    LOOP      Branch if 'Ø'
        LDAA   DREG      Clear flag bit
        JSR    TASK      Perform task
        BRA    LOOP
```

When a clock pulse is detected the CA1 flag bit (bit 7 of the control register) is set at '1'. LOOP tests for this bit by shifting the status word left to move bit 7 to the carry position. A test is made on the carry state and loops back if this is clear. When the clock pulse occurs, the data register of the port is read to clear the flag bit in the control register and then the program jumps to a subroutine which performs the required task that is to occur at each clock pulse. Finally the program branches back to check for the next clock pulse. Here the repetition time is governed entirely by the timing of the external clock and is not influenced by the execution time of the data gathering subroutine, provided that routine is completed before the next clock pulse is due.

A simple data logger could use a scheme such as this with the set of measurements being taken in the TASK subroutine and the external clock set to produce a pulse each time a set of readings is to be taken.

Measuring frequency

The technique for measuring the frequency of some regularly occurring external event is basically similar to that of counting objects moving along a line, except that the number of events is measured over some fixed time period such as one second. In this case the computer has to monitor an input signal whilst simultaneously counting off a specified time delay period. This may be achieved by a routine similar to the following one:

```
            LDA    #TIME
            STA    TCOUNT
            BRA    TLOOP2
TLOOP1      LDA    SIGNAL
            BNE    ONE
NEXT1       BRA    #Ø
            BRA    #Ø
            DEC    TCOUNT
            BNE    TLOOP1
            BRA    DISPLAY
ONE         INC    FREQ
            BRA    NEXT
TLOOP2      LDA    SIGNAL
            BEQ    NEXT1
            BRA    #Ø
            BRA    #Ø
NEXT        DEC    TCOUNT
            BNE    TLOOP2
            BRA    DISPLAY
DISPLAY     ...    Display routine
```

At the start of the routine the number of timing loop cycles required to produce the measuring time period is set up in the variable TCOUNT, and a second variable FREQ is set at 0. This second variable will be used to count the number of cycles of the input signal. Two timing loops, TLOOP1 and TLOOP2, are used in the routine although each provides an identical time delay period and updates the variable TCOUNT. In the first loop an input signal transition from 0 to 1 is detected and this event is counted in the FREQ location, whilst in the second loop the signal 0 state is detected but no alteration is made to the FREQ value. After initial setting up, the program branches to TLOOP2 in order to detect an initial signal 0 condition, after which execution branches into TLOOP1 and cycle counting commences.

In TLOOP1 the input signal is tested to detect a 1 state and if the test fails TCOUNT is decremented and the loop repeats to provide one 'tick' of the timing clock. When the input signal changes to the 1 state the program jumps out of TLOOP1, increments the value of FREQ and then resumes its timing operation again. The INC and BRA instructions used to update

FREQ will alter the length of the current pass of the timing loop, so two BRA #0 instructions have been added into TLOOP1 to balance up the time delay. The BRA #0 instruction merely tells the CPU to execute the next instruction in sequence and its inclusion simply adds four clock cycles to the execution time of the loop.

After the detection of the signal 1 state a different test is required, so a second timing loop TLOOP2 is now brought into play. Again this includes BRA #0 instructions to match its timing with that of TLOOP1. On entry to this loop these extra instructions are bypassed since the delay is provided by the INC and BRA instructions when FREQ is updated. When a signal 0 is detected, the program jumps back into TLOOP1 again in order to detect the next signal cycle.

At the end of the measuring period the number of input cycles that occurred will be held in variable FREQ. The program now branches to a display routine which uses the value stored in FREQ to update a frequency readout display. The whole routine could also be made repetitive so that it takes a new frequency reading and updates the display at regular intervals if desired.

If an external clock is used, this simplifies the program somewhat as follows:

```
          LDAA   #22       Set control mode
          STAA   CREG
START     LDAA   DREG      Clear flag bits
LOOP1     LDAA   CREG      Read port status
          ASLA
          ASLA             Check clock flag
          BCC    LOOP1     Branch if clear
          LDAA   DREG      Clear flag bits
          CLR    COUNT     Set count = 0
LOOP2     LDAA   CREG      Read port status
          ASLA             Check pulse flag
          BCC    NEXT      Branch if clear
          INC    COUNT     Update count
NEXT      ASLA             Check clock flag
          BCS    DISP      Branch if set
          LDAA   DREG      Clear flag bits
          BRA    LOOP1     Do again
DISP      JSR    DISPR     Display routine
          BRA    START     Take new reading
```

Here the external clock is applied to input CA2 whilst the signal being measured is fed in on CA1. A short loop first checks for a clock transition and then the measurement loop (LOOP2) starts. The flag bits are tested by successive left shifts of the status word in the accumulator. When a signal pulse is detected on CA1 the count is incremented and the loop continues.

When the next clock pulse is detected by the BCS instruction, the program branches to perform a display subroutine then goes back to the start to begin a new measurement cycle.

This frequency measuring approach can be used to measure shaft speed by fitting a pulse generator on the shaft. This could be a simple magnetic pick-up giving one pulse per shaft revolution, or might use a phonic wheel scheme where each tooth of the wheel produces a pulse as it passes a magnetic pick-up head. An alternative is to use an optical pulse generator which may consist of a transparent disk mounted concentrically on the shaft with radial black and clear stripes on the disk. A light beam shining through the disk is interrupted by the black stripes to produce a series of equally spaced pulses for each shaft revolution. The pulses generated by one or other of these methods may then be counted over a period of perhaps one second to give a measure of shaft speed in rpm.

Measuring a time period

To measure a time period we need to measure the number of clock pulses occurring between two events. Again we can use the CA1 and CA2 inputs of a 6821 but this time the external clock pulses are counted rather than the signal pulses and the signal frequency is used to start and stop the count. The program now becomes:

```
        LDAA   #22
        STAA   CREG    Set up port mode
        LDAA   DREG    Clear flags
LOOP1   LDAA   CREG    Read port status
        ASLA           Test signal bit
        BCC    LOOP1   Branch if clear
        LDAA   DREG    Clear flags
        CLX            Clear X register
LOOP2   LDAA   CREG    Read status
        ASLA           Test signal bit
        BCS    SAVE    Branch if set
        ASLA           Test clock bit
        BCC    NEXT    Branch if clear
        INX            Update count in X
NEXT    LDAA   DREG    Clear flags
        BRA    LOOP1   Continue counting
SAVE    STX    PERIOD  Store result
```

Here, CA1 is used for the signal input and CA2 for the clock input. The index (X) register is used to hold the count of the number of clock pulses. This allows a 16-bit count total. The first loop detects the start of the period and in LOOP2 the end of the period is detected by the BCS instruction.

Clock pulses are also detected and X is incremented with each clock pulse. At the end of the period the contents of the X register are stored in memory locations PERIOD and PERIOD+1.

The 6840 counter/timer

Most ranges of microprocessor components include some form of counter/ timer chip which is compatible with the microprocessor itself. As an example in the Motorola 6800 range there is a 6840 device which contains three counters and may also be used for timing applications. The basic internal arrangement of this device is as shown in Figure 6.4.

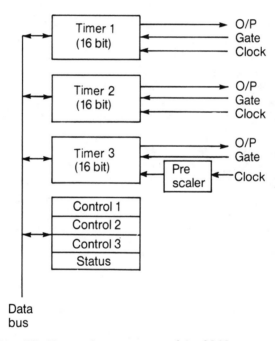

Fig. 6.4 Simplified internal arrangement of the 6840 counter/timer.

Each of the three counters has a 16-bit count register which can also be arranged to operate as two 8-bit registers in some modes of operation. Each counter also includes a gate circuit which allows the incoming pulses to be passed to the counter or blocked according to the state of the gate input. There is also a pre-scaler counter which can be used to scale down the clock frequency used by timer no. 3.

Each counter/timer may be switched to one of four different operating modes. In the continuous mode the counter counts down continuously and produces an output square wave in which each half-cycle counts off a pre-set number of clock pulses. It is also possible to set up a variation of this mode where 8 bits of the counter determine the length of the output '1' period whilst the other 8 bits determine the output '0' period. Thus it is possible to generate a wide range of repetitive square wave and pulse signals.

In its second mode, each counter may be used as a one-shot timer which produces a single output pulse whose length is determined by the pre-set count value written into the counter latch by the CPU. The output pulse may also be triggered by a pulse applied to the gate input.

The third mode of the timer allows the measurement of a period between two high to low transitions of the gate input. This can be used to measure the period of an input square wave. Finally, the fourth mode allows the measurement of the length of a pulse. Here the counter starts counting when the gate input goes low and stops counting when the gate input goes high again.

The 6840 appears to the CPU as if it were eight successive locations in the memory. Six of these are used for the counter latches with two words allocated for each counter. The remaining two memory locations are shared between three control/status registers. One location has two registers allocated to it, and a bit in the third register selects which of the two registers is connected to the bus at any time.

The operation of the 6840 is rather complex and the manual for it needs to be consulted before attempting to use the device. With its three counters which can be cascaded, almost any time period or frequency can be generated. By selecting appropriate modes and using the gate input lines, measurements of frequency and period and pulse length can be made without having to use the CPU at all. When the operation is complete the result may then be read in from the 6840 to the CPU. This device can relieve the CPU of most of the counting and timing operations.

Chapter Seven
Analogue Input-Output

Although the microprocessor works exclusively with digital numbers, most of the signals that we encounter in the real world are analogue in form. This means that the signal level varies in a continuous fashion rather than in discrete steps and may consist of a variable voltage or current in an electric circuit. The output or input voltage or current represents a physical parameter such as pressure, density, length, weight, speed and so on.

In a control system we may require the computer to produce an output in the form of a continuously variable physical quantity such as motor speed, or the force exerted by a solenoid. Let us suppose that we are controlling the speed of a motor. The computer will carry out a series of calculations and end up with a digital number representing the value of motor speed required. The motor itself may require an electrical drive voltage applied to it which is proportional to the required speed. The interface between the computer and the motor must therefore contain a device which converts the digital representation in the computer into a voltage level corresponding to the required speed of the motor shaft. This may take place in two stages. In the first, the digital number is converted into an analogue voltage and, then, the voltage may be scaled or amplified to provide the actual drive required for the motor. The binary digital output data from the computer can be converted into an equivalent analogue voltage or current by using a digital to analogue converter (DAC).

Most of the real world signals that we want to measure using the computer are also likely to be in analogue form. Thus the transducer device used to convert from a physical parameter such as pressure will produce an electrical voltage or current which is proportional to the pressure applied to the transducer. The computer system however requires a signal in digital form as, perhaps, a binary number in a register. Conversion is therefore required between the analogue input signal and the digital binary coded form. This is carried out by some form of analogue to digital (A/D) conversion.

Simple analogue output

Where the analogue output required does not need to be particularly precise, the simplest method of generating the analogue output makes use of a pulse width modulated square wave. We have already seen in Chapter 6 how a variable width pulse at constant repetition frequency can be generated by the microprocessor. If the width of the pulse relative to the total cycle period is varied then the mean DC voltage level of the output signal will change in sympathy thus producing a crude analogue output signal.

The general idea of this technique is shown in Figure 7.1 which shows three possible pulse width conditions. If the output switches on and off for equal time periods as shown in Figure 7.1b then the mean DC level of the output will be $0.5V$ where V is the voltage amplitude of the pulse. Here the ratio between the pulse width and the complete cycle period is 0.5. In Figure 7.1a the pulse width is reduced to $\frac{1}{4}$ of the cycle period and the corresponding mean level voltage output becomes $0.25V$ whilst in Figure 7.1c, for a pulse width of $\frac{3}{4}$ of the period, the output becomes $0.75V$.

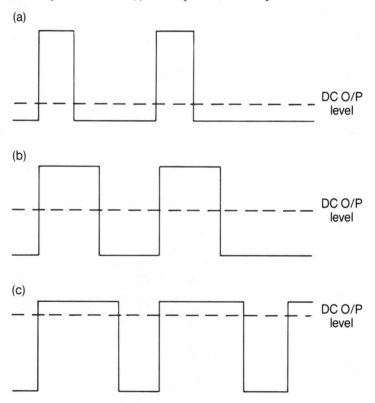

Fig. 7.1 Simple analogue output scheme using variable pulse width to control output amplitude.

The computer produces a continuous stream of pulses at a constant pulse repetition rate. The width of each pulse however is made proportional to the digital value of the variable being output. Here the full-scale digital output is arranged to produce a pulse width which is almost equal to the period between successive pulses. The result is a pulse train where the pulse width is proportional to the digital number being output.

If we consider the mean level of the variable mark–space output waveform, we find that this is given by:

$$V_{\text{mean}} = \frac{V_{\text{max}}\ T_{\text{p}}}{T_{\text{t}}}$$

where V_{max} is the peak voltage level of the pulses, T_{p} the length of the pulse, and T_{t} is the total time period between pulses.

This type of output signal is relatively easy to generate, as we have seen in Chapter 6. The pulse width may be governed by a simple counting loop in the microprocessor program. Whilst this count is in progress the state of the digital output line is set at '1'. At the end of the count the line is reset to '0' and remains at that level until the next output timing cycle starts. The actual output can be generated using any of the basic parallel output port schemes.

In a practical system, the processor will usually have other tasks to perform apart from generating an analogue output, so it is usually more convenient to use one of the counter-type support devices to actually generate the square wave output, leaving the computer free to work on other tasks.

Because the pulse width is determined by a counting operation, the actual width varies in a series of discrete steps and therefore the analogue output will also be produced in steps rather than as a continuously variable output. In a practical system using an 8-bit data word to control the pulse width, the total time cycle would be set at 256 clock periods. The range of pulse widths available runs from 0 to 255 clock periods so the maximum output level is in fact 255/256 of the output '1' voltage level. It would be possible to achieve an output equal to V by turning on the output for the entire cycle period but this would need to be handled by a separate program step since the counter system will only allow the values from 0 to 255 for pulse width. This simple scheme gives an effective resolution in the output signal of about 0.5% of full scale which is perfectly adequate for many tasks.

If the output square wave signal were used to drive an electric heater, for instance, the heat output would be proportional to the mean level of the signal, and the square wave switching component of the signal would be of no consequence. For many applications the pulses in the output signal may affect the operation of the device being controlled. Since we are only interested in the mean DC component of the output, a filter can be added to remove the square wave component and leave only the mean DC voltage level. This can be done by using a simple low pass RC filter as shown in Figure 7.2. For better smoothing of the output, a multi-stage filter might be used and this might be followed by an analogue buffer amplifier to provide a low impedance output.

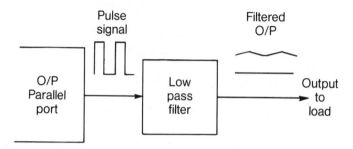

Fig. 7.2 Hardware arrangement for a simple pulse width analogue output.

This form of digital to analogue conversion is easy to implement but the results are not particularly precise. The mean output level depends upon the actual voltage levels produced by the '1' and '0' logic states of the digital output port. These logic levels may vary quite markedly from one device to another, although this could be overcome by having an amplifier with adjustable pre-set gain in the output line. One method of overcoming the problem of variable logic state levels is to use an accurate reference voltage and switch it using an FET switch circuit driven by the port output signal. Another source of error is the time taken for the output signal to switch between its '0' and '1' states. This becomes more important as the pulse or space times become shorter and if the pulse repetition rate is increased.

The output filter introduces a time lag between the output of a signal from the CPU and the output from the filter itself. With a simple resistive capacitive low pass filter the amount of time lag increases as the filtering efficiency is increased. Although this time lag may not be too important if the output is used to drive, say, a heater or a lamp, it can produce problems when the signal is used in a control loop which contains a feedback path.

Weighted current converter

Although the pulse width analogue output scheme is easy to produce, the more popular digital to analogue conversion schemes convert the computer data word directly into an equivalent analogue output by using some form of weighted current system.

If we consider the digital form of the output variable, each data bit may be either on or off (1 or 0) and each has a weighted numerical value (1, 2, 4, 8, etc.). If we set up a series of current generators which produce currents weighted in a binary sequence (1, 2, 4, 8, etc.) and switch these currents to a common load via a series of switches actuated by the bits of the data word, it is possible to build up a total current in the load which is proportional to the value of the digital data. The general arrangement of such a scheme is shown in Figure 7.3.

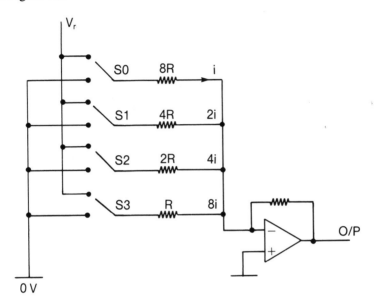

Fig. 7.3 A D/A converter scheme using simple binary weighted networks.

In its simplest form each current generator might consist of a large value resistor, relative to the load resistor, and all may be fed from a common high reference voltage. The resistors are progressively weighted in value so that the current increases by a factor of two in each successive leg of the network. In Figure 7.3 a 4-bit converter is shown where switches S0 to S3 are actuated by bits B0 through B3 respectively in the computer data word. When a bit is set at '1' the corresponding switch is closed, and for a '0' state the switch is open. The resultant current though the load resistor is now the sum of the weighted currents for those data bits that are set at 1 and will be proportional to the actual numerical value of the data word. This produces an analogue voltage across the load which is then amplified to produce the desired output signal.

In this form of converter there is no pulse ripple component so the output does not need to be filtered. There is also virtually no time lag between the application of the digital signal to the current switches and the output of an analogue voltage. Timing is no longer important since the digital data may be transferred from the CPU to a register in the converter device where it is held to produce a continuous analogue output. Thus the computer need only transfer data at intervals to update the analogue output.

The accuracy of the analogue output in this type of converter depends upon the reference voltage, V_r, the values of the weighted resistors or current sources, the load resistor and the gain of the amplifier. The reference voltage and the amplifier gain can generally be adjusted or pre-set to precise levels, but problems can arise in the weighted current network since very precise values of resistance are required in each arm of the network. Thus for an 8-bit converter, the resistor producing the weighted current for half full-scale output needs to be set to an accuracy of better than 0.25% for proper operation of the converter.

If electronic switches are used for S0 to S3 then the series resistance of these switches in the on state, and their leakage in the off state, can also affect the accuracy of the system. The switches are normally set up as change-over types so that the weighted resistor is fed either from V_r or 0 V. This maintains a constant source impedance for the current generating network. If simple on/off switches to the voltage V_r were used, the impedance of the network would change as the digital data changed and this could produce a non-linear output characteristic.

An 8-bit converter provides a step resolution of 256 steps, so the current generation arms must provide weighted currents to an accuracy of better than 0.5% of full scale. This means that resistors of perhaps 0.1% to 0.2% precision are needed and the switch circuits need to be carefully matched if the device is to provide the required 8-bit precision at its output. This may be practical in a discrete component circuit where small trimming resistors may be used to accurately set the weighted currents. For resolution levels better than 8 bits, this type of conversion network can be very difficult to set up and maintain to the desired degree of accuracy.

Ladder network converters

Whilst the weighted resistor system is easy to understand it is not generally used for modern D/A converters. Suppose instead of using a series of weighted value resistors to produce the weighted currents for the converter we use a ladder network scheme as shown in Figure 7.4.

The ladder network itself consists of resistors with one of two values, R or $2R$. The impedance of the network is R ohms at any point along the chain when the network is properly terminated. The network itself acts as an attenuator in which each section provides an attenuation factor of 2. If a voltage, V, is applied at one end, the voltage produced at each node (A, B, C, D) is half that at the previous node. By switching the reference voltage to the legs of the network, a binary weighted output signal is produced and this may be amplified to the desired output level by a buffer amplifier following the conversion network.

The R–$2R$ ladder network is particularly useful for converters where the resistors are to be fabricated on a silicon chip or on a thin film substrate. In the chip or substrate it is difficult to produce precise values of resistivity in the film or silicon material but it is possible to produce very precise geometry

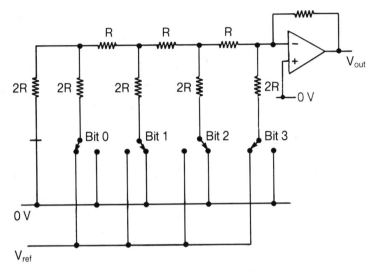

Fig. 7.4 A D/A converter using a ladder network.

in the mask which produces the resistive elements. Thus it is easy to achieve very precise ratios between resistors but difficult to produce precise resistor values. In the $R-2R$ network scheme, it is the ratio between the arms that is important rather than the values of the resistors themselves, so this approach is ideally suited for use in thin film or solid state fabrication of the conversion network. Problems with linearity due to loading can also be overcome if the network is properly terminated since the impedance remains constant irrespective of the states of the data switches.

Linearity and monotonicity

Ideally a D/A converter should produce an analogue output which is exactly proportional to the digital input number. If this were so then by stepping through the digital numbers in sequence we would produce an absolutely linear increase in analogue output from zero to full scale. In practice, due to component tolerances and the characteristics of the buffer amplifier used at the output of the converter, the analogue output will not be exactly linear in relation to the digital input. The degree of deviation from linearity is usually measured by taking the largest difference between the actual output of the converter and an ideal straight line output. This deviation from linearity is usually expressed as a percentage of the full-scale output.

A second linearity characteristic which is important in a D/A converter is the differential linearity or monotonicity. In a switched weighted current type converter the steps should ideally have exactly the same size throughout the range. In practice a small error in the weighted current of one of the higher value data bits can cause a marked disturbance in the output analogue signal at the point where that bit is switched. This is shown in Figure 7.5. Here, for step 3 the analogue output is produced by the sum of the weighted currents for bits 0 and 1. For the next step, bit 2 is turned on and the other bits are switched off. A weighting error in the current for bit 2 could however cause that bit to produce an output equal to or even less than the output for the previous step.

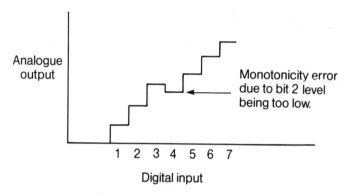

Fig. 7.5 The effect produced when a converter suffers from monotonicity errors.

Commercially-produced D/A converters will normally be monotonic over their entire output range under normal operating conditions, but monotonicity problems may occur if the converter is operated under nonstandard conditions.

Precision and resolution

The basic resolution, or step size, of the analogue output is governed by the number of bits in the input data and by the way in which the digital input is coded. Thus an 8-bit converter using a binary coding scheme will provide a resolution of 256 steps over the full scale range giving an output signal resolution of approximately 0.4% of full scale. When the BCD code is used the resolution for 8 bits falls to 100 steps and output resolution becomes 1%.

A 10-bit binary converter gives 1024 steps and 12 bits increases the resolution to 4096 steps. In practical systems the 12-bit resolution is generally about the highest used because of the difficulties encountered in handling analogue output signals to this degree of resolution which is about 0.025% of full scale. When full scale is perhaps 10 volts, this gives a step size of only 2.5 mV.

Although the resolution of a converter determines the number of steps in the output, the actual size of the steps will determine the precision with which the analogue output is produced. This is determined by the accuracy of the reference voltage in the converter, the resistor network ratios and the gain of the buffer amplifier. In practice D/A converters normally have a scale adjustment facility so that the actual analogue output for a particular digital input can be set precisely. This adjustment may in fact be divided into two steps. One adjustment is made to set the zero level whilst a second sets up the scale factor and is usually adjusted at the full-scale output condition.

Glitches

An important failing of the switched current type converters is the presence of 'glitches' in the output analogue signal. These take the form of sharp spikes and are caused by differences in the switch on and switch off times of the switches used in the converter. Figure 7.6 shows the effect produced in the output waveform. The largest glitches are likely to be produced when the most significant bit is being switched.

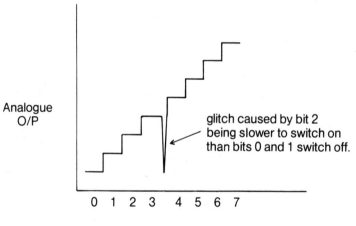

Digital input increasing with time

Fig. 7.6 A glitch at the output of a D/A caused by differences in on and off switching times in the D/A converter switch.

To minimise glitch problems it is important that the digital inputs themselves switch rapidly and provide no overlap between adjacent bits. Power supply decoupling around the converter needs to be carefully laid out and adequate for the pulses involved. Most modern converters tend to be reasonably glitch-free but when they do occur it is usually possible to remove their effects by inserting a low pass filter in the analogue output path. If the converter forms part of a closed control loop any filter used to suppress glitches must be taken into account in designing the overall control loop.

Amplifier characteristics

In many cases the D/A converter module will consist of the conversion network, switches and reference voltage but the user will be required to supply the amplifier.

An important characteristic of the amplifier is its 'slew rate' since this will limit the speed at which conversions can be carried out. The slew rate defines the maximum rate at which the output of the amplifier can change and is often quoted in volts/microsecond.

Stability

The accuracy of the analogue output levels is determined by the voltage reference, ladder network and any buffer amplifier used to provide output drive capability. All of these may change their characteristics slightly with temperature and the stability of the converter is normally quoted in terms of percentage of full-scale output per degree Celsius temperature change. The voltage reference diode is usually chosen to have a reference voltage in the region of 5.6 volts since this seems to provide the minimum drift of reference voltage with temperature. In a ladder network system the resistors in the ladder are normally all on the same substrate and therefore tend to change value in sympathy so that the R to $2R$ ratio tends to remain unaffected and output remains constant. The other main source of drift is likely to be in the output amplifier. In a bipolar type of converter the offset bias can be a source of drift in the output level. Here the mean output level drifts rather than the slope of the output signal.

Temperature stability of the scaling of the converter is usually quoted in parts per million per degree Celsius and a typical figure is often 5 ppm/°C. Thus, even for a change of some 50° C the scale will have changed by about 1 part in 4000, so that on a 12-bit converter the scaling will be out by about one least significant bit.

Analogue to digital conversion

For instrumentation, the computer system will be required to deal with analogue input signals and for this purpose some form of analogue to digital converter (ADC) will be required. There are a number of different techniques available for converting an analogue input signal into the digital form needed for input to a microcomputer. We shall look at some of the more popular schemes used for this purpose.

Single ramp converters

Perhaps the simplest approach for dealing with an analogue input signal is to generate a reference signal whose voltage level starts at zero and then rises linearly with time. This linear analogue ramp signal is then compared with the input signal that is to be measured. The length of time between the start of the ramp and the point where the ramp and input signals are equal will be proportional to the DC level of the input signal as shown in Figure 7.7.

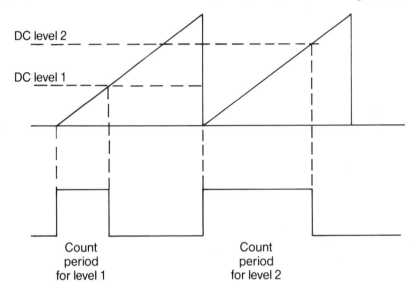

Fig. 7.7 Basic principles of a single ramp integrating type converter.

The comparator circuit is basically a very high gain balanced amplifier with one of the signals to be compared fed to each of its inputs as shown in Figure 7.8. When signal A is lower than signal B the amplifier transistor Q2 is turned on to saturation and the output voltage is low. As the signal A reaches and rises above input B, the amplifier rapidly switches its state and Q2 cuts off to give a high output. Since the ramp voltage is proportional to time elapsed then, by measuring the time from the start of the ramp to the point where the comparator switches its state, we can generate a digital signal equivalent to the analogue input. The time period can be easily measured by using a counter and if desired this function could be performed by the CPU itself. In effect this conversion scheme is the inverse of the variable pulse width scheme for producing analogue output, since here we are producing a variable width pulse from the comparator which is proportional to the analogue input being measured.

For accurate results the ramp reference signal must rise linearly with time and its rate of increase must be consistent from one measurement cycle to another. The usual process for generating the reference ramp is to use a

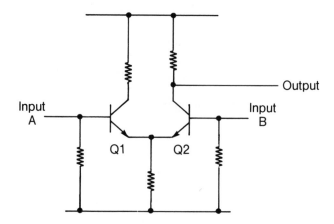

Fig. 7.8 A simple comparator circuit that might be used for an analogue to digital conversion.

capacitor which is charged from a constant current source. The voltage across the capacitor is given by:

$$V = Q/C$$

or

$$V = (I \times t)/C$$

so that for a constant current, I, and fixed capacitance, C, the voltage will be directly proportional to t, the elapsed time to give:

$$V = kt$$

where k is a constant.

The conversion system becomes as shown in Figure 7.9. Here, the constant charge current may be produced by a transistor circuit controlled by a precise reference voltage which may be derived from a Zener diode. A transistor switch connected across the capacitor is closed before the conversion cycle starts and this discharges the capacitor so that the reference ramp starts at a known voltage level, which is generally zero. The discharge circuit is disabled and the counter is allowed to start counting clock pulses to measure the time interval. The ramp voltage and the analogue input signal are fed to the two inputs of an analogue comparator circuit which is basically a very high gain analogue amplifier. When the ramp voltage is less than the input, the comparator output will be hard over to one of its limits. When the ramp voltage passes through the same voltage level as the input signal, the comparator output switches rapidly to the opposite limit condition and this transition is used to trigger the control logic which stops the counter and provides a signal to the computer to indicate that conversion is complete. At this point, the count value stored in the counter is directly proportional to the input signal and may be read into the computer via a digital input port or by direct access via the CPU data bus.

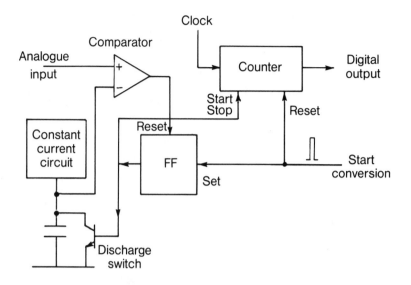

Fig. 7.9 Circuit arrangement for a single ramp type A/D converter.

In a practical system, the counter may be built up from discrete logic devices or it may be one of the counter/timer type support chips such as the 6840. Some single-chip microcomputer devices incorporate counter timer facilities and these may be used to control the conversion process.

Dual slope converters

A major limitation of the simple timing ramp converter is that the accuracy of the converted data depends upon a number of relatively imprecise factors. The time period itself depends upon the actual charging current and the exact value of the capacitor. Measurement of the time period itself depends upon the accuracy of the timing clock. If any of these parameters change with time the scaling factor, k, which relates analogue input and digital output, also changes so that the digital reading becomes inaccurate. By adopting a modified technique, however, it becomes possible to eliminate most of these problems.

The scheme uses two periods of integration instead of one and such converters are usually referred to as 'dual ramp' converters. The basic arrangement of such a converter is shown in Figure 7.10. A feedback type integrator using an operational amplifier is used with the time constant determined by the values of R and C. The input voltage applied to the resistor R determines the charging current and hence the rate of change of the integrator output voltage, V_o.

The integrator input is initially switched to the signal being measured, V_i, and its output, V_o, is allowed to increase for a fixed time period T_1, as shown

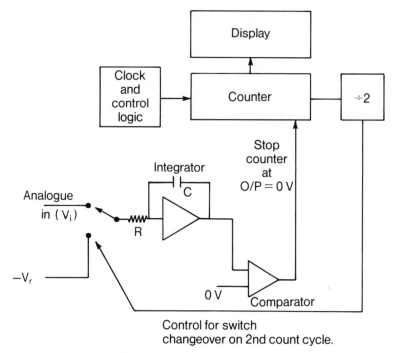

Control for switch
changeover on 2nd count cycle.

Fig. 7.10 Circuit arrangement for a dual ramp A/D converter.

in Figure 7.11. Since the integrator output rises linearly with time at a rate directly proportional to the input voltage, V_i, the final level of V_o after time T_1 is:

$$V_o = k T_1 V_i$$

where k is a constant.

At the end of this period, a fixed reference voltage is applied to the integrator input. This reference voltage is arranged to have the opposite polarity to the signal being measured. Now the integrator output will fall at a constant rate and this is allowed to continue until the output voltage, V_o, reaches zero. For this second integration phase we get:

$$V_o = k T_2 V_r$$

where T_2 is the time taken for V_o to fall to zero and V_r is the reference voltage.

This value for V_o can be substituted in the previous equation to give:

$$k T_1 V_i = k T_2 V_r$$

and this can be rearranged to extract T_2 as follows:

$$T_2 = T_1 V_i / V_r = k_1 V_i$$

so that T_2 is in fact directly proportional to the input signal being measured since T_1 and V_r are constant for all measurements.

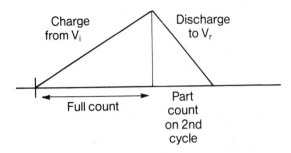

Fig. 7.11 Principles of operation of a dual ramp A/D converter.

At the start of the first ramp period, a counter is set running. This counter is driven by a constant timing clock and is allowed to go through its complete count cycle. During this time the integrator output rises to a level V_o which is proportional to the input V_i. When the count recycles to zero the input signal is disconnected and the reference V_r is applied to the integrator. The counter continues to count up from zero on its second count cycle. Now the output of the integrator falls at a rate determined by V_r. A comparator is used to detect when the output of the integrator reaches zero. At this point the counter is stopped and the indicated count will be proportional to the value of the input voltage V_i.

Because the time constant for the integrator is the same for both ramp cycles, the precise values for R and C have no effect upon the accuracy of the output reading since any change of the value of C would change both ramps to exactly the same extent. Since the same clock signal is used to drive the counter during both integration periods, the exact clock frequency becomes unimportant provided that it remains stable throughout the conversion period.

The dual ramp converter responds to the mean level of the input signal over a period of time so this type of converter tends to be immune to the effects of spikes and random noise on the input signal. By choosing the time constant of the integrator and the time period of the input integration, it is also possible to eliminate the effects of periodic noise such as pick-up from the supply mains. To achieve this the integration period should be made equal to an integer number of cycles of the signal to be suppressed.

The integrating dual ramp converter does have one disadvantage when used in conjunction with a computer type system. The actual time taken for a complete conversion cycle is governed by the level of the input signal. Most of these converters are arranged to be free running so that at the end of one conversion cycle a new one starts immediately. For use with a computer system, an output latch could be incorporated into the system so that at the end of each conversion cycle the counter contents would be transferred to an output register where they would remain stored whilst the next conversion is taking place. The output register would then update to a new value at the end of each conversion cycle. If the system were used with a computer the update pulse could be used as a signal to the computer to indicate that a new reading of V_i is ready. The computer can detect this signal and read the register contents which represent the latest value for the analogue input.

Dual ramp converters are basically slow measuring devices. The resolution is governed by the total count carried out during the first integration period. Thus, for a 12-bit precision (about 0.025%), the count would be 4096 clock pulses, and assuming a 1 MHz clock, the conversion time would range from about 4 to 8 milliseconds depending upon the input signal level. Many of these converter devices are designed to drive digital readouts and the counter system is usually arranged to count in BCD format to make interfacing to the displays more straightforward. In this case it is important to remember that the inputs to the computer must be treated in BCD format also.

The most popular application for dual ramp converters is in digital panel meters where the device drives a display directly. One type which is specifically designed for interfacing to a microprocessor bus system is the Intersil ICL7109 which provides a 12-bit dual slope converter in a 40-pin dual in line integrated circuit package. Maximum operating speed is about 30 conversions per second for this device.

Counter-type converters using a DAC

Instead of using an analogue technique for generating a reference ramp voltage, we can alternatively employ a digital counter which drives a D/A converter as shown in Figure 7.12. Once again a comparator is used to compare the input being measured with the reference ramp and when the

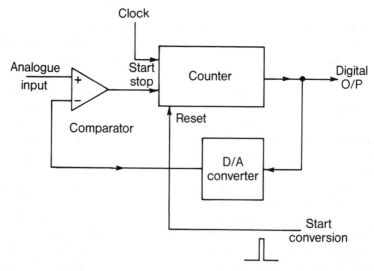

Fig. 7.12 Counter-type A/D converter with feedback from a D/A converter.

two become equal the output from the comparator is used to stop the counter and end the conversion cycle.

At the start of the conversion cycle the counter is firstly reset to zero and then allowed to start counting upwards from zero. The output of the D/A converter also starts at zero and then, following the counter data, produces a linear staircase voltage which is compared with the analogue input voltage. When the two voltages become equal the output of the comparator is used to stop the counter. At this point the digital value of the count is proportional to the input signal and may be read into the computer. This system is more complex than a dual slope version, since a D/A converter is used to generate the reference ramp, but it does have the advantage of being easier to set up and, being a single ramp system, gives a shorter conversion time.

Tracking converters

A major disadvantage of the simple counter type converter with a DAC feedback loop is that it has to carry out a counting cycle proportional to the input each time a conversion is made. An alternative approach to this feedback type of conversion makes use of an up–down counter instead of a simple up counter. The general arrangement is as shown in Figure 7.13.

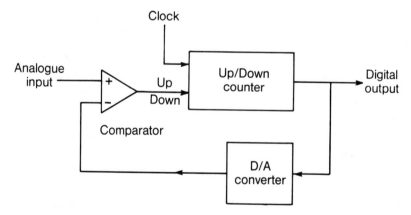

Fig. 7.13 Basic arrangement of a tracking-type analogue-to-digital converter.

In this circuit the output of the comparator is used to determine whether the counter increments or decrements on each clock pulse. If the input voltage is larger than the feedback voltage from the DAC, the counter mode is switched so that its count value increases, thus increasing the DAC voltage level. When the input is lower than the DAC reference level then the counter is switched to its count down mode and the DAC output starts to fall. When the DAC signal is approximately equal to the input voltage the counter will spend most of its time just oscillating back and forth by one count step. As the input changes the counter and the DAC voltage will simply follow it to a new digital counter reading. In effect the digital output from this type of converter will continually follow the input and for this reason it is called a 'tracking' converter.

The advantage here is that when a digital readout is required there is no need to wait for a conversion cycle since the counter contents already represent the most recent value of the input signal. The counter contents are simply read by the CPU. This type of converter does however have a disadvantage since the rate at which it can follow a rapidly changing signal is limited and, ideally, the input should not change by more than one resolution step in one counter clock period. The maximum slew rate of the input is therefore given by:

$$SR = \frac{V_m}{N_s T_c}$$

where SR is the slew rate in V/s, T_c is the clock period in seconds and N_s is the number of resolution steps for full scale. The value of N_s is 2^n where n is the number of data bits in the digital output word. Thus for a 12-bit converter (N_s=4096 steps) with a 1 MHz clock rate and a full-scale output of 10 V the maximum slew rate is:

$$SR = \frac{10 \times 10^6}{4096 \times 1} = 2500 \text{ V/s}$$

which means that the maximum frequency sine wave that it can follow is about 80 hertz assuming that the sine wave has a peak to peak amplitude of 10 volts.

An example of a tracking type converter is the Datel ADC856 which provides a 10-bit conversion and can handle signals up to 300 hertz. This device is packaged as a 28 lead integrated circuit and can fairly easily be interfaced to a microprocessor system.

Successive approximation converters

The simple counter type converter using a D/A network works very well when the number of bits required from the digital output is relatively small, say up to 8 bits, or there is ample time available for carrying out the conversion. If we consider a 12-bit converter, the maximum count will be 4096 clock cycles and, even using a 1 MHz timing clock, the conversion time will be in the region of 4 milliseconds, which for many applications is very slow. Increasing the clock rate can present problems with reliable operation of the comparator, and possibly the D/A circuits, so some alternative scheme of deriving the required output data must be used. The most popular method is that of 'successive approximation'.

The technique used is similar to that of using a set of scales to find the weight of an object. The unknown object is placed in the pan on one side of the scales and weights of known values are then added to the other scale pan until the scales come into balance, at which point the weight of the object being measured is equal to the sum of the known weights in the second pan.

The logical method of weighing the object is to add the known weights, in sequence, heaviest first. If the scales tilt towards the pan with the known weights, (i.e. the object being weighed is lighter), the weight last added is replaced with the next lowest weight in the set. This is repeated until the scales tilt towards the unknown weight: now the unknown weight is the heavier. When this happens, add the next heaviest known weight to those already in the pan and continue the above procedure until the scales balance.

The electronic scheme works in much the same fashion. The counter of the earlier type of converter is replaced by a special register and control logic called a successive approximation register. At the start of conversion all of the bits in this register are set at '0'. The first step is to set the most significant bit of the register to '1'. This action causes the output of the D/A converter to rise to about half the full-scale analogue level. The output of the comparator is examined and if it indicates that the input is less than the D/A signal, the bit in the register is reset to '0'. If the analogue input is greater then the bit is allowed to remain set at '1'. The next significant bit in the register is then set at '1' and the process is repeated as shown in Figure 7.14. This action continues for each bit in turn until all of the bits in the register have been operated upon. At this point, the output of the D/A converter should be approximately equal to the input signal and the digital value for the input signal will be set up in the successive approximation register. Conversion is now complete and the data may be read into the microcomputer system as desired.

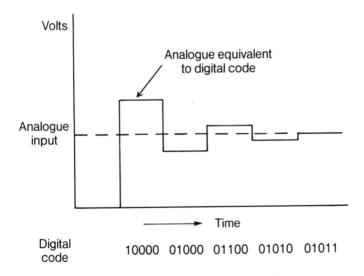

Fig. 7.14 Principle of the successive approximation-type converter.

In the successive approximation technique the number of steps in the conversion process is the same as the number of bits required in the digital output. Thus a 12-bit converter would require just 12 clock cycles to complete its conversion and, using a 1 MHz clock, this would give a conversion time of only 12 microseconds compared with some 4 milliseconds for a counter-type converter. In fact most of the faster A/D converter devices use this successive approximation technique.

Nearly all of the popular A/D converters which are designed to be interfaced to microprocessor systems are of the successive approximation type.

Missing codes

One important fault condition in the analogue to digital conversion system is that of missing codes. This will normally occur only in the successive approximation types of converter and is the converse of the monotonicity problem in a D/A converter. If the step size of the individual bits is not accurate, generally due to poor monotonicity in the DAC used within the converter, then it is possible that some output codes may be missed out altogether.

Other parameters of an A/D converter such as linearity, scaling accuracy, resolution and stability are measured in the same terms as those of a D/A converter.

Coding schemes

In practical D/A converter devices the digital input may be coded in various different ways and the analogue output signal may be either unipolar or bipolar. In a unipolar converter, the output signal is always positive (or always negative) over the range of digital inputs as shown in Figure 7.15. A bipolar converter permits both positive and negative analogue outputs. Normally bipolar converters are set up so that the positive and negative limit outputs are approximately equal in magnitude.

In a unipolar converter the simplest coding scheme is pure binary code and, for an 8-bit converter, the digital input codes will range from 0 up to a maximum value of 255. Where the computer is operating on binary coded decimal (BCD) numbers it may be more convenient to have the D/A converter accept a BCD format input. In this case the 8 data bits may be arranged in two groups of 4 as shown in Figure 7.16. Now the lower 4 bits represent units whilst the upper 4 represent tens. Inside the converter two separate ladder networks are used, one for the tens bit group and the other for units. The output of the units network is then scaled down by a factor of ten before it is added to the output of the tens network as shown in Figure

Binary code	Analogue output
1111	3.75 V
1110	3.5 V
1101	3.25 V
1100	3.00 V
1011	2.75 V
1010	2.5 V
1001	2.25 V
1000	2.00 V
0111	1.75 V
0110	1.5 V
0101	1.25 V
0100	1.00 V
0011	0.75 V
0010	0.5 V
0001	0.25 V
0000	0 V

Fig. 7.15 Unipolar binary coding scheme used on both A/D and D/A converters.

BCD data code		Analogue voltage
Tens	Units	
1001	1001	9.9 V (full scale)
1000	0100	8.4 V
0101	0101	5.5 V
0010	0100	2.4 V
0001	0000	1 V
0000	1000	0.8 V
0000	0010	0.2 V
0000	0000	0 V

Fig. 7.16 BCD coding for A/D and D/A converters.

7.17. One important consequence of using the BCD coding scheme is that the resolution of the converter has been reduced. In the BCD format the converter can only resolve 100 output levels corresponding to digital values from 0 to 99, as compared to the binary version which is capable of resolving 256 steps from 0 to 255. Despite this loss of resolution, the BCD format converter can often be useful in systems where it is more convenient to use BCD rather than binary coding in the computer data.

When the range of outputs is to be bipolar, several options are available for the arrangement of the digital input coding. The simplest is known as

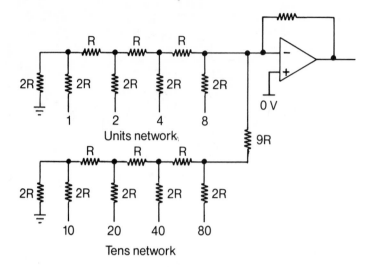

Fig. 7.17 Arrangement of the tens and units registers in a D/A or A/D converter.

offset binary coding. Here the input to the converter is a simple binary code from 0 to 255, as for a unipolar device, but the analogue output has an offset bias applied so that zero output occurs when the input data value is 128. Now inputs below 128 will produce a negative output voltage whose magnitude increases as the digital input falls toward the 0 level. Input values above 128 produce a positive output which increases in sympathy with the digital level as shown in Figure 7.18.

Binary code	Analogue output
1111	+1.75 V
1110	+1.5 V
1101	+1.25 V
1100	+1.0 V
1011	+0.75 V
1010	+0.5 V
1001	+0.25 V
1000	0 V
0111	−0.25 V
0110	−0.5 V
0101	−0.75 V
0100	−1.0 V
0011	−1.25 V
0010	−1.5 V
0001	−1.75 V
0000	−2.0 V

Fig. 7.18 The offset binary code.

An alternative form of digital coding is signed binary. In this case the most significant data bit is used as a polarity indicator. When this bit is at 0, the analogue output is positive whilst if the bit is set at 1, the analogue signal is negative. The magnitude of the analogue output is determined by the lower 7 bits of data and there will be a total of 128 steps. This type of signed binary format is easy to understand but is not particularly compatible with the arithmetic operations within the CPU which normally use complemented binary format. In this form the most significant bit again acts as a sign or polarity indicator but the magnitude of the negative values is represented in twos complement form as shown in Figure 7.19. Where BCD coding is used, one bit, usually the most significant bit of the highest significant BCD digit, may be used as a sign bit.

Binary code	Analogue output
1111	−0.25 V
1110	−0.5 V
1101	−0.75 V
1100	−1.0 V
1011	−1.25 V
1010	−1.5 V
1001	−1.75 V
1000	−2.0 V
0111	+1.75 V
0110	+1.5 V
0101	+1.25 V
0100	+1.0 V
0011	+0.75 V
0010	+0.5 V
0001	+0.25 V
0000	0 V

Fig. 7.19 Complemented binary coding scheme used on many types of A/D or D/A converters.

In general the data coding arrangements of analogue to digital converters follow the same pattern as for digital to analogue conversion. The main types are usually pure binary coded with either unipolar coding or with bipolar coding using either sign magnitude or offset formats. It is also possible to obtain binary coded decimal formats with both unipolar or bipolar coding.

Choice of a converter

The type of conversion process chosen for a system will depend upon the requirements of the data acquisition scheme. The main factors involved are speed, conversion accuracy and cost.

For high-speed conversion the choice will usually be the successive approximation type of converter which will give typical conversion times of the order 10–15 microseconds or better for a 12-bit converter. This type of converter may need a sample hold circuit to ensure that the input remains constant throughout the conversion period. In general the cost of this type of converter has fallen in recent years with the availability of fully integrated or hybrid converter modules.

The tracking-type converter can be very useful since this is continuously converting the input signal and therefore the effective conversion time is merely the time taken to read the current value of the internal counter. The digital accuracy is not as good as in a successive approximation type since the results are + or − one bit as against the half-bit accuracy of the other types. The tracking converter does not need a sample hold circuit. If several channels are to be read in sequence it may be wise to use holding registers so that the outputs of all of the A/D circuits can be latched at one time and then read at leisure into the computer. If this were not done the readings would effectively be staggered in time.

Where speed is not too important the counter or dual ramp type converters may be more useful. These are generally less expensive to implement although they may have no advantage in terms of size. The dual slope converter is particularly useful with noisy signals because of its integration characteristic. By choosing an integration time equal to, say, the period of the power supply AC input, it is possible to cancel any effects due to pick-up of the mains frequency signal in the analogue inputs. This type of converter also tends to be virtually immune to the effects of noise spikes on the inputs because of its integration action. Most digital panel meters use some form of dual slope conversion technique.

For very high-speed conversion, such as the digitisation of video signals, special types of converter may be used. These use a bank of separate comparators operating either in parallel or in a ripple through mode. Conversion times for such devices may be as short as 100 ns for 12-bit precision.

Interfacing to the CPU

Where a D/A converter is to be used in a microcomputer system some means of interfacing it to the computer data bus is required. The converter ladder network and switches will need a continuous digital input applied whereas the data on the computer bus is multiplexed and therefore continually changing. Some form of data register external to the computer system will be required which can retain the digital data from the computer to provide the drive for the converter.

The drive for a D/A converter can be readily produced by using a parallel data output port as shown in Figure 7.20. To output a signal to the D/A converter the computer addresses the appropriate output port and data is transferred via the data bus to the output register in the data port. This digital signal is then applied to the switch drive inputs of the D/A converter device. In the computer program a data transfer instruction is inserted each time the analogue output is to be updated. Usually this will occur at regular time intervals and the updating of all output channels both analogue and digital may be performed by using an interrupt service routine triggered by an external clock signal.

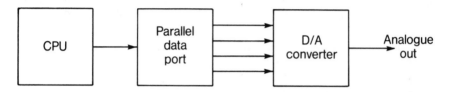

Fig. 7.20 Simple approach to interfacing a D/A converter to a CPU using parallel ports.

Many of the newer designs of D/A converter have a built-in data register which may have external data clocked into it as shown in Figure 7.21. Where this type of converter is used its input data lines may be connected to the CPU data bus directly. To output data to the D/A converter an address

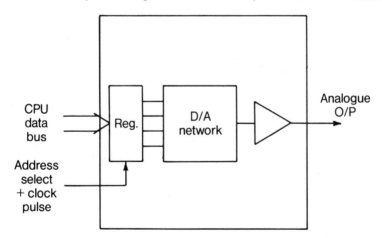

Fig. 7.21 Arrangement of a D/A converter which is designed to be built into a computer bus system.

decoder is used to select a particular combination of data on the address bus and the CPU R/W and clock lines. When this combination is detected the data gates are activated and the data word is transferred via the data bus to the D/A register. Sometimes a clock pulse is required for the

D/A register and this can be obtained from the same address decoder circuit. Some modern D/A converters are designed for use in micro-processor systems and will have the gates and register built in. These may simply be treated as an output port device and are activated by a specific memory address and a STORE instruction to the CPU. In a general purpose microprocessor system it is often convenient to use only partial address decoding so that the converter will in fact respond to a whole block of addresses in the memory map.

An interesting situation occurs when a 12-bit D/A converter is to be interfaced to a microprocessor system. If the microprocessor has a 16-bit data bus there is no real problem since the converter data can be transferred from the lower 12 bits of the data word. When an 8-bit data bus is used however the data must be transferred as two data words and some care is needed in arranging this transfer. The usual scheme is to incorporate a temporary data latch as shown in Figure 7.22. The temporary register is used to hold the upper 4 data bits. The first step in producing an output is to transfer the upper 4 data bits to the latch. When the lower 8 bits are transferred from the microprocessor data bus, the upper 4 bits are transferred into the converter register at the same time so that all 12 bits are presented to the D/A conversion network simultaneously. If this were not done, then, for a brief period, the upper 4 bits would have been updated whilst the original values for the lower 8 bits remained present and a serious step of incorrect analogue output could easily result, particularly where the signal level is near one of the major changeover points in the digital data pattern.

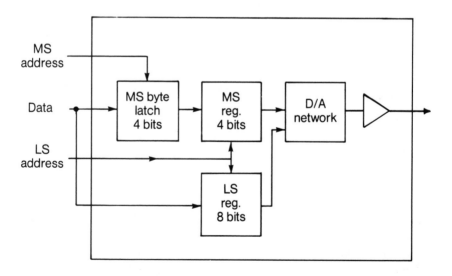

Fig. 7.22 Latching arrangement used to get 12-bit data for a D/A converter.

The actual choice of which part of the data word is latched depends upon the way in which the CPU will handle a double length data word. In the Motorola series converters it is usual to store the more significant word first with the lower significant word in the next memory address. Since the input–output on these processors is memory mapped it is convenient to maintain the same convention. The double length word can in fact be output using just one instruction by making use of the index register. If the data word is set up in the index register and then written to memory using an STX instruction the processor will automatically store the two 8-bit segments in successive memory addresses. In this case the strobe pulses for the DAC data registers are derived from the address and processor clock pulses so that, as each address is set up on the address bus, the data will automatically be routed to the correct register in the DAC system.

Handshake lines are not normally required when interfacing a D/A converter to the computer bus since the requirement is simply that the computer output some data to the converter which, in turn, will produce the corresponding analogue output voltage.

A few D/A converters are designed to accept a serial input data signal rather than direct parallel data. This has some advantages in reducing the number of interconnecting wires and may be useful where the D/A converter is located in a remote position or in an area where only a limited number of wires may be used for the link to the computer. Three signals are normally required for such a system as shown in Figure 7.23. The serial data and an associated train of clock pulses are fed to a shift register in the D/A device. Data is clocked out from the computer in serial form and shifts through the shift register. When the last bit of the serial has been transferred, an enable or transfer pulse is sent along a third wire and this causes the data in the shift register to be transferred in parallel to the main data register of the D/A converter where it generates the required analogue output.

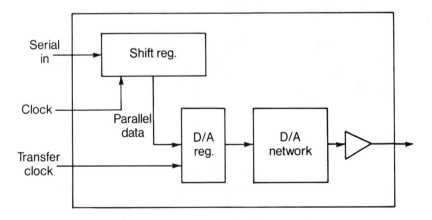

Fig. 7.23 Serial interface to a DAC.

A/D converter interfacing uses a similar approach to that for interfacing a D/A converter except that data is read from the converter rather than written to it. There is however an additional requirement which may involve the use of handshake signals.

Most A/D converters will need an input signal which initiates the conversion process. When the A/D converter is directly interfaced to the bus system a popular method of dealing with this requirement is to use a dummy write instruction to the memory address used by the converter. An address decoder which is gated to operate when the R/W control line is in the 'write' state is used to detect the dummy write instruction and generates a pulse which initiates the conversion process. If the A/D converter is interfaced to a parallel data port a strobe handshake output may be used to initiate the conversion.

Once the conversion has been initiated, the A/D converter will take some time before it presents a valid digital output and the CPU must wait for a period before it tries to read data from the converter. Where a data port is used, a further handshake line may be used to tell the CPU that conversion is in progress. At the end of the conversion time the CPU detects the change in the status condition and reads in the data. With a memory-mapped converter the CPU can be placed in a delay loop which allows sufficient time for the A/D converter to complete its conversion process. At the end of this delay the CPU reads in the digital data. With fast successive-approximation converters, the required delay may be only a few microseconds and is readily achieved by inserting one or two dummy instructions between the ADC initiation command and the instructions that read the data. A typical A/D converter read routine using this approach might be as follows:

STAA	ADC1	Initiate conversion
NOP		No operation (delay)
NOP		No operation (delay)
LDAA	ADC1	Read MS byte
LDAB	ADC1+1	Read LS byte

In this case NOP instructions are used for the delay but these might equally well have been CLRA (Clear Accumulator) or some other instruction which takes up time but does not upset the program sequence or any data that is currently held in the CPU.

Test routines

In order to check that the A/D or D/A converter devices are operating correctly it is useful if some test routines are built into the software of the microcomputer system. Perhaps the most effective test for a D/A converter is that of generating a linear sawtooth output waveform. The sawtooth is produced by incrementing the digital input to the D/A converter through its entire range and repeating this process continually. The sawtooth waveform analogue output from the D/A converter may then be examined by displaying it on an oscilloscope or by using a chart recorder. Examination of the displayed waveform will reveal problems such as missing data bits, monotonicity errors and non-linearity. Failure of a data bit signal, where the bit remains permanently on or off, produces discontinuities and displacement of sections of the sawtooth. Monotonicity errors will normally produce a small kink in an otherwise linear output waveform.

Non-linearity of the analogue output may be seen as curvature of the ramp output although for most converters the non-linearity will need to be quite severe before it becomes obvious in the output display. Before checking non-linearity in a D/A converter using this method, it is important to check that the display device itself has a linear response.

Glitches may be detected by examining the output using an oscilloscope. Because the spikes produced in the output waveform are extremely short in duration they may be difficult to see unless an expanded or dual timebase facility is available on the oscilloscope. The most important glitches in terms of their potential amplitude are likely to be found at the quarter and half full scale transitions. An alternative means of detecting glitches is to feed the D/A converter output to a logic analyser. It will also be useful to feed the digital input signals to the same logic analyser since they can provide a position reference which will show where in the sawtooth the glitch occurs.

The program needed to generate a linear sawtooth output is a repetitive counting loop which cycles through all of the digital values and then repeats the cycle indefinitely. This may be set up as a test subroutine which may be selected from the main program. As an example of this type of test program the following machine code routine might be used:

```
START    LDAA    #255      Set full scale o/p
         STAA    COUNT
LOOP     JSR     DELAY     Time delay routine
         LDAA    COUNT
         STAA    DAC       Output data to DAC
         BEQ     START     Cycle complete?
         DEC     COUNT     Decrement output
         JSR     CHRIN     Read from keyboard
         CMPA    #13       Carriage return?
         BNE     LOOP      No, continue test
         RTS               Yes, exit routine
```

Here the output to the D/A converter is held as a variable called COUNT and this is set at full scale at the start of the routine. A time delay routine is called to determine the timing between output steps to the D/A converter. The current value of COUNT is then written to the converter which, in this case, has the variable address called DAC. After the data has been output a test is made to see if COUNT has reached zero and if it has the program returns to the start of the routine to begin a new output cycle. When COUNT is not zero its value is decremented and the program runs round the inner loop returning to the DELAY routine before outputting a new digital value to the D/A converter.

One problem with this type of continuous loop is that it would normally run for ever, so some form of exit routine must be included. The simplest approach is to check for a character input from the keyboard after each output step to the D/A converter. This is done by calling a subroutine (CHRIN) which reads a character from the keyboard and places its ASCII code into the accumulator. If a character is detected a check is made to see if it is a 'carriage return' (ASCII code value 13). When this test fails the loop returns to LOOP and starts the next time delay period but if the character detected is a carriage return the subroutine exits back to the main program. Any desired character may be used to initiate the exit from the test routine by inserting the appropriate ASCII character code into the compare (CMPA) statement.

Testing an A/D converter is a little more difficult. The most convenient approach is to make the A/D converter operate at regular intervals, then let the CPU read data from the A/D converter and immediately output the data via a D/A converter to produce an analogue output. The analogue output can then be compared with the analogue input that is being applied. As with the D/A converter a convenient waveform for test purposes is a linear sawtooth or triangular waveform which may be generated by a suitable external waveform generator. The rate at which samples are taken, and the timing of the test waveform, must be adjusted so that the A/D converter can produce all of its possible digital output values during each cycle of the input wave. Thus for an 8-bit converter (256 levels), if the sampling interval is say 100 microseconds then the minimum cycle period for the sawtooth input must be 256×100 microseconds or 25.6 milliseconds giving a sawtooth frequency of about 40 hertz.

The analogue output from the D/A converter channel may be compared with the input waveform by using a dual-beam oscilloscope or dual-trace pen recorder. Once again faulty data bits, missing codes and non-linearity may be detected by examining the output analogue waveform. Missing codes in the A/D converter will produce a similar effect to monotonicity errors in a D/A converter. It is important that the D/A converter is checked for non-linearity and other errors prior to the test on the A/D converter.

The program routine for this test might be arranged as follows:

```
START    JSR     DELAY      Time delay
         STAA    ADC        Start conversion
         NOP                Delay to allow ADC
         NOP                to convert data
         LDAA    ADC        Read ADC data
         STAA    DAC        Output to DAC
         JSR     CHRIN      Read keyboard
```

```
CMPA   #27      Test for ESC code
BNE    START    No, continue loop
RTS             Yes, exit routine
```

Here again a keyboard test routine has been included so that the test can be terminated by inputting a character code from the keyboard. In this case the test looks for an ESC (Escape) control code which has the decimal value 27 (hex value 1B). The ESC key is a convenient one for this purpose because it is usually located at a corner of the keyboard and is a key that is not normally used when entering information from the keyboard.

Setting up routines

In a typical D/A converter the tolerances on the analogue sections of the circuit mean that some adjustments are required to set up the overall sensitivity and take out any zero offset. The sensitivity is controlled by a potentiometer which varies the gain of the analogue buffer amplifier. The zero setting is controlled by a second potentiometer which applies an offset bias to one of the amplifier inputs.

To facilitate the setting up of these adjustments we need a simple computer routine which alternately applies a zero and a full scale input to the digital side of the converter. The analogue output of the converter may be connected to a digital voltmeter and the gain and offset adjustments may then be made until the analogue output readings are correctly set up.

A simple repetitive loop may be used for this purpose and each digital output level is applied to the converter for a period of say one or two seconds. In many converter schemes the two adjustments interact with one another so the alternate switching from one state to the other should allow the two adjustments to be completed satisfactorily. In some converter systems, where the output is bipolar, the adjustment sequence may need to alternate between full scale negative and full scale positive for proper setting up so the converter data sheet should be consulted to determine the best sequence for the setting up routine.

An A/D converter will also have zero offset and gain adjustments which need to be set up for proper operation. Here the analogue input is applied from an accurate DC voltage source. The computer routine is required to initiate conversion and read the digital result at regular intervals of perhaps one second. The output can conveniently be displayed as integer numbers on the display screen of the terminal that is used to communicate with the microprocessor system. With zero input applied the zero offset is adjusted until the desired digital reading is obtained. Full scale, or near full scale, input is then applied and the gain adjustment is set up. Once again the two adjustments may need to be repeated alternately and readjusted until satisfactory results are obtained.

Like the test routines these calibration and setting up subroutines are arranged as continuous repetitive loops and must include a test which checks for an input from the keyboard and, on recognising a specified character code, will cause the subroutine to terminate and return program control to the main program in the microcomputer.

Chapter Eight
Data Acquisition

So far we have looked at ways in which analogue or digital signals may be input to or output from a microprocessor system. In most intrumentation and control applications of a microprocessor we shall want to acquire data from a number of input sources, process the data and then store or output the results. We shall now look at some of the aspects of data acquisition which will influence the design of the processor system.

Signal sampling

The signals occurring in the real world outside the computer may take a variety of forms. In general these signals will be analogue types and will have an infinite number of possible values within their range limits. When the computer takes a reading of an input it effectively samples the instantaneous value of that input at the time of measurement. The results obtained from a data acquisition program are very much dependent upon the frequency at which the samples are taken and the characteristics of the signal being measured.

Perhaps the simplest signals are those which remain essentially constant or change very slowly with time. Examples of such signals might be measurements of the water level in a tank or of the ambient temperature. Sampling rates of perhaps one reading per minute or even one per hour may be perfectly adequate for these slowly varying signals, since they are unlikely to change significantly between successive samples. There is little point in using a high sampling rate, such as 10 samples per second, since this will merely produce strings of virtually identical readings and result in a mass of redundant and basically useless data which fills the available memory space in the computer.

Let us suppose that we are monitoring a simple sine wave signal with a frequency of 100 hertz. If the sampling rate is set at, say, 10000 per second then there will be 100 samples for every cycle of the input signal. If these sample values were now plotted against time the result would be a graph which would be a virtually perfect reproduction of the original sine wave.

If the sample rate is now reduced to, say, 1000 per second there will be only 10 samples per cycle of the signal waveform. If these are plotted they will still lie on a sine curve but will not define the curve as well as the high sample rate. This is shown in Figure 8.1. If the points are joined by straight lines, the sine wave is still recognisable and the straight line interpolation will introduce a relatively small error.

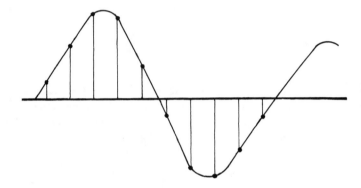

Fig. 8.1 Effect of sampling a sine wave with about 10 samples per cycle.

If the data obtained using 10 samples per cycle were spectrum analysed by using a Fourier analysis technique, the result would still show a fundamental sine wave at 100 hertz with a small harmonic content. The original waveform could also be reproduced reasonably successfully from the sampled data points, albeit with some percentage of distortion.

If the number of samples per cycle of the input signal were reduced further, the original waveform becomes increasingly difficult to reconstruct. At two points per cycle it is still theoretically possible to reconstruct the original value of the sine wave component by using a Fourier analysis technique. This however assumes that the two points have non-zero values.

Reducing the sample rate below two samples per cycle will cause the sampled point on the input signal to creep through the sine wave cycle on successive samples as shown in Figure 8.2. If the points are now joined they will appear to indicate a waveform of a different frequency from the original input wave and the data obtained becomes invalid. Now it may no longer be possible to reconstruct the original sine wave signal.

This is in fact the basic finding in the theory for sampled data signals and the frequency where there are two samples per cycle of the input waveform is called the Nyquist frequency. The criterion for choosing the sampling rate is that there must be at least two non-zero samples for every cycle of the highest frequency input signal that is to be resolved. Obviously all lower frequency signals will be sampled more than twice per cycle and therefore must be resolvable.

Therefore the minimum sampling frequency f_s must be:

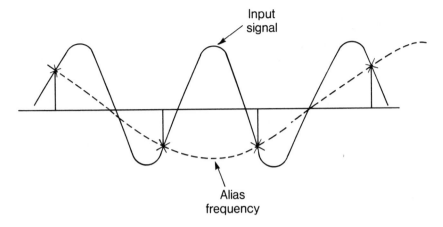

Fig. 8.2 Effect of sampling a sine wave with 1.5 samples per cycle.

$$f_s = 2 \times f_h$$

where f_h is the highest data frequency required. Working in terms of the time period between samples we get:

$$T_s = 0.5\ T_d = \frac{1}{2f_h}$$

where T_s is the sampling interval and T_d is the period of the input data.

Aliasing

When the sampling frequency is reduced below two samples per cycle of the input frequency we have seen that a lower frequency now appears that was not present in the original input. This new false signal is called an 'alias' signal.

When a signal is sampled the result is similar to that produced by amplitude modulating a train of pulses with the input signal, as shown in Figure 8.3, where the height of each sample varies in amplitude in sympathy with the signal frequency.

In amplitude modulation, using sine wave signals for both the carrier and the modulating signal, the amplitude of the resultant waveform is given by the product of the two signals f_d and f_s to give:

$$V = A(1 + \cos 2\pi f_d t) \cos 2\pi f_s\, t$$

where V is the resultant signal, f_d is the data frequency, f_s is the sampling frequency and A is an amplitude constant. Here it has been assumed that the data signal, f_d, modulates the sample frequency f_s fully (i.e. 100% modulation). Multiplying through gives:

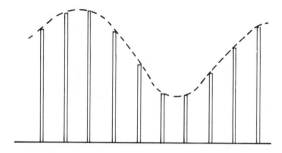

Fig. 8.3 The modulated pulse waveform produced by a sampling process.

$$V = A\cos 2\pi f_s t + A\cos 2\pi f_s t \cos 2\pi f_d t$$

Substituting

$$\cos A \cos B = (\cos A{+}B)/2 + (\cos A{-}B)/2$$

we get:

$$V = A\cos 2\pi f_s t + 0.5A\cos(2\pi f_s + 2\pi f_d)t + 0.5A\cos(2\pi f_s - 2\pi f_d)t$$

Thus the sampling process produces not only the original components, f_d and f_s, but two new signals which have frequencies equal to the sum and difference respectively of f_d and f_s. This is shown in Figure 8.4.

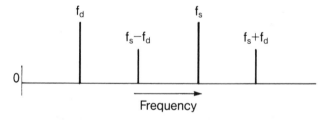

Fig. 8.4 The sum and difference frequency components.

   In a practical system the input signal will cover a range of frequencies and is conveniently shown as a band of signals ranging from zero (DC) up to some frequency f_h. Generally the amplitude of the signal components will tend to fall off smoothly with increasing frequency as shown in Figure 8.5. Because the sample component is actually a pulse it can be represented by a fundamental frequency, f_s, and a series of harmonic components, $2f_s$, $3f_s$, $4f_s$ and so on. Each of these components will produce sum and difference frequencies with the input signal to give a spectrum similar to that shown in Figure 8.5.

   We have assumed so far that the input signal contains no frequencies higher than f_h which is the highest we are interested in measuring. In practice this is extremely unlikely since there will always be a certain amount of random noise present and the frequency components of this noise will extend beyond the frequency f_h. Let us suppose that we have selected a

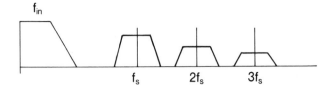

Fig. 8.5 Frequency spectrum produced by a sampled data signal.

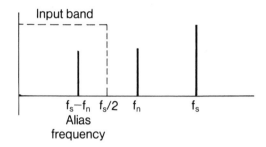

Fig. 8.6 The production of an aliasing frequency component when a signal falls at a frequency greater than $f_s/2$.

sampling frequency, f_s, which is twice f_h but that a higher frequency input signal, f_n, is also present as shown in Figure 8.6.

The difference component, f_s-f_n, lies below frequency f_h and therefore appears to be a new input frequency within the band of frequencies that we are accepting as valid data. This frequency f_s-f_n is an 'alias' frequency since it did not exist in the original input and has been produced solely by the sampling process. The computer is unable to detect the difference between the 'alias' signal at frequency f_s-f_n and a real signal at that frequency, so it will produce false results in any analysis of the sampled input signal.

To avoid problems with alias signals we need to eliminate any input signals with frequencies between $f_s/2$ and f_s which could produce 'alias' components. This can be done by passing the input signal through a low-pass filter before it is sampled. In our example, where $f_s = 100$ hertz, this means that all frequencies above 50 hertz need to be removed by the filter without affecting the valid input signals in the 0 to 50 hertz range. Theoretically, any filter used must give no attenuation up to $f_s/2$ and virtually infinite attenuation at all frequencies above $f_s/2$. In practice such a filter characteristic is not achievable so some form of compromise must be accepted. The usual solution is to limit the input data bandwidth in comparison to the sampling frequency, f_s, when it becomes possible to produce a filter that gives minimal attenuation of the wanted signal whilst giving a good rejection of signals above $f_s/2$. In a practical system with $f_s = 100$ hertz the filter might be designed to have a cut-off frequency (3dB point) of say 20 hertz. The filter will still need to have a rapid roll-off characteristic beyond the cut-off frequency if it is to provide enough attenuation at and above the 50 hertz point.

The type of filter characteristic needed and the degree of attenuation in the stop band will depend upon the anticipated level of noise or spurious signals that might occur in the band between $f_s/2$ and f_s. Ideally the filter must reduce these components to less than one step of resolution in the binary data. Thus for an 8-bit data word, if we assume that the noise signal is of the same amplitude as the data signal, the attenuation factor needs to be about 250 to 1, so the filter must provide a stop band attenuation of some 48 dB. A more realistic signal to noise ratio might be say 20 to 1 so the attenuation requirement would fall to perhaps 22 dB. With practical filters this usually means that the data pass band has to be limited to perhaps $0.2f_s$.

Multiplexed channel operation

So far we have considered the case of a single input data channel, but in a practical system it is likely that several different input signals will need to be measured simultaneously. If the signals are already digital in form and can be switched on to the computer bus system then it is quite a straightforward matter to take the samples from the channels in sequence. Each channel is allocated a different memory address and the CPU is told to read data from each input address in sequence. If the input signals are analogue in form then a separate analogue-to-digital converter is included in each input line to provide a digital signal that may be read into the CPU, so that we may have a system similar to that shown in Figure 8.7.

The next consideration is to decide whether to read the signals into the CPU in one short burst or to spread out the sample times over the complete

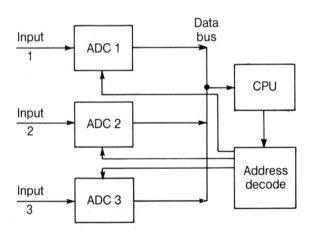

Fig. 8.7 A multi-channel analogue input system using separate A/D converters in each channel.

multiplex cycle as shown in Figure 8.8. The advantage of the burst method is that the samples are taken at virtually the same time so that there will be little phase shift error between the samples on different channels. In a system where the multiplexer is driven by external logic it may be more convenient to use the equally spaced sampling points. If this is done then it is best to acquire all of the data on all channels at the same point of the cycle and then hold the channel outputs steady throughout the sampling cycle.

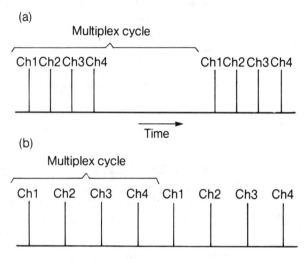

Fig. 8.8 Multiplexing schemes using burst and evenly spaced sampling techniques.

Analogue multiplexing

One disadvantage of multiplexing the digital signals is that a separate A/D converter is required for each analogue channel. Although modern A/D converter devices are relatively cheap, this method becomes unattractive when a large number of analogue channels are to be used. A further disadvantage is that the A/D converter may be a relatively large device and space may be limited. Instead of using a separate A/D converter for each analogue input, an alternative solution is to use a multiplex switch to select each analogue input in turn and apply it to a common A/D converter device which then produces the corresponding digital signal for input to the CPU, as shown in Figure 8.9.

Analogue multiplexers generally fall into two basic types. The simplest is the mechanical switch or relay which provides low series resistance and large signal handling capacity but is relatively slow in operation. The alternative is a solid state switch which will generally employ field-effect transistors. The solid state switches can be extremely fast in operation but generally have a significant 'on' resistance and will usually have only a limited voltage range. The choice of solid state or mechanical switches will depend upon the application and the type of signals being handled.

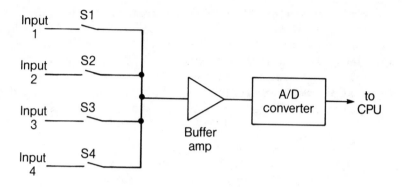

switches S1–S4 selected by CPU

Fig. 8.9 Multi-channel analogue input arrangement using an analogue multiplexer.

The analogue multiplexer using solid state switches will take the form shown in Figure 8.10. The individual switches may be selected by using separate output lines from a digital data port and setting each output line to the '1' state in sequence to select the analogue channels. Some multiplexer

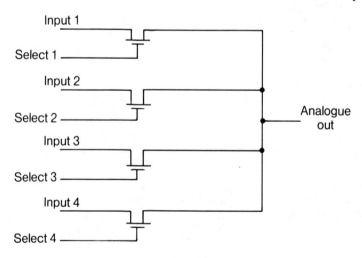

Fig. 8.10 Typical solid state multiplexer arrangement.

switch devices are arranged in groups of four or eight switches and a built-in address decoder is included. For these types, the switch may be selected by using signals from the CPU address bus and treating each switch as if it were a memory location. To take a data sample from an input channel the multiplex switch must first be selected by the CPU and then, after a short period to allow the signal to settle to a stable level, the A/D converter is given a convert command. When conversion is complete the digital data word is read into the computer.

The characteristics of the buffer amplifier used between the multiplex switches and the A/D converter are very important when designing a system. One important factor is the rate at which the output of the amplifier can change. Suppose one analogue input is at maximum signal level and the next is at the minimum level. After the multiplexer has switched, the amplifier output will have to slew through the entire input signal range. Suppose the range is 10 volts and the amplifier is a standard 741-type device. The slew rate of the output of a 741 amplifier is $0.5 \text{ V}/\mu\text{s}$, so the time taken to slew through 10 volts will be 20 microseconds and the A/D converter command pulse must be delayed by at least 25 microseconds after the command to the multiplex switch.

The total time taken for the buffer amplifier, multiplex switch and A/D conversion will limit the rate at which the samples can be taken if the burst reading mode is used. If the samples are spread out equally through the sampling interval this will generally allow much more time for data switching and conversion on each channel.

Supermultiplexing

In some systems the frequency range of the input signals will vary from channel to channel with some channels having virtually constant signal levels and others varying at high frequencies. Although it is possible to sample all channels at a sufficiently high sample rate to cover the highest expected signal frequencies, this can result in a lot of redundant information on those channels with slowly varying signals. If there are only a few channels with high frequency data this situation can be improved by using a supermultiplexing scheme. In this arrangement the high frequency channel is sampled several times in each multiplex cycle as shown in Figure 8.11. Here the slower channels are sampled once per multiplex cycle but for high frequency channels, extra samples are taken and interleaved with data for slower channels at evenly spaced intervals through the cycle. Suppose eight samples are taken and interleaved in this way. The effective sampling rate of the high frequency channel is now eight times that of the other channels and its effective frequency range is therefore increased by eight. This high frequency signal is said to be 'supermultiplexed'. It is possible to have a second supermultiplexed channel with say four samples taken during a normal multiplex cycle to give a four-fold increase in frequency range. These two different supermultiplex channels may be combined with normal channels as shown in Figure 8.11.

Ground returns

When connecting up any system of analogue and digital circuits, the

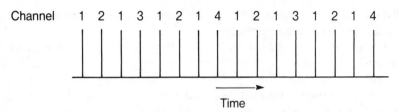

Channel 1 2 1 3 1 2 1 4 1 2 1 3 1 2 1 4

Time

Fig. 8.11 Interleaving of supermultiplexed and normal channels within a common multiplex cycle.

arrangement of the ground return wiring can be vitally important. This becomes especially true if the analogue signals being measured are of small amplitude, or if a high resolution A/D converter is being used.

The ground return wire for the digital parts of the system can carry quite large current pulses, as the load current changes when several digital gates change state at the same time. If the digital circuits are properly decoupled on the circuit board most of the very fast switching spikes will not get on to the power lines, but the logic power supply rails are generally quite noisy as will be seen if they are examined with an oscilloscope. If the 0 V return wire for a digital power supply is made common with the analogue ground return, then any noise developed along the common return wire will be added to the analogue input signal to produce noise and possible data errors.

To avoid problems with cross-coupling between digital and analogue circuits it is important that the only common ground point between the analogue and digital parts of the system should be made at the A/D converter itself. In fact an A/D converter will normally have separate connections for its analogue signal ground and its digital logic ground. The signal grounds for the analogue multiplexer and any amplifiers or filters in the analogue chain must be routed directly to the analogue ground on the A/D converter and not to a local power ground. When screened cables are used and the screen is used as a signal return, this can present problems since, ideally, all of these screens should be kept separate from the main ground and from one another and only joined at the single signal ground point on the A/D converter.

One useful technique when the equipment is used in an electrically noisy environment is to employ balanced signal circuits for the multiplexer and filters, as shown in Figure 8.12. Any noise picked up on the analogue wires due to, say, electrical or magnetic coupling with other circuits, will tend to be in phase on both analogue signal lines relative to the common signal ground, whereas the desired signals are balanced relative to ground. The noise and interference signals will cancel out in the buffer amplifier whilst the required signals are passed through to the A/D converter.

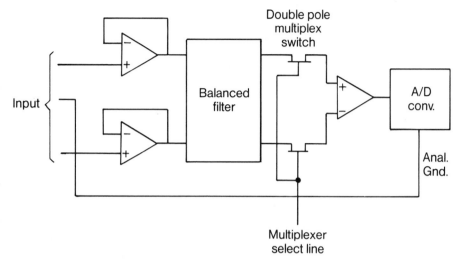

Fig. 8.12 A balanced input scheme which might be used where the analogue signal lines are in a noisy environment.

Anti-aliasing filter choice

The type of filter required to remove aliasing problems depends very much on the way in which the resultant data is to be used or analysed.

If the system is used for data acquisition and it is important that the relative phase relationships of the signals on different channels be correct, then the phase characteristics of the filters need to be carefully matched from one channel to another. If the signals are to be spectrum analysed and again the phase relationships of the frequency components of the signal are to be correctly reproduced, it is important that the filter has a predictable phase/frequency characteristic. Unfortunately a filter with a smooth phase response relative to frequency is likely to have amplitude characteristics in the pass band which are less desirable although the high frequency roll-off may be good. The problem can however be eased by increasing the sampling frequency so that only part of the pass band of the filter is used for the wanted signal but potential aliasing components are kept to a minimum. The disadvantage here is that the noise will tend to be increased giving a reduced signal to noise ratio.

If accurate amplitude measurements are required for the input signal frequency components then the optimum filter would be a Butterworth type which has a fairly flat amplitude response through the pass band but its roll-off beyond the pass band is only moderately steep, as shown in Figure 8.13. If a better high frequency rejection is required, the Tchebychev type of filter will produce a more rapid roll-off in the response above the cut-off frequency, as shown in Figure 8.14. The disadvantage with the Tchebychev filter is that there is a ripple in the amplitude response in the pass band which may affect the accuracy of the measurement of signal amplitude

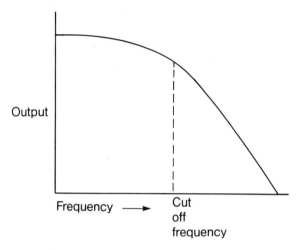

Fig. 8.13 Frequency response of a Butterworth-type low pass filter.

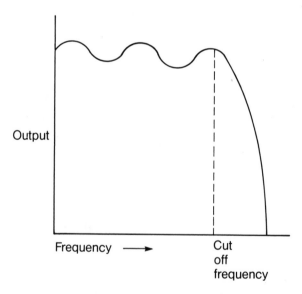

Fig. 8.14 Frequency response of a Tchebychev-type low pass filter.

The rate at which the filter response rolls off above the cut-off frequency can be improved by cascading several filter sections as shown in Figure 8.15 where simple low pass R-C elements are used. The number of filter sections required is governed by the anticipated level of unwanted signals around the frequency $f_s/2$ in relation to the expected signals in the pass band. The object of the anti-alias filter is to reduce signals at the frequency $f_s/2$ to a level which is less than the resolution of the A/D converter being used.

In the extreme case where the potential alias signal is of full-scale input amplitude and the converter system has a resolution of 10 bits, the unwanted

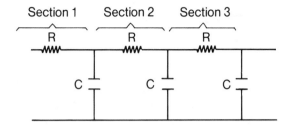

Fig. 8.15 Circuit arrangement for a simple multi-section R-C low pass filter.

signal must be reduced by a factor of 1024 in voltage terms. This requires a filter attenuation of some 60 dB which will be extremely difficult to achieve with an analogue filter whilst still maintaining a reasonable response in the pass band. One solution to this problem might be to use a relatively straightforward low pass filter combined with a notch-type rejection filter centred on the $f_s/2$ frequency as shown in Figure 8.16. This combination should produce a frequency response similar to that shown in Figure 8.17.

In practical systems it is not normally a requirement to reject a full-scale noise signal since, hopefully, this can be avoided in the first place. Thus the filter may need to deal with only a relatively small noise component and a rejection of perhaps 25–30 dB at the $f_s/2$ frequency may be more than adequate.

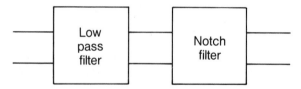

Fig. 8.16 Using a combination of a notch and a bandpass filter to achieve better rejection of alias components near the $f_s/2$ frequency.

One important point to remember in any multiplexed system is that the filtering must be carried out before the sampling process takes place. In a system with an analogue multiplexer this must be before the multiplexer switch, but in a system with separate A/D converters for each channel it must be before the A/D converters. Digital filtering within the computer itself cannot deal with the alias components since the CPU has no way of distinguishing real inputs from alias components after sampling has occurred.

If a much higher sampling frequency is used for the initial sampling process, together with alias filters as appropriate, then it is permissible to use a digital filter routine to process the signals prior to a second sampling process at the final desired sampling rate. Digital filters can be designed to have very good attenuation and roll-off characteristics and, of course, all channels can be processed by an identical filter algorithm to give matched

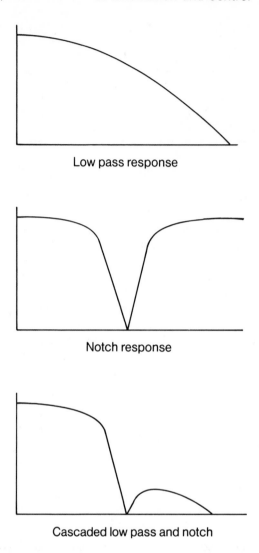

Low pass response

Notch response

Cascaded low pass and notch

Fig. 8.17 Frequency response of a combined low pass and notch rejection filter.

channel characteristics. In severe conditions this two-stage filtering process may provide better performance than a single-stage scheme with analogue filtering. The disadvantage here is the need for the high initial sampling rate and consequently more expensive multiplexer and A/D components.

Sample/hold circuits

When a number of channels are multiplexed by analogue switching into a common A/D converter, there must inevitably be some delay between the times at which the actual samples are taken by the converter since it is time shared between all channels. In many cases we actually want to record the signals on all channels at the same point in time. If the signals are changing relatively slowly and follow some form of regular pattern, then it may be acceptable to predict the correct readings on all channels by interpolating the readings relative to, say, the last two readings for that channel and taking into account the time delay in the conversion and multiplex process.

Where signals may change rapidly or in an unpredictable manner, an alternative solution is required and one possibility is to include a sample/hold circuit in each channel at a point before the analogue multiplexer switch. This circuit is basically an analogue switch feeding into a capacitor and followed by a high impedance buffer amplifier, as shown in Figure 8.18. When transistor Q1 is on, a sample of the analogue signal is taken since, assuming that the source is of relatively low impedance, the capacitor will charge to a voltage equal to the input signal. When transistor Q1 is off, the capacitor remains charged since the leakage impedance across it is very high. In practice, of course, the charge will slowly drain away but for a short period the capacitor effectively stores the analogue input. If we arrange that the sample/hold circuits for all of the channels are sampled at the same time and then placed in the hold state, then the values seen by the A/D converter as each channel is multiplexed will represent the reading at the sample point and all signals will be correctly in phase.

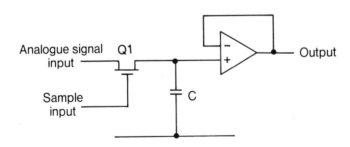

Fig. 8.18 Basic principles of a sample/hold circuit.

In a sample/hold circuit there is a time period required for taking the sample and this is normally referred to as the aperture time. The other important characteristic of the sample/hold circuit is the hold decay rate, since this determines the maximum permissible hold time for maintenance of the required analogue accuracy. Sample/hold circuits also suffer to some extent from temperature drift but this may not be significant for the short values of hold time likely to be encountered in a typical acquisition system.

Digital filtering

Normally the anti-aliasing filters used in a data acquisition system are simple analogue types, but rather better filter characteristics can sometimes be achieved by using digital filtering. In digital filtering the action of the filter is produced by calculations made on the sampled digital signal. The first requirement is that the sampling rate must be increased since the filter algorithm needs at least two samples per cycle at its nominal roll-off frequency. Some analogue anti-aliasing filters will still be required prior to digitisation to remove effects of high frequency noise.

Let us consider the digital implementation of a simple R-C low pass analogue filter whose circuit arrangement will be as shown in Figure 8.19. The output voltage V_o is also the voltage across the capacitor C and this is given by:

$$V_o = \frac{1}{C} \int i dt$$

where C is the capacitance and i is the current flowing through capacitor C.

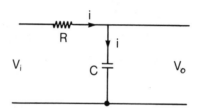

Fig. 8.19 Circuit for a simple low pass R-C filter.

The voltage drop across the resistor is given by iR, where R is the resistance and i is the same current that flows in the capacitor. Thus we get:

$$iR = V_i - V_o$$
$$\text{or} \quad i = \frac{1}{R} (V_i - V_o)$$

and substituting i in the previous equation we get:

$$V_o = \frac{1}{RC} \int (V_i - V_o) dt$$

Differentiating both sides gives:

$$\frac{dV_o}{dt} = \frac{1}{RC} (V_i - V_o)$$

which can be rearranged as:

$$V_o + RC \frac{dV_o}{dt} = V_i$$

The value RC is a constant and is usually replaced by the term T_1 which is called the time constant for the circuit.

Using Laplace notation this equation can be written as:

$$V_o (1 + SRC) = V_i$$

where S represents the operation d/dt.

This can be rearranged to give the relationship between the output and the input (V_o/V_i) of the filter which is known as the transfer function and is given by:

$$\frac{V_o}{V_i} = \frac{1}{1 + ST_1}$$

where T_1 the time constant is equal to the product RC.

To calculate this using the computer and a set of sampled data we need to use the differences between successive samples and it is convenient to start from the basic equation

$$V_o + T_1 \frac{dV_o}{dt} = V_i$$

which can be written in difference form as:

$$V_{o(n)} + \frac{T_1\; V_{o(n)} - V_{o(n-1)}}{T_s} = V_{i(n)}$$

where $V_{i(n)}$ is the current data sample, T_s is the time between samples, $V_{o(n)}$ is the calculated output and $V_{o(n-1)}$ is the result of the calculation for the previous sample time. This equation can now be rearranged as follows:

$$T_s\, V_{o(n)} + T_1\, V_{o(n)} - T_1\, V_{o(n-1)} = V_{i(n)}\, T_s$$

$$V_{o(n)}(T_1 + T_s) = V_{i(n)}\, T_s + V_{o(n-1)}\, T_1$$

$$V_{o(n)} = \frac{V_{i(n)}\, T_s}{T_1 + T_s} + \frac{V_{o(n-1)}\, T_1}{T_1 + T_s}$$

$$= K_A V_{i(n)} + K_B V_{o(n-1)}$$

where

$$K_A = \frac{T_s}{T_1 + T_s}$$

$$K_B = \frac{T_1}{T_1 + T_s}$$

From this we see that the new value is calculated by adding a small increment to the last calculated value and this small increment is related to the difference between the new sample reading and the last calculated output for the filter.

The statements for calculating the output from this type of filter would be similar to the following:

```
READ VI
VO = (KA * VI) + (KB * VOL)
VOL = VO
OUTPUT VO
```

where VI is the current input signal and VOL is the output signal calculated at the last sample time. After calculating a new value for VO the variable VOL is updated ready for the next calculation cycle. This sequence of calculations is repeated at time intervals of TS seconds when a new value of VI is read in and a new value for VO is output.

The constants KA and KB are calculated before starting the repetitive real time loop using the equations

$$KA = TS/(TS + T1)$$
$$KB = T1/(TS + T1)$$

where TS is the time interval between samples and T1 is the time constant for the filter.

If we apply a step input to this filter calculation the result is the typical exponential output produced by the analogue version of the filter circuit and the output will tend to approach the input step level V_i after some period of time. At the time T_1, the output will have reached $0.707 V_i$ as shown in Figure 8.20.

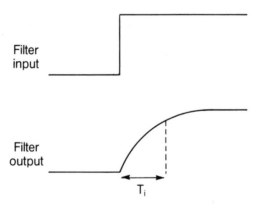

Fig. 8.20 Response of a digital low pass filter to a step input.

This same basic approach for calculating filter output for each input sample value can be applied to any filter design by starting with the Laplace form of the transfer function and converting it into difference form and then relating this to current and previous sampled or calculated values as appropriate. The Laplace operator S is normally replaced by the function d/dt when converting the equation into the difference form.

Averaging

A function similar to integration is that of calculating the mean value of a signal. This can be done fairly simply by taking the sum of the individual samples taken over some number of sample periods, N, and then dividing the result by N. This process effectively smooths out variations due to high frequency noise to give a relatively smooth mean reading. One disadvantage of this process is that the numbers involved in the integration process will steadily increase during the period of time where samples are being summed and may exceed the limits of the computer's arithmetic system.

An alternative scheme is to calculate a running average. We might start by taking, say, four successive samples of the input to produce the integral value and this is then divided by four to give the current average. After this point when each new sample is added to the integral sum the oldest sample is subtracted so that the sum represents the total of the last four samples taken. Once again the average is produced by dividing the current sum value by four. This technique limits the magnitude of the integral sum whilst giving a realistic average value over the most recent four samples. The more samples that are included in the running average the more accurate the average will be, but the limitation here is the permissible size of the sum in relation to the arithmetic capabilities of the processor.

This running average technique can be useful in filtering noisy data prior to carrying out calculations since it will tend to remove high frequency variations of the signal whilst maintaining the average value and slower changes in signal level. Some variations on this general theme give different weights to the samples in the group to give a better averaging action.

Software aspects

An important part of the design of a microprocessor-based data acquisition system is the software used to control the operation of the system. A microprocessor-based system will usually perform a number of other tasks apart from that of simply reading data from transducers and the software is usually divided into a number of modules each of which deals with one operating mode of the system.

In a simple data acquisition system based on conventional logic the unit will do little more than take readings of the data and perhaps record these on say a magnetic tape. The recorded data is then taken to a computer for analysis at a later time. If this approach is adopted in a microprocessor-based system then little use will be made of the processing capability of the microprocessor. Apart from a brief burst of activity at each sample time, the CPU will spend most of its time waiting for the next sample time to come around. In a practical system the CPU may be used to provide monitor readouts of the data being recorded. Even in a simple system of this type some additional software will be required to set up the input and output ports and to allow the data-acquisition section to be tested and calibrated. Further facilities may be provided for recording the data on magnetic tape. Extra information may be inserted in the recorded data to label each experiment run and may include details of the experiment conditions that will be useful during later analysis.

In many cases the microprocessor may be used to provide some degree of post-run processing of the data that was acquired during an experiment run. This may simply provide an average or RMS value, or may analyse the peaks and troughs of the record to give perhaps an indication of the frequency of peaks at various amplitude levels. In some cases the entire analysis of the records may be carried out by the microprocessor by calling up a data analysis program which uses the data which has just been acquired. In other cases the data may be partially processed prior to recording for later analysis. Here the object may simply be to reduce the amount of data that needs to be recorded.

Since the actual acquisition of data will usually take up little of the available processing time, it may well be possible to carry out some or all of the data processing as the data is being acquired. This is quite feasible for calculating mean signal levels or for counts of peaks and troughs during the run. In some cases several of the input parameters may be used in an analysis calculation and here the calculations may be made by the processor as each set of readings is taken. Other processing which may go on whilst data is being acquired will include any scaling conversions and the detection of limit or fault conditions in the experiment. Thus if the results being monitored are potentially useless the experiment may be aborted.

In some types of experiment each run will produce just one point on the final analysis plot and here it is useful if the microprocessor can at least give an approximate value for that point so that the experimenter can decide how the next few runs should be conducted. This may be important where an unexpected result is obtained and where perhaps a series of additional runs may be inserted into the planned program to examine more closely the results in that area of the experimental conditions.

In any microprocessor system it is important to include some software which will allow the user to check that the system is operating correctly and perhaps to provide some degree of fault detection and diagnosis.

Typical software design

The basic software for a data acquisition system will usually consist of a mainline program block which initially sets up the system and will then interface with the user to allow the various operating modes to be selected and the various operating parameters of the system to be set up.

At the start of the main program there will normally be some form of initialisation routine which sets up the input and output port devices, starts any timer devices and then displays messages on the terminal screen to indicate that the system is ready. This section of the program may also include a simple check of the operation of the read/write memory and may provide an indication of any fault conditions detected during the initialisation process.

Once initialisation of the system is complete the interaction with the user can commence. Perhaps the most convenient scheme is to use a menu-driven dialogue with the user. In such a scheme the CPU will present the user with a display giving a selection of options, generally referred to as a menu, and the user is invited to select an option by pressing a key on the terminal keyboard. For a data acquisition system the menu display might be similar to the following table:

Key	Option
1	Calibration mode
2	Data acquisition
3	Post run analysis
4	Record data on tape
5	Diagnostic routines

Press key to select option

Having produced the display the CPU monitors the keyboard and when a key input is detected the program will jump to an appropriate subroutine module which provides the selected mode of operation. If the key detected is not one of those specified, the display may simply be rewritten or some form of error message may be presented to indicate that the key selected is not valid.

When an option is selected, the subroutine may present a new menu giving the user further options and selection of these will lead to further subroutines within that section of the overall program. When the program has all of the information it needs, a jump is made to a subroutine which performs the selected function. In some cases, such as in setting up constants, when the operation is complete the program returns to the menu from which the function was selected. Each of the lower level menus must have an escape option which allows the user to return to the main menu so that other operations of the system may be selected. Thus the program structure will be on the lines of that shown in Figure 8.21.

The dialogue with the user should be designed so that it guides the operator through the setting up and selection of operating conditions and tests should be included so that if some of the parameters needed have not yet been selected the menu for setting them up will automatically be presented before the system will allow the user to select an operating mode. The messages used in the menu displays will take up a fair amount of memory and many early microprocessor-based systems used cryptic messages and error codes because available memory was limited. Today

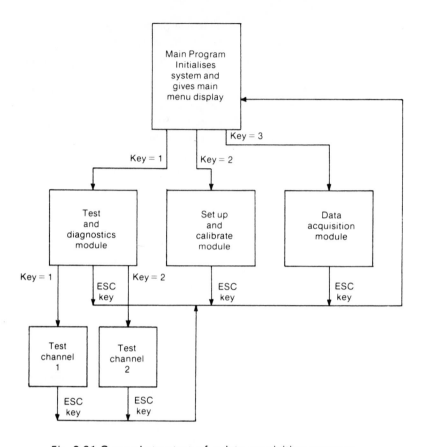

Fig. 8.21 General structure of a data acquisition program.

memory is usually plentiful on a CPU system so it is as well to include full messages to make operation of the system easier for an inexperienced user.

Test and calibration routines

An important part of the software for a data acquisition system is that which provides the setting up, test and calibration procedures for the data input channels.

Analogue input channels will normally include an A/D converter and in most systems this is likely to be one of the successive approximation type. To test the operation of the converter and its associated analogue input channel, one convenient test is to apply a sawtooth or triangular waveform and examine the output by displaying it on an oscilloscope or chart recorder. If there is a D/A converter available in the system then this can conveniently be used to generate the sawtooth or triangle waveform and the analogue signal can then be connected to the input channel being tested. The test signal may be routed to the input channel under test by using the CPU to switch a series of analogue gates to re-route the analogue output of the DAC to the appropriate channel input. The CPU may also generate sine wave or step outputs from the DAC if these are more suitable for test purposes.

Scaling factors

In a basic data-logger system it may be acceptable to record the integer binary output from the A/D converter onto a magnetic tape. At some later stage this data may then be read into a larger computer system for analysis. When the data is in the larger computer however it will need to be converted into values which are equivalent to the real world parameters that were measured.

In most applications involving data acquisition it is likely that some simple analysis may be required either whilst the data is being acquired or immediately after an experimental run. In some cases the data acquisition system will be used to drive monitor displays which indicate the real world quantities being measured. In all of these cases the output binary data from the A/D converter on analogue channels, or the digital data from digital transducers, must be related to the real world parameters that it represents and this involves applying some scaling factors to the acquired input data.

Suppose we are using a simple potentiometer to measure the angle of rotation of a shaft relative to some reference position. The potentiometer itself will produce an output voltage which is proportional to shaft rotation in degrees. For example, a rotation of 1 degree might produce a voltage of 0.1 V so we have a scaling factor of 10 degrees per volt. Assuming that the A/D converter in use has a 12-bit resolution and is bipolar with a range of $+5$ V to -5 V, we might set it up so that 2000 increments in the digital output would equal 5 V input. Thus we get a sensitivity of 5/2000 or 2.5 mV per digital increment. To find the overall scaling factor we can combine these two factors as follows:

$$\frac{\text{Deg.}}{\text{Step}} = \frac{\text{Deg.}}{\text{Volt}} \times \frac{\text{Volt}}{\text{Step}} = \frac{10}{1} \times \frac{5}{2000}$$

$$= 0.025 \text{ degrees per step}$$

Now if the output of the A/D converter is multiplied by this constant the resultant variable will represent degrees of shaft rotation.

A similar process can be applied to a D/A output channel to convert from the real value stored in the computer to an appropriate voltage output which will produce the equivalent real world output from the device being driven by the analogue output.

Chapter Nine
Control Systems

One area of industrial electronics to which microprocessors can be applied is that of control systems and process control. In this chapter we shall examine the principles involved in control systems and then go on to see how digital techniques and microprocessors may be used in this application.

Open loop control systems

The simplest form of control system, whether microprocessor-based or not, is an 'open loop' system which is shown in Figure 9.1.

At the centre is the process which is being controlled which might, for example, be a tank containing fluid which must be maintained at a specified temperature. The state of the process is governed by a controller unit which actuates valves or motors to govern the state of the process. In the case of our tank of liquid, the controller might be used to regulate the flow of steam through a heater element immersed in the process liquid. The controller itself responds to an input signal which in this case might be manually controlled by an operator.

In order to check on the state of the process some form of monitoring system must be provided. This might consist of a temperature sensor

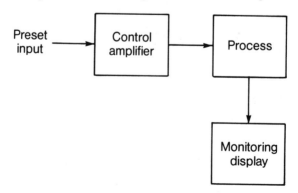

Fig. 9.1 A basic open loop control system.

immersed in the fluid tank and coupled to a measuring instrument which displays the temperature of the liquid.

If we assume that all conditions such as ambient temperature, fluid density and so on remain constant then it should be possible for the operator to adjust the input so that the temperature of the liquid is at the desired temperature and the heat input produced by the steam exactly balances the heat loss from the fluid to the surrounding environment. By measuring the input settings required for stable operation at a number of different temperatures, it would be possible to calibrate the input control in terms of fluid temperature so that the operator could select a specified temperature at will by adjusting the input control to the appropriate setting.

In practice the fluid may be flowing through the tank and changes in the flow rate will affect the operating temperature. These changes may, however, be corrected by the operator who monitors the actual temperature reading and adjusts the input control to compensate for changes in the running conditions of the process. The operator in effect closes the loop around the control process by adjusting the input in response to measured temperature in order to maintain the specified running conditions. We can readily derive from the temperature readout, a signal which represents the error between the actual liquid temperature and the specified temperature and, if this signal can be made to govern the input of the controller, we can remove the human operator and have a 'closed loop' automatic control system as shown in Figure 9.2.

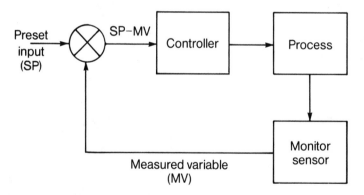

Fig. 9.2 A simple closed loop automatic control system.

On/off control

The simplest form of 'closed loop' control system is an 'on/off' type controller in which the controlling signal is switched on or off in response to an error signal derived from the difference between the measured and desired state of the process being controlled.

Consider the example of a tank of liquid which is to be maintained at a pre-set temperature, T_p. The liquid temperature is monitored by a suitable sensor and gives a measured temperature, T_m. Voltage signals proportional to these two temperature values are fed to a comparator circuit whose output goes high if $T_p > T_m$ and remains low for all other states. Thus when the measured temperature is lower than the specified level the controller opens the steam valve to provide maximum heat flow into the tank. The liquid in the tank now heats up and when the measured temperature, T_m, reaches the pre-set level T_p, the comparator switches state and the steam is completely cut off.

With the valve shut and no steam being input, the heat losses from the tank will cause the temperature to fall and this continues until T_m once again falls below T_p when the steam is again turned on. In practice the measured temperature will overshoot the pre-set level, T_p, because, although the steam input is shut off, some heat energy will continue to be transferred from the steam already in the heater unit to the liquid in the tank.

The resultant action of the temperature and steam valve will be as shown in Figure 9.3.

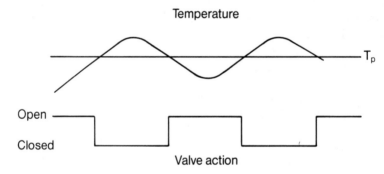

Fig. 9.3 Changes in temperature and action of the steam valve in a simple on/off temperature controller.

One problem with a simple set-up like this is that when the temperature of the room is approximately correct the valve will tend to oscillate continuously between its on and off states as the temperature fluctuates around the pre-set level. If the sensitivity of the comparator circuit is increased to try to improve the temperature control, the valve oscillation will become more violent and more rapid causing undesirable valve wear and noise.

The continual switching action of the valve can be stopped by building some 'hysteresis' into the system. This may be done by having different temperature levels for turning the valve on and turning it off. This is shown in Figure 9.4. Here the valve is turned off when the upper temperature limit is reached and remains off until the temperature falls below the lower temperature limit. The two limit levels are set above and below the desired

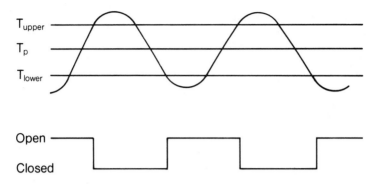

Fig. 9.4 Characteristics of an on/off controller with hysteresis.

temperature level. In this case, once the temperature has reached the upper limit the control system effectively shuts down until the measured temperature falls below the lower limit when a further burst of steam is injected into the system. The area between the limits is in fact a 'dead zone' where the system is not effectively in control.

On/off controllers are essentially crude systems but can be effective where the dead zone can be tolerated and where precise control is not essential. Simple examples of such systems are thermostatically controlled irons and the simple float-operated ball valve used in a cistern.

Proportional feedback

Instead of using a simple on/off switch scheme actuated by the error signal we can use a slightly more sophisticated approach. In this, the amount of control applied is made proportional to the error between the ordered state and the measured state of the process being controlled. The basic arrangement of the system now becomes as shown in Figure 9.5.

The error signal E, in this case, is obtained by taking the difference

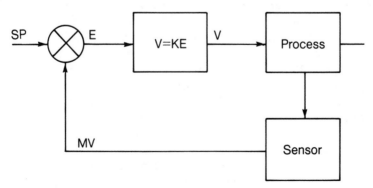

Fig. 9.5 Block diagram of a proportional feedback controller system.

between the ordered temperature, T_p, and the measured temperature, T_m, as follows:

$$E = T_p - T_m$$

Thus the output signal from the controller will be:

$$V = KE$$
or $\quad V = K(T_p - T_m)$

where V is the controller output and K is a constant which represents the gain of the controller. The amount by which the valve is opened will now be proportional to the controller output V which is in turn proportional to the error input E.

When T_m rises higher than the required value, T_p, the value of E falls and the valve will start to close, thus reducing the heat input. If T_m is lower than T_p the error E increases and this opens the valve to let in more heat and raise the temperature T_m.

As the value of K is increased, the amount of change in the setting of V relative to the error increases. There will in practice be finite limits to the range of the valve position V. When V reaches a limiting value, further increases in E will have no effect. The range of E over which proportional control of V is maintained is generally referred to as the 'proportional band' and is often quoted as the percentage change in error needed to move the valve through its full range. The proportional bandwidth is inversely proportional to the gain constant K, so that a narrow band system has a high gain and a wide band system has a low gain. The higher the gain becomes, the more nearly the controller will approach the characteristics of a simple 'on/off' controller.

To implement this type of controller on a microcomputer the basic calculation required is:

$$V = K(SP - MV)$$

where V is the output to the actuator which controls the process. MV is the measured variable and SP is the set point at which the process is required to operate. The constant K is the control loop gain.

For the calculations inside the processor it is usually best to scale the values of V, SP and MV in terms of real world variables such as temperature, pressure, speed and so on. This involves conversions of the input variables from voltage levels or binary numbers to real variables. At the end of the calculations the result V must be converted from some real variable such as a valve angle or a heater power level into a control voltage that will produce the required result from the actuator in the process system.

As an example we might measure the temperature with a sensor which produces an output $k_1 T$ in volts. In the computer this can be converted into a temperature value and this is compared with the set temperature value which may have been entered into the computer as a simple numerical value.

The output may be calculated as a percentage opening of the steam valve and must be converted into a voltage or current level that will in fact move the steam valve by the desired amount.

Offset error

In the temperature controller, if we assume that for $V = 0$ the valve is fully closed and that for some other value, $V = V_m$, the valve is fully open, then in order to produce the temperature T_p the valve must be partly open so that V must be greater than 0. This would mean that E must also be greater than 0 and therefore T_m cannot equal T_p.

It would be possible to manually pre-set the steam valve so that for $V = 0$ the valve is open just enough to produce the desired temperature, T_p, under average operating conditions. Ideally we should arrange this so that the valve was half open in this state. Now under average operating conditions V, and hence E, will be zero and therefore the measured temperature T_m will be equal to the desired temperature T_p.

If a change occurs in the process conditions, perhaps due to change in the flow rate of the liquid through the tank, then the measured temperature, T_m, will change and an error signal, E, will be produced. The error signal E moves the valve to a new position in an attempt to correct the temperature change but since an error E must exist in order to move the valve to its new position the new value for measured temperature T_m will not quite be restored to the desired value T_p. Thus any disturbance caused by a change in the process conditions will always give rise to a small error in the final value of T_m which is called the 'offset error'.

Suppose that if the loop were open the temperature change caused by the flow rate alteration was T_c. When the loop is closed the change in the measured temperature will be given by:

$$T_m = KE + T_c$$
$$= K(T_p - T_m) + T_c$$

But since T_p is constant, this becomes:

$$T_m = -KT_m + T_c$$
$$\text{or} \quad T_m(1+K) = T_c$$

which gives:

$$T_m = \frac{T_c}{1 + K}$$

Thus any disturbance due to a change in the load conditions on the process will be reduced by a factor $1/(1+K)$ but can never be reduced to zero.

Stability

In any practical control system there will always be a time lag between a change being made at the input of the process and the corresponding change occurring at the output. There may also be a time lag in the measuring instrument as, for example, in a dual slope A/D converter.

Suppose we have a system where measurements are taken once a second and where the process has a time lag of one second. Suppose we have the system balanced with zero error and then apply a change in load which causes an error E. We will assume that the overall gain around the loop is 0.5.

The first measurement gives an error signal E which produces a controller output of $0.5E$. At the next sample time, this will produce a correction and

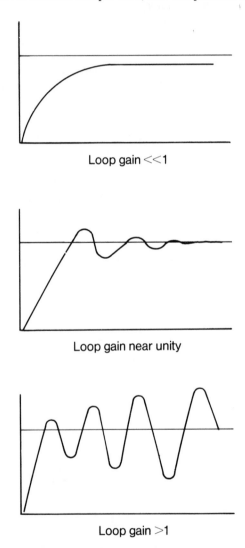

Loop gain ≪1

Loop gain near unity

Loop gain >1

Fig. 9.6 Effect of altering the overall loop gain of a controller in a system which has a built in lag component.

the new error measurement will be 0.5E. This produces a control signal of 0.25E. At the second sample time we have an error of E and a correction of 0.25E, so the new error is now 0.75E. As this process continues it will produce a damped oscillation centred around an error of 0.5E.

If the loop gain were increased to 1, the system would go into oscillation and if the gain were greater than 1, the amplitude of the oscillations would build up until limited by the output capability of the controller. The frequency at which oscillations occur will be governed by the time lag of the overall loop and the loop gain.

Figure 9.6 shows the effect of increasing the loop gain in a system which has time delays in the loop. At low gain figures the response to the error is delayed. As the gain is increased the output overshoots and performs a damped oscillation. In designing a simple proportional feedback system therefore a compromise must be made between a low loop gain with a slow response and large offset but good stability, and high loop gain with a small offset and faster response but a tendency to oscillate.

Integral feedback

Instead of making the controller output V proportional to error E, we could arrange that the rate of change of V is proportional to E. This is represented by the equation:

$$\frac{dV}{dt} = K_i E$$

and if we integrate both sides this gives:

$$V = K_i \int E dt$$

where K_i is a constant. The control loop is now as shown in Figure 9.7.

The transfer function of this type of controller can be written in Laplace form as:

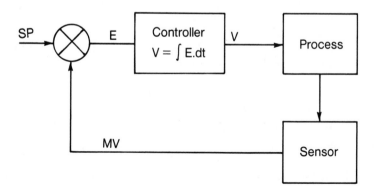

Fig. 9.7 Control loop using integral feedback.

$$\frac{V}{E} = \frac{K_i}{ST_i}$$

where T_i is the integration time constant and S is the Laplace operator.

The integration process is in effect a summation and if calculations are made at discrete time intervals, T_s, then the controller output, V, increases by a small fraction of the error, E, at each time step. In the computer this is done by adding a small increment to the output variable V at each iteration of the control loop calculations as follows:

$$V_{(n)} = V_{(n-1)} + K_i E_{(n)}$$

where $V_{(n)}$ is the new value for V and $V_{(n-1)}$ is the value for V calculated in the previous time period.

If only integral feedback is applied to the controller, the output signal V will rise in a roughly exponential fashion with the rate of rise flattening out as V approaches the value needed to completely cancel the error E. In the integral feedback equation, when E has fallen to zero the output V stops changing but remains at some constant level which is sufficient to maintain E at zero, so the system does not produce an offset error. The integral feedback is useful for dealing with slow drift in the state of the process.

The PI controller

We saw that a proportional controller always produces an offset when it tries to correct an error condition whereas the integral feedback controller will cancel an error completely. If we combine the two types of feedback then it should be possible to achieve the fast response of the proportional controller with the resetting capability of the integral controller to give a system which has no offset error. We can in fact combine the two types of feedback to produce a 'two step' controller.

Usually, a combination of proportional and integral feedback in the system will give a better performance than a simple proportional feedback system. By combining the two transfer functions we now get the transfer function for a PI (Proportional + Integral) controller by simply adding the two components together to give:

$$V = KE + K_i \int E.dt$$

Now it would be more convenient if we could use a common constant, K, to represent the gain of the controller so we shall try to find the value of the integration constant, K_i, in terms of the proportional gain constant K.

On a proportional controller the constant K is given by V/E. In an integral controller, if we assume that the error E is constant, the output V will change linearly with time and after some time period, T_i, will have changed by an amount equal to the error E as shown in Figure 9.8. During

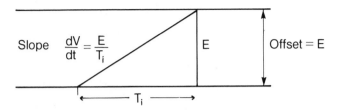

Fig. 9.8 Derivation of the value of the integration constant using the slope of the output signal (V).

the time between samples T_s, the integral term changes by an amount $K_i E$ so the rate of change of V due to integral feedback is:

$$\frac{dV}{dt} = \frac{K_i E}{T_s}$$

and from Figure 9.8 we see that the slope of the graph of V over the period T_i is given by:

$$\frac{dV}{dt} = \frac{KE}{T_i}$$

therefore:

$$\frac{K_i}{T_s} = \frac{K}{T_i}$$

giving:

$$K_i = \frac{KT_s}{T_i}$$

and we can now rewrite the equation for the PI controller as:

$$V = K(E + \frac{1}{T_i} \int E.dt)$$

Using Laplace notation the transfer function becomes:

$$\frac{V}{E} = K\left(1 + \frac{1}{ST_i}\right)$$

and the block diagram of the controller will be as shown in Figure 9.9.

The program for implementing a PI controller using a microprocessor would calculate the proportional and integral elements of the controller output separately and then add them together to produce the desired output. The sequence of operations might be as follows:

$$
\begin{aligned}
E &= SP - MV \\
VP &= K * E \\
VI &= VI + (KI * E) \\
V &= VP + VI
\end{aligned}
$$

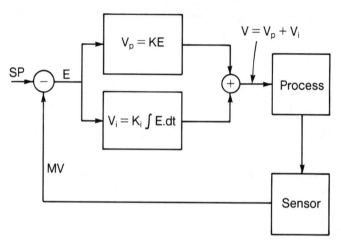

Fig. 9.9 Block diagram of a Proportional + Integral or PI controller.

In the second term the new value for VI is found by adding the increment (KI * E) to the existing value for VI which was calculated at the previous sample time.

The constant KI is calculated from:

$$KI = (K * TS) / TI$$

where TI is the integration time constant, TS is the time between samples and K is the controller gain. This calculation is made before the program begins the real time calculations of the control loop thus reducing the amount of time needed to compute new values for V.

When the error term E is positive the integral term VI will steadily increase with each iteration; when E is negative the VI term decreases with each iteration.

Derivative feedback

One problem with the proportional feedback system is that to avoid problems with severe overshooting, or even oscillation, the gain figure is limited and this in turn limits the rate at which the system can respond to a step at the input. The integration system is inherently slow in response. In order to achieve a more rapid response to changes in the input or set point conditions we can use derivative feedback. In this form of feedback the output of the controller is made proportional to the rate of change of the error signal. Thus we get the equation:

$$V = K_d \frac{dE}{dt}$$

As in the case of the integral gain constant we can relate the value of K_d to the proportional gain K and a derivative time constant T_d to give the result:

$$K_d = K T_d$$

So the controller equation can be written as:

$$V = K T_d \frac{dE}{dt}$$

and in Laplace form the transfer function for the controller becomes:

$$\frac{V}{E} = K_d T_d S$$

where T_d is the derivative time constant and K_d is the derivative gain constant.

The derivative term is produced in the computer by taking the difference between the current value of the error signal and the previous reading and dividing the result by the time interval between samples, T_s. Thus we get:

$$V = \frac{K T_d (E_n - E_{n-1})}{T_s}$$

In the computer program this becomes:

```
E   = (SP − MV)
VD = KD * (E − EP)
EP  = E
```

where VD is the component of the output due to differential feedback, KD is a constant and EP is the value for E measured at the previous time interval. After the calculation of VD is complete the value of EP is updated to the new value for E ready for the next iteration. The constant term KD would be calculated using the statement:

```
KD = (K * TD)/TS
```

before starting the real time control loop calculations.

With this form of feedback the response to a step change in the input condition is a very large inverse control signal which then falls away with time to a steady level depending upon the rate at which the output signal is changing. This type of feedback is not particularly useful by itself but is generally combined with proportional and integral feedback to improve the performance of the controller.

An important problem with derivative feedback, particularly if a high gain is used, is that the system will become very sensitive to high frequency noise, and to any transient spikes in either the measured output state or the input control signal. This can become something of a problem with digitised data since it inevitably contains steps and these will translate into large spikes in the control loop unless some form of low pass filtering is used.

The PID controller

We can combine all three forms of feedback to form what is generally referred to as a PID (Proportional + Integral + Differential) controller. This will have the Laplace transfer function:

$$\frac{V}{E} = K \left(1 + \frac{1}{ST_1} + ST_2\right)$$

where K is the controller gain, T_1 is the integral (or reset) time constant and T_2 is the derivative (or rate) time constant. The block diagram of the controller is as shown in Figure 9.10 where the three terms are derived separately and then added together to produce a combined output V.

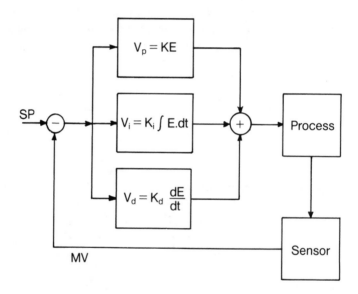

Fig. 9.10 Block system arrangement for an ideal PID controller.

In the microprocessor version of this controller the three components of the output signal are calculated separately and then they are added together to produce the final output V. The sequence of program steps carried out at each successive time interval would be as follows:

```
E    = SP − MV
VP   = K * E
VI   = VI + (KI * E)
VD   = KD * (E − EL)
EL   = E
V    = VP + VI + VD
```

As before the constants KI and KD would be calculated and the values of VI and EL would be set to zero before starting the repetitive control loop calculations. It should be noted that the real time controller loop must also contain statements to read in the values of MV, SP and any other input variables and after the calculations the value V must be output to the device being controlled. Each iteration will also include statements to introduce the required time delay or detect the next clock input from a timing clock which determines the time period TS.

Real PID algorithms
In the ideal PID controller scheme discussed above the three forms of control feedback are independent of one another. In the typical transfer function for an analogue type controller system this is not generally the case and the three types of feedback interact with one another. This characteristic is usually determined by the physical nature of the controller system and this type of transfer function is usually referred to as an interactive or 'real' PID controller.

In most real controller transfer functions some form of low pass filtering is often incorporated to limit the rate of change of the error term applied to the controller proper. As a result the transfer function of such a controller may take the form:

$$\frac{V}{E} = K \left(1 + \frac{1}{T_1 S}\right)\left(\frac{1 + T_2 S}{1 + K_2 T_2 S}\right)$$

where the final term is a derivative function whose denominator provides the rate limiting or filter action. The middle term is effectively a PI type controller whilst the constant K represents the overall gain of the controller.

In the computer program it is convenient to deal with the derivative term first and then use the result of this calculation as the error input for the PI controller term.

Let us call the output of the derivative calculation X which gives:

$$\frac{X}{E} = \frac{1 + T_2 S}{1 + K_2 T_2 S}$$

or rearranging:

$$X(1 + K_2 T_2 S) = E(1 + T_2 S)$$

which becomes:

$$X + K_2 T_2 \frac{dX}{dt} = E + T_2 \frac{dE}{dt}$$

Converting this to difference form gives:

$$X_n + K_2 T_2 \left(\frac{X_n - X_{n-1}}{T_s}\right) = \left(E_n + T_2 \frac{E_n - E_{n-1}}{T_s}\right)$$

and rearranging gives:

$$T_s X_n + K_2 T_2 X_n - K_2 T_2 X_{n-1} = T_s E_n + T_2 E_n - T_2 E_{n-1}$$
$$X_n = \left(\frac{T_s + T_2}{T_s + K_2 T_2}\right) E_n - \left(\frac{T_2}{T_s + K_2 T_2}\right) E_{n-1} + \left(\frac{K_2 T_2}{T_s + K_2 T_2}\right) X_{n-1}$$
$$X_n = K_a E_n + K_b E_{n-1} + K_c X_{n-1}$$

where

$$K_a = \frac{T_s + T_2}{T_s + K_2 T_2}$$

$$K_b = \frac{- T_2}{T_s + K_2 T_2}$$

$$K_c = \frac{K_2 T_2}{T_s + K_2 T_2}$$

X_n = Current output
X_{n-1} = Previous output
E_n = Current error input
E_{n-1} = Previous error input
T_s = Time between samples
T_1 = Integral time constant
T_2 = Derivative time constant
K_2 = Rate limiting constant

The various K and T constants would be calculated or input to the program before starting the real time repetitive control loop calculations. This greatly reduces the computation time in the real time program loop.

When X_n has been calculated it is used as the error input for the PI controller section of the transfer function. The integral term is calculated first from:

$$I_n = I_{n-1} + \frac{T_s X_n}{T_1}$$

then the final output is found from:

$$V_n = K(E_n + I_n)$$

Thus the iterative part of the computer program would have the form:

```
X = (KA * E) + (KB * EL) + (KC * XL)
I = I + (TS * X)/T1
V = K * (E + I)
EL = E
XL = X
```

Here EL and XL are the values calculated at the previous iteration and are updated at the end of each calculation loop. The initial values of EL, XL and I would be set to zero before starting the iterative control loop calculations to give the proper start-up conditions for the controller.

Other variations of real PID transfer functions can usually be processed in a similar way by converting the differential equations into difference form and then calculating the current output in terms of current and previous values of the other variables.

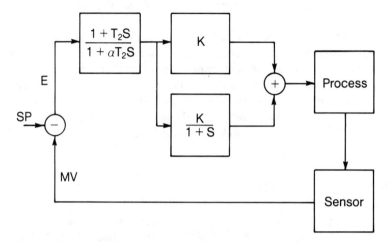

Fig. 9.11 Real PID controller scheme based on the designs normally used in analogue implementations of the controller.

Bumpless controller

One problem that can occur in a conventional PID system is that, with a large error, the integral term may well saturate the controller system and this can cause difficulties. There is also the problem that at start-up, unless the process is already pre-set to the nominal conditions so that the start-up error

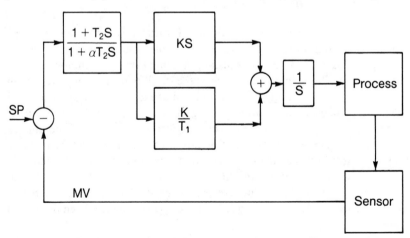

Fig. 9.12 Modification of the block system of a PID controller to give 'bumpless' operation.

is small, there will be a transient 'bump' whilst the system settles down. This can be avoided by careful choice of start-up conditions in the controller equations, but by using a slight variation of the PID scheme it can be eliminated completely.

If, in the P and I terms, we differentiate both signals and then, to get the correct results, we integrate the summed output, the equations effectively work with a rate of change of error rather than actual error. In this case the integral term simply produces the current error multiplied by a constant. For the proportional term we need to use both the previous sample value and the one before that in order to calculate the required result.

Fig 9.12 shows the basic block layout for this type of controller.

Multiple loop controllers

Actual controller systems may be quite complex since the controller may in fact use PID algorithms applied to perhaps three or four different variables in order to derive a control signal. Thus a system may have to respond to both pressure and temperature changes whilst maintaining a constant rate of flow of a fluid. In an aircraft autopilot the attitude and height of the aircraft would be affected by both the elevator settings and the power applied to the engines. The control system might be designed to maintain height whilst limiting the pitch angle of the plane to acceptable levels for passenger comfort.

Controller program design

In an actual controller system the values for the constants K and the time constants T_1 and T_2 should be readily variable either by inputting values from a keyboard or by having adjustable analogue or digital inputs to set the constants up. This is important because the stability of the complete system depends not only upon the transfer function of the controller but also upon the transfer function of the process being controlled and any lags introduced by the monitoring system. The process control engineer may be able to produce an approximate transfer function for the process, in which case it may be possible to calculate the required controller transfer function to provide stable operation. In most cases, however, only some rough estimates for the constant values are likely to be available and the system will need to be tuned experimentally for optimum performance when the loop is closed.

This may be done by applying a step input to the controller to see how the system responds. An overdamped system which has too little gain will provide stable but slow response. Increased gain will produce an overshoot and some tendency to oscillate. The relative amounts of derivative and integral control may then be adusted to produce a fast response with minimal overshoot and cancellation of the proportional offset error.

In general the overall software for a controller system is likely to follow along similar lines to that for a data acquisition system, with a small mainline program and a number of sub-modules which perform such functions as system initialisation, running the controller, test and setting up routines.

For a simple dedicated controller the initialisation will be done at switch-on and the equations and constants used may be fixed. Some input facility for setting up the set point conditions (SP) and for reading the measured variable input or inputs must be provided. A further input may be used to start and stop the operation of the control action.

When the characteristics of the controller are to be variable and selected by an operator then a menu driven dialogue with the operator can be employed to allow selection of various modes of operation and for input of constants which determine the operating conditions. These might include test facilities for applying a sine wave or step input function to the control loop in order to test its response.

Dynamic compensation

In a simple feedback controller the response to a change in either load or set point can be improved by increasing the gain of the controller. The major limitation in this approach is that, as the gain is increased, the system will become less stable and this can lead to uncontrolled oscillation if the overall loop gain reaches unity at some frequency.

The stability of the control system can be improved by inserting a lag network in cascade with the controller as shown in Figure 9.13. This lag network is a simple low pass filter with the transfer function:

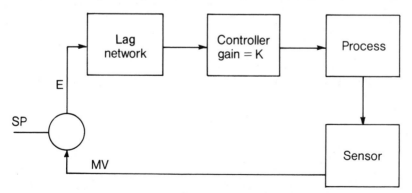

Fig. 9.13 Addition of a cascaded lag network to a controller to provide dynamic compensation.

$$\frac{V_o}{V_i} = \frac{1}{1 + T_1 S}$$

where T_1 is the filter time constant.

This has the effect of altering the phase characteristics of the loop and will generally allow a higher gain to be used in the controller before stability problems are encountered. Although the system becomes more stable and the higher gain can reduce the proportional offset the overall response of the system to changes in operating conditions will become slower.

If the process being controlled has a lag characteristic then the response of the system can be improved by adding a lead or phase advance network into the loop.

The phase advance network can be represented by the transfer function:

$$\frac{V_o}{V_i} = 1 + T_2 S$$

where T_2 is the time constant of the network.

In practice it is usually convenient to build in both phase lag and phase advance networks and these may then be adjusted to produce an optimum level of dynamic correction to the controller system. The combined transfer function for the lead plus lag network can be expressed as:

$$\frac{V_o}{V_i} = K\left[\frac{1 + T_2 S}{1 + T_1 S}\right]$$

where T_1 is the lag-time constant, T_2 is the lead-time constant and K is a gain factor.

These three terms can be calculated in cascade. Starting with the lead network term $(1 + T_2 S)$ and substituting d/dt for the operator S we get:

$$X = E + T_2 \frac{dE}{dt}$$

which in difference form gives:

$$X_n = E_n + T_2\left[\frac{E_n - E_{n-1}}{T_s}\right]$$
$$= \left[1 + \frac{T_2}{T_s}\right] E_n - \frac{T_2 E_{n-1}}{T_s}$$
$$= K_A E_n + K_B E_{n-1}$$

where

$$K_A = 1 + \frac{T_2}{T_s}$$
$$K_B = \frac{-T_2}{T_s}$$

E_n = Current value of input E
E_{n-1} = Previous value of input E
X = Current value of output

T_s = Time between samples
T_2 = Lead-time constant

The lag term has the transfer function:

$$\frac{V}{E} = \frac{1}{1 + T_1 S}$$

which gives

$$V + T_1 \frac{dV}{dt} = E$$

and converting to difference form we get:

$$V_n + \frac{T_1}{T_s}(V_n - V_{n-1}) = E_n$$

Rearranging gives:

$$(T_1 + T_s)V_n = T_s E_n + T_1 V_{n-1}$$

or

$$V_n = K_C E_n + K_D V_{n-1}$$

where

$$K_C = \frac{T_s}{T_s + T_1}$$

$$K_D = \frac{T_1}{T_s + T_1}$$

V_n = Current output
V_{n-1} = Previous output
E_n = Current input E

In this case the value used for E would be the value of X obtained from the lead section calculation. Finally the value obtained from the lag calculation is multiplied by the gain factor K to produce the required output.

Note that for both the lead and lag calculations the result from the previous sample is used and these two results need to be stored in the computer as separate variables which will be updated to the new calculated values at the end of the calculation loop. The program statements will follow similar lines to those of the earlier examples in this chapter. In this case the output from the lead lag calculation might then be applied as an input to the actual controller calculations.

Optimal controllers

When we are using a digital control system where samples are taken at regular intervals and the controller output is calculated from some controller algorithm, there is an alternative approach to the design of the controller. This scheme assumes that it is possible to calculate or measure the transfer function of the process that is being controlled.

If we know the transfer function of the process then we can work back from the output and calculate what input signal must be applied to the controller in order to completely correct the output change. Suppose we measure an error E at sample time T_n. If we wish to cancel the output error at the next sample time then we have to predict what input, E_n, will produce the required output change at time $T_{(n+1)}$.

If the error is measured at one sample time then, by using the known response of the process, it is possible to work back to find an input signal which, when applied to the process, will exactly cancel the error at the next sampling time.

Whilst it might appear that an optimal controller might be the best choice for use in a control system, this is not always true. The problem is that an optimal controller can be designed, for instance, to correct very effectively for changes in the process conditions due perhaps to alteration of the load on the process but will generally be very poor at correcting for a change in the set point conditions. Similarly, a controller that can handle set point changes may not perform very effectively when confronted with load changes or with noise signals. As in the case of the PID controller, the design tends to be a compromise but the range of conditions which a PID controller can cope with is likely to be much broader than that for an optimal controller which, after all, is designed to produce optimal control under certain specified conditions.

Chapter Ten
Interrupts and Real Time Operation

In many applications where control of external devices is involved the microprocessor system must be able to detect and react in real time to the signals from the outside world.

When looking at schemes for input and output data transfers, we have so far examined techniques in which the program software is designed to monitor and react to external events. In cases where the program itself requires data from an external device before it can proceed with further processing, the usual arrangement is to make the computer wait in a loop-type operation until the external data is available. This idea is shown in the flow chart of Figure 10.1 where the computer is waiting for an input from a keyboard. The program checks the state of a keyboard status line which will indicate when a key has been pressed. If no key press is detected the program loops back and repeats the test until eventually a key press is detected and the key data may be read into the CPU. In such a system a warning message is displayed before the testing loop commences and this informs the operator that an input is required. In an automatic system an action request signal is output to the remote device. Thus, in the case of, say, a printer this will tell the printer that data is ready and if the printer is ready it will then respond with a ready signal which is detected by the test loop and the program continues by transferring data to the printer.

Although this type of monitoring scheme provides a rapid response to the external device it has the disadvantage that the CPU does no useful work while it is waiting for a response from the external device. Let us suppose that the program is going to output a block of 100 text characters to a printer. We shall assume that the printer can operate at a rate of 50 characters per second so that it prints one character every 20 milliseconds. If the CPU is a typical general purpose 8-bit type, its average instruction execution time is likely to be of the order of 5 microseconds and only one or two instructions are required to carry out the data transfer. In the 20 ms waiting time while the printer deals with the character, the CPU can execute about 4000 instructions. The net effect is that whilst the CPU is outputting the 100 characters to the printer it is only working at about 0.025% efficiency.

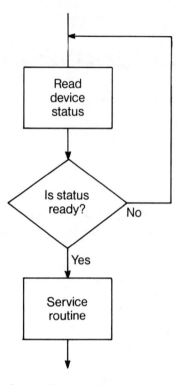

Fig. 10.1 Flow chart for a poll-and-wait scheme for checking the status of a peripheral device.

This situation can be improved by building a buffer memory into the printer system so that the CPU can dump the 100 character data codes very rapidly into the buffer memory and then go on with its program execution. The printer then deals with the contents of the buffer memory at its own speed.

In a system where the main program runs as a repetitive loop it is possible to adopt an alternative strategy. An example of this type of program might be that used for a control system where the calculation loop repeats at regular intervals to update the state of the control loop. The program can now be arranged as shown in Figure 10.2. Here, the test of the status of the remote device is made as before but this time if the external system is not ready the program continues round the main program loop. When a ready status is detected the program branches off to a subroutine which services the needs of the external device before the main program loop is resumed.

Here, there is little loss of processing time if the external device is not ready since the main program does not wait for a response. The disadvantage is that if the external device becomes ready just after a test has been performed it will have to wait for another pass through the main program loop before it is serviced. With slow-acting external devices where

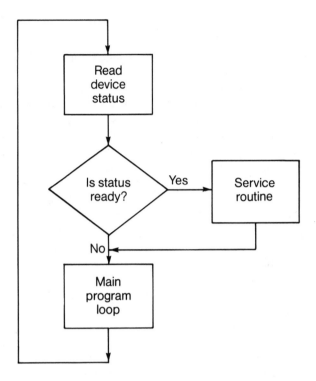

Fig. 10.2 Cyclic polling scheme that may be used in a repetitive main program loop to check for readiness of a peripheral.

the data remains relatively constant this need not be a significant problem. Some external devices will, however, need a more immediate response if the system is to work properly. This can be achieved by repeating the status check at a number of points spaced through the main program loop, or alternatively the main loop has to be made shorter so that tests occur at more frequent intervals. The effect of this is to increase the amount of program time taken up in testing for readiness in the external device in order to achieve a sufficiently rapid response.

Neither of these program controlled methods for sensing the status of input–output devices is ideal where a fast response is required without seriously reducing the program efficiency. What is required is some method by which the CPU hardware will respond automatically to a signal from the external device. There is a way of achieving this more desirable state of affairs and it makes use of a technique known as 'interrupt' operation.

All of the currently available types of microprocessor and microcomputer devices provide some form of interrupt facility. Some of the more sophisticated general purpose microprocessor chips provide two or more independent interrupt input lines and may also include automatic logic to determine the priority given when several interrupts occur simultaneously.

Basic interrupt action

The interrupt operation is controlled by a special input control line to the CPU which is generally called the interrupt request or IRQ input, although on some processors this line may be called simply the interrupt (INT) input. Usually the IRQ line is held high when not in use. If an external device pulls this IRQ input to the '0' level, the CPU will automatically go into an 'interrupt sequence' where it will complete the instruction that it is currently executing and then save the contents of the program counter. After this the program execution jumps to an 'interrupt service routine'. This service routine carries out the required data transfers and any other operations required to deal with the needs of the external device that initially caused the interrupt. At the end of the service routine the contents of the program counter are restored and the main program resumes with the next instruction after the one where the interrupt occurred. In effect this service routine is very much like a subroutine except that the branch to it is caused by a hardware signal rather than by a BSR or JSR instruction. At the end of the service routine there is a special return from interrupt (RTI) instruction which restores the original state of the program counter from the stack and the main program then resumes execution at the point where it was interrupted.

The interrupt system does not rely on the computer waiting in a test loop whilst it checks for an input but instead provides a virtually immediate response to the interrupt request signal from the external device at any point in the execution of the main program. As an example of the use of this interrupt facility we may have the CPU performing some long calculating or analysis task but we may still want it to take readings from a transducer at one second intervals. If the interrupt line is driven by a pulse from an external timing clock, so that the interrupt is triggered once per second, then the calculation program halts temporarily whilst the transducer reading is taken and then resumes for another second. To achieve this without an interrupt facility would involve a rather complex programming task.

Saving the CPU status

When the CPU jumps out of the main program to a subroutine we know exactly when the jump to the subroutine will occur within the program sequence. If we want to use one of the CPU registers during the subroutine and do not want to lose its current contents we can readily arrange to store the register data in memory or on the stack for recall later. When an interrupt system is being used the interrupt input signal may occur at any time because it is initiated by an external device and its timing is not governed by the program that is running in the CPU. As a result we have no way of knowing in advance when the interrupt will occur in the program sequence. The problem here is that the interrupt might occur in the middle of some important calculation.

If the program were simply allowed to jump off to the interrupt service routine, the contents of the CPU registers may well be altered by the actions of the interrupt service routine. On returning to the main program we could now find that some vital intermediate result that was being held in the accumulator has been overwritten and lost. Obviously some action is needed to save the state of the various CPU registers at the time the interrupt occurs so that after the interrupt service routine has been completed the CPU can be restored fully to its state at the time the interrupt occurred.

In some computers such as the Motorola 6800 this process of saving the CPU register contents is carried automatically when the interrupt is received. If the CPU is in the middle of executing an instruction when the interrupt occurs, that instruction is completed and then the CPU goes into an interrupt sequence in which it pushes the contents of the various CPU registers on to the stack before branching off to the interrupt service routine. The PC register goes on to the stack first and is followed by the index register, the A and B accumulators and finally the status register. As the interrupt service routine starts, the contents of the stack will be as shown in Figure 10.3. When the interrupt service routine ends and the RTI instruction

SP	Free	Top of stack
SP+1	Status	
SP+2	ACCB	
SP+3	ACCA	
SP+4	IX (MS)	
SP+5	IX (LS)	
SP+6	PC (MS)	
SP+7	PC (LS)	

Fig. 10.3 Stack contents of a 6800 CPU at the start of an interrupt service routine.

is executed, a recovery sequence is carried out in which all of the CPU register contents are restored to their original state by pulling the data back from the stack. Finally when the PC register contents are restored the main program resumes and the CPU has all of its original data intact.

The 6809 processor has several more registers within its CPU but, like the 6800, when it is activated by an IRQ interrupt input it also stacks away the contents of the CPU registers and the state of the stack will be as shown in Figure 10.4 at the start of the interrupt service routine. The 6809 has two stack pointer registers. One of these called the S register is used by the CPU to control its program stack and it is to this S stack that the data is pushed when an interrupt occurs. The second stack pointer controls the user stack and is called the U register. This stack may be used by the programmer for holding or manipulating data so its pointer is automatically saved during the

SP	Status	Top of stack
SP+1	ACCA	
SP+2	ACCB	
SP+3	Page	
SP+4	X (MS)	
SP+5	X (LS)	
SP+6	Y (MS)	
SP+7	Y (LS)	
SP+8	U (MS)	
SP+9	U (LS)	
SP+10	PC (MS)	
SP+11	PC (LS)	

Fig. 10.4 Stack contents of a 6809 CPU at the start of an interrupt service routine.

interrupt sequence. The 6809 has two index registers, X and Y, and another register that is saved to the stack during an interrupt is the direct page register which provides the upper byte of the address in some direct addressed instructions.

Whilst the automatic saving of all CPU register contents is a nice fail-safe feature, it does mean that the processor will take some time before it actually starts to process the interrupt. In a 6800 CPU this process takes up 10 CPU clock cycles, whilst the 6809 CPU uses up 15 clock cycles before it starts to deal with the interrupt request. If the contents of some of the registers are not important this means that time is wasted on saving useless information with the result that the response to the interrupt is delayed. A similar delay in resuming the main program occurs at the end of the service routine whilst the contents of the CPU registers are restored. It might be useful in some cases if the processor did not save all of the register contents automatically.

Some processors, such as the Intel 8085, treat an interrupt as if it were a call to a subroutine and as a result only the PC register is saved on the stack to provide a return address to get back to the main program after the interrupt has been serviced. In this case the programmer must include instructions to save any CPU registers at the beginning of the interrupt service routine. At the end of the service routine the CPU register contents are restored by pulling data from the stack before the return instruction is performed to return operation to the main program.

The 6809 CPU has a fast interrupt facility which is triggered by applying the interrupt request signal to the FIRQ (fast interrupt request) input on the CPU instead of using the IRQ input. This FIRQ interrupt causes only the PC and status register contents to be pushed to the stack when the interrupt is processed, thus reducing the response time to just 6 CPU cycles and the delay at the end of the interrupt routine is also reduced to 6 cycles.

Interrupt vectors

After an interrupt occurs and the appropriate CPU register contents have been saved, the program execution must branch to the start of the interrupt service routine. When a subroutine is being called the jump to the start of the subroutine instructions is achieved by using the operand of the BSR or JSR instruction to generate the address for the next instruction to be executed. In the case of an interrupt the CPU is not responding to an actual instruction and therefore there is no operand to produce the required address. In most systems this situation is dealt with by using a 'vectored' address scheme.

In vectored addressing the address of the first instruction in the interrupt service routine is placed in a specific location or pair of locations in the memory. When the interrupt is processed the contents of the CPU are saved and then the start address of the interrupt routine, which is called the 'interrupt vector', is loaded into the program counter so that the next executed instruction will be the start of the service routine. As an example, in the case of the Motorola 6800 CPU the interrupt vector for a simple IRQ interrupt is located at the top of the memory in addresses $FFF8 and $FFF9. Other types of CPU may have the interrupt vectors located at the bottom of the memory map. In either case the start address of the interrupt service routine must be stored in the appropriate interrupt vector locations in memory.

In the Intel 8085 CPU, the interrupt operation is a little more complicated. When an interrupt is received the current instruction is completed and then the CPU outputs an interrupt acknowledge signal (INTA) to the external device. The CPU now expects to receive an opcode for its next instruction and this must be provided by the external device. Usually the opcode will be a CALL to a subroutine but alternatively a RESTART instruction may be used. Having received the CALL instruction, the CPU will expect a further two bytes of data representing the address for the start of the subroutine, which in this case will be an interrupt service routine. After the external device has delivered the operand for the CALL instruction, the CALL will be executed and the program counter is saved as for a normal subroutine before execution jumps to the first instruction of the interrupt service routine.

The 8085 CPU does also have a vectored interrupt facility which uses three inputs called RST5.5, RST6.5 and RST7.5. When one of these inputs is activated it causes the PC contents to be pushed to the stack and then jumps to the interrupt service routine whose start address is held in a pair of fixed locations at the bottom end of the memory. This is similar in action to the FIRQ operation of a 6809 CPU except that the status register contents are not saved automatically.

Handling two separate interrupts

It is quite likely that there will be more than one external device which needs to be able to interrupt the operation of the CPU in order to transfer data or receive some other attention. The simplest way of dealing with this requirement is to connect the interrupt lines of all external devices in parallel to the IRQ input of the CPU. This input is normally arranged to have a 'wired OR' configuration. This means all devices connected to the IRQ input must have open collector transistor outputs. Any device may pull down the interrupt input to the '0' state but none of them will be able to drive the input to a '1' state, thus avoiding the possibility of damage to the output stage of external devices if two became active together. A pull up resistor is normally included, as shown in Figure 10.5, so that when all external devices' outputs are turned off the IRQ level will be in the '1' state.

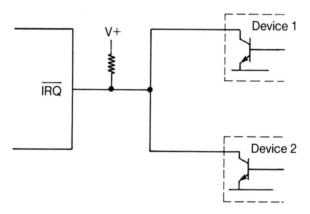

Fig. 10.5 The wired OR configuration normally used for IRQ inputs.

Now if device 1 on the system triggers an interrupt, the CPU will jump to an interrupt service routine and start to process the interrupt. The problem with this arrangement is that the two external devices are likely to need different routines to service their interrupt request. For instance, device 1 may be a printer whilst device 2 is a keyboard. The CPU needs to be able to identify which device on the system has caused the interrupt and then the appropriate service routine can be selected. This can be done by using a polling system.

Each device connected to an I/O port will normally have some form of status register associated with it. If the input is made via a PIA device such as the 6821, the control register of the PIA also acts as a status register and, in fact, bits 6 and 7 of the control register act as interrupt flag bits which indicate if an input has occurred on the handshake input lines C1 and C2 respectively. So if we have a device connected to the PIA we can arrange that when it wants to interrupt the CPU it places a signal on the C1 input control line of the PIA. This input to the PIA causes bit 7 in the PIA control register to be set to '1' and the PIA will also send an IRQ signal to the CPU.

To find out which device caused the interrupt, a polling routine can be placed at the start of the interrupt service routine. In this polling routine the CPU reads the status register for each input or output port in turn in some pre-arranged sequence. A test is made of the interrupt flag bit or bits in each port register and when a '1' is detected it indicates that that particular input or output needs attention. At this point a simple branch to a subroutine can be used to select the appropriate service routine for that device. If no flag bit is detected the program goes on to test the state of the next device and so on. The general idea is shown in the flow chart of Figure 10.6 where the external devices are defined as a keyboard and a printer.

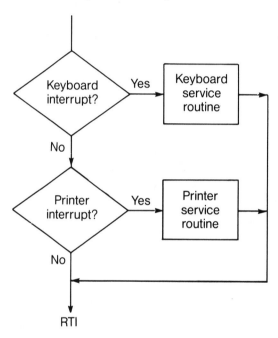

Fig. 10.6 Program flow for a simple interrupt polling routine.

If both devices have requested attention then, after the first device has been serviced, the program operation returns to the polling routine and will check the remaining devices to see if any others need attention. As each device is serviced its interrupt flag is reset. This is done automatically in a 6821 PIA when the data register is selected for a read or write data transfer and at the same time the IRQ output from that port is set back to the '1' state so that it is no longer requesting an interrupt. Most other interface chips use a similar scheme.

At the end of the interrupt service routine all of the devices requesting an interrupt will have been serviced and the main program is resumed until a new interrupt occurs.

Masking the interrupts

In the simple situation described above the two interrupts occurred together and are then processed by the interrupt routine. Suppose, however, that a new interrupt occurred whilst the interrupt routine itself was in progress. In theory this would cause the interrupt routine to stop and a new interrupt to start, but we may not want the servicing of the interrupt to be interrupted. This situation is dealt with by means of an 'interrupt mask' bit in the CPU status register.

In the 6800 CPU the interrupt mask or I bit in the status register is normally set at '0' and under these conditions the CPU will respond to an interrupt request on its IRQ input. When an interrupt occurs the CPU state is saved on the stack and then the I mask bit is set to '1' before the jump is made to the start of the interrupt service routine. When the I bit is set at '1' the IRQ input is ignored so any further interrupt inputs will not trigger a new interrupt sequence. This is called 'interrupt masking' and this type of interrupt operation is called a 'maskable interrupt'.

Now if a new interrupt occurs whilst the first is being serviced it will be ignored. At the end of the interrupt service routine when the RTI instruction is executed the I bit will be reset to its '0' state thus enabling the interrupts again. If the IRQ input is still at the '0' level a new interrupt operation starts and the interrupt service routine is repeated. Thus, in our example, if the printer raised the first interrupt it would be serviced by the interrupt routine. If during this time an interrupt were received from the keyboard it would be ignored until the end of the printer routine and then when the I status bit in the CPU is cleared to '0' the keyboard interrupt will be processed.

On the 6809 CPU both the IRQ and FIRQ interrupt input lines will generate a maskable interrupt and both use the I bit in the CPU status register as a mask control bit.

Non-maskable interrupts

In our simple interrupt scheme with the printer and keyboard both using the IRQ input for interrupts, we can have the state where the printer causes an interrupt and is being dealt with by its interrupt service routine. Now the printer may be a relatively slow device so that it takes some time for the service routine to complete. During this time any input from the keyboard is ignored but we may want the CPU to respond immediately to an input from the keyboard.

One way of dealing with this situation is to have a different interrupt input line which is not affected by the interrupt mask bit and will therefore react immediately. Such an interrupt is called a 'non-maskable' interrupt and in the 6800 series devices it is triggered by an input line called NMI. When this interrupt is activated it saves the data in the CPU registers in the same way as an IRQ interrupt and sets the I bit in the CPU status register to '1', but it jumps to a different vector address from the one used by the IRQ interrupt. In a 6800 CPU the start address for the NMI interrupt service routine is held in locations $FFFC and $FFFD. The service routine will end with an RTI instruction and the return to the main program proceeds in the same way as for an IRQ interrupt.

The NMI facility is particularly useful for handling, say, a real-time clock input which must be processed immediately it occurs rather than waiting for other interrupt routines to finish. An NMI interrupt will automatically mask any following IRQ interrupt until the NMI interrupt has been completely serviced. Only one external device is normally connected to the NMI input to avoid possible conflicts in timing, since any other device triggering the NMI input could interrupt the NMI service routine that is in progress.

Software interrupts

The third type of interrupt facility provided on microprocessors is the software interrupt. Unlike the other interrupts this one is actually triggered by an instruction in the program. In the 6800 CPU the software interrupt instruction is SWI and it has no operand.

In some ways this particular interrupt may seem a bit superfluous since its action is very much the same as that of a subroutine. When the SWI instruction occurs it causes the interrupt mask bit to be set in the status register and then the CPU registers are saved on the stack as for a normal interrupt. The program then branches to the start of an interrupt service routine by picking up its start address from a vector location at the top of the memory. The vector address for an SWI instruction with a 6800 CPU is stored in locations $FFFA and $FFFB. At the end of the service routine an RTI instruction recalls the CPU status and returns execution to the main program. Apart from saving the CPU registers, the action is similar to that of a subroutine.

One difference between SWI and, say, BSR is that the SWI instruction needs no operand. The other point is that the routine to which it jumps can readily be selected by altering the address stored at the vector location without having to alter the program itself.

Software interrupts are often used in program debugging routines. If the program is held in the read/write RAM it is fairly easy to change an instruction operand to SWI. Now when the program is run and it reaches the SWI the program can be made to branch to a routine which allows register contents to be examined or altered as desired. The SWI can then be removed and the original instruction replaced; then the SWI can be moved to a new point further along the program where the next test is to be made.

In this way it is quite easy to break into and test a program without having to rewrite it to incorporate the tests.

In some processors the software interrupt can be invoked when certain specified status conditions exist in the CPU. This allows the possibility of trapping error conditions and then dealing with them in an interrupt routine rather than having to write in error detection routines at various points in the program.

Interrupt priority

So far we have seen that if we have a device which must have immediate attention it can use the NMI input which will always interrupt any interrupt routine that has been started by an IRQ interrupt. Suppose that we have three units in the system which need to have interrupts processed. One may be the printer, another the keyboard and perhaps the third might be a real-time clock. We can easily give the clock its priority by allowing it to use the NMI input, but the keyboard and printer will have to share the IRQ input line.

With the normal scheme of things, if the printer starts an interrupt sequence then the keyboard is effectively locked out until the printer has been dealt with. Of course, if both interrupts occur together and we always poll the keyboard first then the keyboard will get priority over the printer. What we need is the ability for the keyboard to interrupt the printer routine so that it can be serviced immediately.

One way of allowing the keyboard to gain priority would be to feed its interrupt input to the non-masked NMI input line. The NMI input is not affected by the mask bit in the CPU status register so now an input from the keyboard will cause an interrupt even if the printer interrupt service routine is running. At the end of the keyboard service routine the program execution will return to the printer routine. In fact the keyboard could interrupt the printer routine several times before the printer completes its operation.

Suppose we are already using the NMI line and want to use an ordinary IRQ input for the keyboard. Now the solution is that we need to be able to switch off the mask bit in the CPU status register and this can be done by using a CLI instruction. So now at the start of the routine that services the printer we can first of all clear the interrupt flag in the PIA that feeds the printer by reading its data register. If the printer is the only device requesting attention this will clear the input on the IRQ line. The next step is to use a CLI instruction which resets the mask bit and enables the IRQ interrupt system. Any new interrupt request will now interrupt the printer service routine so when the keyboard demands attention it will interrupt the printer processing and be serviced. When the keyboard has been dealt with the printer routine resumes. In fact the keyboard may interrupt the printer routine several times before the printer routine eventually completes.

Suppose now that the keyboard has raised the only IRQ interrupt and is being serviced when the printer puts an interrupt request on the IRQ line. If there is no CLI in the keyboard service routine then the mask bit will prevent the printer from interrupting the keyboard routine, so all will be well and the keyboard processing will not be held up by the printer.

When there are more than two devices on the IRQ line, things get a little more complicated. If there were three devices we could poll them in order of priority with the highest priority first. The top priority device would leave the mask bit set so that its operation could not be interrupted by the others. Devices 2 and 3 would both have to have the mask bit cleared at the start of their service routines but this could mean that number 3 with the lowest priority could still interrupt the servicing of device 2. The solution to this problem is to disable the interrupt line of the lowest priority device at its output port when the service routine for device 2 starts and before the IRQ input is enabled on the CPU.

Most port devices, such as the 6821 PIA, have a facility for disabling their interrupt request output to the CPU. In the 6821 this can be done by setting bit 0 of the control register to '0' to disable interrupts caused by the C1 input line, or by setting control register bit 3 at 0 to disable interrupts caused by the C2 input line. So now at the start of the interrupt sequence for device number 2 the control register for device 3 is altered to disable its IRQ output then the mask bit is cleared so that device 1 can still interrupt the service routine. At the end of the service routine for device 2, the mask bit is set and then the control register for port 3 is altered again to restore the IRQ output. If device 3 has requested an interrupt the IRQ output of its port will now go to '0' and start a new interrupt request from the CPU.

Hardware priority schemes

Although it is possible to handle interrupts with different priorities by using a software polling scheme and using the masking and disabling of the interrupt signals, an alternative approach is to carry out the priority selection using hardware logic. Special devices called interrupt priority controllers are available which provide the required logic for managing a series of interrupts with different priority levels.

The basic arrangement for such an interrupt priority controller is shown in Figure 10.7. An input register is used to hold the current states of, say, eight interrupt input lines. A second register is used to indicate those interrupt lines that are currently being serviced by the CPU. On all but one of these the interrupt service routine will have been suspended whilst the current highest priority interrupt is being dealt with. A further block of logic is used to determine the highest priority input being requested and to check to see if this has a higher priority than the one currently being serviced. If the

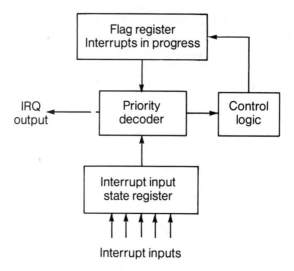

Fig. 10.7 Internal organisation of a hardware interrupt priority controller.

new interrupt has a higher priority then an interrupt request is sent to the CPU so that the new interrupt is dealt with immediately, and its associated bit is set in the register for currently running interrupts. As each interrupt routine completes, its flag bit is reset in the current interrupt register and the next highest priority interrupt is then determined. If this is already running its interrupt routine is resumed, but if a new high priority input is present then a new routine is started. The main advantage of the hardware priority decoder system is that it works more rapidly than any software priority resolution scheme.

In the Intel 8259 Priority Interrupt Controller there is a facility for handling up to eight interrupt inputs. The controller will automatically generate the CALL opcode required by an 8085 CPU in answer to its interrupt acknowledge signal and will also provide an address for the start of the interrupt service routine. Eight different addresses may be generated which may be spaced either four or eight locations apart in the memory map. Normally the memory will contain some form of jump instruction at these addresses and this will send the program to the actual start address of the service routine. Thus, when any device places an interrupt on one of the input lines of the priority controller, it will be checked to see if it has high enough priority to be accepted and then the jump will be made to the appropriate memory address generated by the priority controller, and from there another jump may be made to the appropriate service routine.

Planning a real-time system

If the system being designed has to work in real time, the first decision that needs to be made is whether to use interrupts or not. For some systems the simple software polling of peripheral devices at intervals through the program may be perfectly adequate and may present less problems for the programmer. As an example, a real-time controller may be operating at a sampling rate of perhaps two per second and the operations within the calculation loop may complete in perhaps a quarter of a second, so that for a large part of the time the CPU is simply waiting for the next timing clock pulse from an external clock running at 2 hertz. Other operations required may be the ability to input new parameters to the system or to read out the current state to a display on command. The software polling for these functions can be performed at the end of each sampling loop and, providing the request can be serviced before the next clock pulse is due, no problems are likely to arise.

In many cases software polling will not be practical so some form of interrupt system will be needed. Before starting to design this, each of the tasks or devices that are likely to cause interrupts must be defined and then placed in order of priority. A decision needs to be made for each activity about whether it can be interrupted by other tasks or not. At this point it is possible to sort out the routine for the highest priority task and then the others can be resolved working down the levels of priority. In each case it is important to work out some estimate of how long each interrupt service routine is likely to take to see whether it will affect any other routines, and the priority ranking of the routines may then need to be adjusted accordingly.

Remember that the NMI input can be used for the highest priority task unless there are periods when that task needs to be disabled, in which case it will have to use a maskable interrupt. For the lower level tasks, inhibiting of the interrupt facility in individual I/O ports may be required to maintain the priority system but do not forget to restore these at the end of the higher priority routine.

If a number of routines are nested it is possible that the lowest priority routine may never complete or may be delayed excessively. Here it may be desirable to build in some form of time-sharing feature so that if the lowest priority routine has been running for some specified length of time it will set the mask bit or disable some of the other interrupts in order to complete its service routine. This situation is also true of the mainline program since it is possible for interrupts to occur sufficiently frequently that the main program makes little progress between interrupts.

Multitask operation

In mainframe and minicomputer systems it is fairly common to find the machine operating with several different programs running at the same time. This mode of operation is referred to as multitasking. This type of operation could be implemented on larger microprocessor systems particularly where the latest 16- and 32-bit word CPUs are used.

In a multitasking system all of the programs that are to run are loaded into the computer memory at the same time. Where the available memory space is limited, however, some schemes keep only a segment of each program in memory and will call up new segments as and when they are required. Each program is allocated a priority level and the computer will normally execute the program which has the highest priority level. All of the programs share the same peripheral resources such as printers, disk memory, input–output channels and so on.

Let us suppose that there are two programs or tasks to be executed. The high priority task, which is usually referred to as the foreground task, will execute until it is held up by the need to wait for a data transfer to or from a peripheral device. At this point the foreground task is suspended and program execution branches to the second program which is called the background task. This low priority task now executes until the data transfer for the foreground task can be completed. At this point the background task is interrupted and suspended whilst the foreground task is resumed. This process continues with small sections of the background task being executed each time the foreground task is held up. When the foreground task completes, the background task will be allowed to execute continuously unless another higher priority task is loaded into the machine. There may in fact be several high priority foreground tasks operating at one time and the execution will work down the priority levels as each task becomes held up by a peripheral. Often the hold up will be caused because the peripheral required by one of the lower priority foreground tasks is already being used by the highest priority task. The supervisor program which controls the allocation of peripherals and the switching from task to task can be very complex. If a large number of tasks are set up concurrently it is possible that the whole system will grind to a virtual halt because the CPU will spend most of its time swapping tasks and less time actually executing them.

In most microprocessor applications, where the basic computer systems are relatively inexpensive, it may be more sensible to use a separate computer for each task rather than using one large machine. This leads to a system in which several microprocessors may be linked together and may in fact share some of the peripheral resources or share the computing load.

The RESET function

When a CPU is first switched on, the contents of its internal registers, including the program counter, will be random data patterns. If the CPU were simply allowed to start operating it would therefore start by taking an instruction from a random memory location and executing it. This situation is most unsatisfactory, since what we want the CPU to do is to start execution with the first instruction of the program that has been placed into its memory. The function of starting up the operation of the CPU in an orderly fashion is performed by an additional interrupt-type operation which is generally given the name RESET.

When the RESET input of the CPU is pulled low it triggers an interrupt operation and the CPU will call up a vectored address from memory. This address is the memory location of the first instruction of the program that is to be executed. Unlike the other interrupt operations RESET does not store any CPU register contents on the stack. In fact RESET causes all of the internal registers of the CPU to be cleared, then the program counter is loaded with the start address for the program and instruction execution commences.

The RESET input should ideally be triggered when power is initially applied to the CPU so that the system starts up automatically. On the 6800 CPU the restart sequence is initiated by a transition from the '0' to the '1' state at the RESET input. At power on, the RESET line must be held at '0' for about 8 clock cycles before being allowed to go to '1' to start the RESET operation. One simple approach that is often used is the circuit shown in Figure 10.8. Here the capacitor between the RESET terminal and ground is

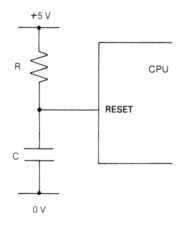

Fig. 10.8 Typical circuit for power on RESET operation.

initially discharged so the RESET input is at 0 V. When power is applied the capacitor will start to charge through resistor R and if the value of R is sufficiently high there will be a short delay before the RESET input rises to the '1' state. During normal operation of the CPU, the RESET input remains at the '1' level. It is, of course, possible to reset the CPU by applying a pulse going to '0' to the RESET input at any time. This reset action may be used to restart the program or to get the CPU out of a fault condition produced by an error in program operation. An example might be where, because of an error in programming, the CPU is placed into an endless loop operation and the only way to get it out of this situation is to use the RESET operation which initialises the CPU.

In the 6800 CPU the address of the instruction which is executed after a RESET sequence is contained in memory locations $FFFE and $FFFF. The RESET operation will override all other interrupts or actions of the CPU that may be in progress.

Direct memory access

Normally when data is to be transferred between a peripheral device, such as a disk memory, and the main computer memory it has to be transferred byte by byte through the CPU of the computer. If a large block of data is to be moved this can tie up the CPU for some time and it would be useful if we could have some means by which data could be transferred between the peripheral device and the memory without using the CPU at all. This can be achieved by a process known as direct memory access or DMA. The data links between the CPU, memory and peripheral device for the normal mode and the DMA mode are shown in Figure 10.9.

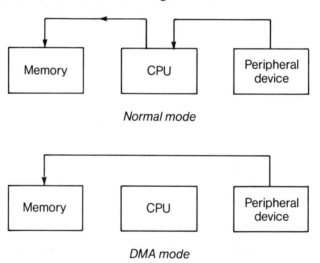

Fig. 10.9 Normal and direct memory access data paths in a microprocessor system.

When a direct memory access transfer is required, the CPU is placed into a HALT condition where processing of the program instructions is temporarily suspended. When in the HALT state the CPU releases control of the address and data buses. These two buses are now taken over by the peripheral device that wishes to transfer data to or from the memory. The peripheral device places memory addresses on the address bus and reads or writes data via the data bus as required. When the data transfer operation is complete the peripheral device releases the bus system and the CPU is taken out of the HALT state to resume control of the system and execution of the program.

There are two basic methods by which the DMA data transfer may be made. In one which is known as 'cycle stealing' the CPU is halted for one instruction cycle whilst a byte of data is transferred through the DMA channel. Thus a single cycle may be stolen once every ten or so instruction cycles so that the program execution is only slightly slowed down. This is useful if a large amount of data is to be transferred without too much disturbance of the program and where the rate of DMA transfer need not be very high.

The alternative DMA mode is the burst mode where the CPU is halted and then a short block of data bytes is transferred between the memory and the peripheral. This provides very fast data transfer but does hold up program execution whilst the transfer is made. The choice between the modes must be made according to the relative priority of transferring the data quickly or maintaining program execution.

The timing and control of DMA transfers is generally linked with the timing of the CPU and usually the CPU clock will be used as a timing reference. Special DMA controller devices are available which will automatically generate the control and timing signals needed and may also automatically generate the sequence of memory addresses needed for transferring a complete block of data. In this case the CPU will have written some data to the DMA controller to tell it how many data transfers are required and where in memory the data will be located. When the block transfer mode is used the DMA transfer itself will often be initiated by using an IRQ interrupt and the service routine will then start the DMA operation in the DMA controller device. The detailed operation of the DMA data transfer mode will depend upon the type of CPU being used and the operating characteristics of the DMA controller chip, so a study must be made of the relevant data sheets or application manual when the DMA section of the system is being designed.

Chapter Eleven
Software Development

For any microprocessor system to work effectively it must have a program stored in its memory system to provide the instructions that the CPU will execute. Whereas the physical components used to make up the microcomputer system are called the hardware, the list of program instructions is generally referred to as the software. In dedicated systems, where the program is held in a ROM, the software may be referred to as firmware.

One of the more important stages in producing any microprocessor-based system is that of designing, writing and testing the software which will govern the operation of the hardware system. In many applications the hardware used will consist of ready-built circuit cards, or possibly a ready-built computer system. Thus the performance of the hardware will already be proved and the success or failure of the project will depend upon the performance of the software that has been written to control it. In this chapter we shall look at some of the aspects of the design and development of the software.

The basic design process

The first step in software design is to decide exactly what the system is required to do. This can be done by first defining the broad requirements of the system. Thus, in a control system, we need to be able to monitor a number of different parameters and to calculate the control functions which will govern the process being controlled. The system may also be required to carry out some analysis of the monitored readings and perhaps display the results on a display screen. Other factors to be considered are facilities such as the ability to enter control constants from a keyboard or some other device and the provision of automatic calibration or fault detection schemes.

Once the basic requirements of the system have been written down, it should be possible to divide the various tasks required into groups. Some of these need to be included in a continuously running part of the program.

Examples of these would be the monitoring and control calculations. Other activities may be required only when requested by an operator. These would include facilities such as the ability to change control or calibration constants or to run a test or calibration routine.

When the various tasks have been identified each can be treated as a separate program or subroutine. Individual tasks may now be more closely defined by being broken down into calculation or processing steps. This may involve further subdivision of the section of program into subroutines some of which may be common to other program modules. For instance, some mathematics routines may be used by several different modules. Having defined the relationships between the various modules and any data transfers between them, each module may be worked on by a different programmer or team of programmers provided that some liaison is maintained to ensure that the modules will remain compatible.

Evaluation and development systems

In order to test the software when it has been written, some form of software development system will be required. This must provide facilities for generating the actual machine code data that the CPU will work with and for running the program under controlled conditions so that any errors or 'bugs' in the software can be detected and eliminated.

At the lowest level, most microprocessor manufacturers provide evaluation cards for their particular types of CPU. These cards usually contain a minimal microcomputer system based around a particular CPU and will usually contain RAM, various input and output ports and perhaps other facilities such as programmable timer devices. Also included in the system will be a ROM which contains a simple control program called a 'monitor'. The monitor is essential since it provides the routines that allow the user to communicate with the CPU from, say, a terminal and to place data into the system memory or read the contents of the memory. Thus it becomes possible to input the machine code version of the user's program into the development system memory and then execute the program. The system will usually provide some limited diagnostic aids for finding and fixing problems in the user's software.

In general the evaluation systems are intended primarily as an introductory tool to allow users to familiarise themselves with the operation of the particular CPU. The facilities on an evaluation system are, however, very limited and development of serious software on such a system, although possible, is not recommended except in the case of very simple projects.

The next level up in software development tools is the full-scale hardware and software development system. These systems are basically quite complex microcomputers intended to allow the development and testing of the software for a particular type or make of CPU. Examples of such systems are the Motorola Exorciser system for 6800 and 6809 processors or the Intel Intellec system for use with Intel processors. The system will normally consist of a CPU, a large memory of perhaps 32 or 64 kilobytes, input and output channels of various kinds and a built-in operating system with full facilities for writing and developing programs for the particular CPU around which the system is based. Some systems may handle a range of different processor types from the same manufacturer. The system is usually based around a set of plug-in modular cards and a different processor card may need to be installed in the system to match the type of processor for which the software is being written. Development systems normally have a floppy-disk-based mass memory system which allows a wide range of applications programs to be used, and the various versions of the user's program can also be held on disk files for future reference.

There are some so-called 'universal' development systems available which allow a wide range of processors from different manufacturers to be used and software to be developed for them. In most cases these use plug-in CPU cards to select the type of processor for which the software is being developed but the memory and other facilities are common for any type of CPU. Other systems use a single CPU type in the system and emulate the target CPU purely by using software.

For many applications in control and instrumentation it may be more practical to use a personal computer system to provide the microcomputer hardware. These systems are in fact working microcomputers and come complete with an operating system and, in most cases, high level programming facilities. Programs written for use on a personal computer can generally be debugged and tested by using the facilities provided in the computer's own operating system.

Assemblers

For a dedicated microcomputer system, the program which is written into the RAM or ROM and which the CPU executes will simply consist of a string of data words which represent instructions and operands. Writing programs directly in machine code is just not practical so it is usual to employ a mnemonic code scheme for writing the initial or 'source' program. In order to produce the machine code data needed by the CPU some form of translation program is required. This translation program is called an 'assembler' and it takes the mnemonic form 'source' code and converts this into the required machine code data that will be written into the system memory. This final machine code is usually called the 'object' code. All of the development systems will provide some form of assembler program.

The assembler program will generally operate in two different modes. One mode is basically a text editor which is designed to allow the mnemonic instructions to be typed into a file to form the source code. Text editors can range from very simple line editors to full screen editors and it is well worthwhile checking the facilities of the editor provided since a good editor system can save a lot of time in generating the original source code.

A line editor will normally allow a correction to be made on one statement line as it is entered. Lines may also be deleted or inserted into the text file but, generally, the method of operation tends to be slow and sometimes rather complicated if corrections have to be made. A full-screen editor allows the cursor on the screen to be moved to any point in the source program listing and corrections may be made simply by typing new data over the old data. Screen editors tend to be much easier to use and allow more rapid entering and correction of a source program text file, thus saving time and making life a little easier for the programmer.

Once the source program has been satisfactorily entered as a text file, it is usually stored on a floppy disk for future reference. At this stage the translation mode of the assembler program may be brought into play.

The translation phase of an assembler takes each statement and translates its instruction mnemonic into the corresponding numerical opcode required by the CPU. The required operand for each instruction is then generated and placed in the next one or two bytes of the translated data stream. The assembler automatically keeps track of the current memory address where the eventual program will be loaded ready for execution. The data file produced by the translation process is a string of data bytes which is identical to the data that will be used when the assembled program is executed. This output data is called the 'object' code and is also stored on tape or disk for future reference.

Most assemblers use a two-pass system where they first read through the mnemonic list and convert all of the opcode mnemonics into actual opcode numbers. A futher pass is then made which ties up all jump and branch addresses and does a final check for possible program errors. At the end of the conversion stage, if no errors have been detected, an object code file is produced and may be saved on disk. If errors are detected, the assembler will print out various error messages on the terminal and these should allow the programmer to detect and correct the errors in the source program and then re-run it through the assembler. The assembler will normally allow a listing of the source program to be produced and in many cases this listing, if done after the translation stage, will include the actual object code data and details of the memory addresses that it will occupy in the microprocessor system.

As well as dealing with the instruction mnemonics for the CPU, the assembler program also handles some additional mnemonic codes which are called 'directives'. Unlike the CPU opcode mnemonics, these do not produce instruction codes for the CPU but merely tell the assembler itself to do something. Typical directives might reserve one or more memory locations for use in storing variables and allocate a variable name to them.

One of the directives will tell the assembler what the memory address for the first instruction has to be, so that when the object code is produced and loaded into the memory it will be located in the correct addresses in memory.

Assemblers fall into two main types, one of which produces absolute object code output whilst the second type produces relocatable object code. The simple assemblers produce an absolute object code which is designed to execute when stored in a specific area of memory. The start address is defined by the user and the resultant machine code program can be simply loaded into memory in the target processor system and executed. One disadvantage of these absolute assemblers is that any changes in the program will require that the whole program be reassembled in order to ensure that the final object code is correct and ready to be loaded into the target computer.

Relocatable assemblers
Sometimes it would be useful if the program code could be moved to any position in memory without having to go through altering all of the specified addresses. This is particularly true if we have a subroutine that might be used in several different programs but will be located at different points in memory in each case. This problem can be overcome by using what is known as a 'relocating' assembler. This type of assembler does not generate actual absolute addresses in its object code but maintains an index of addresses required for its variables. The program address is simply referred to the start of the section of program or subroutine being assembled. Special instructions at the start of the code sequence tell the assembler which variables are required and whether they are specified by another section of the program or not. During assembly the program keeps a table of address references but at this stage does not actually generate values for instruction operands.

Each module of program can be assembled to produce what is known as 'relocatable object code'. The various modules may then be joined together by using a 'linker' program. The linker is told where the complete program is to be located in memory when it is executed. The linker may also be told which area of memory is to be used for variable storage. As the linker is executed it allocates absolute memory addresses to the program instructions and to the variables, to eventually produce an executable version of the machine code which may then be loaded into the memory, ready for execution.

The advantage of a relocatable system is that if parts of a program are modified, only those parts need to be reassembled. The other sections of the program will automatically be relocated in memory and all of the instruction operands will be adjusted as required by the linker routine. This feature can be very useful in large programs where different programmers may be working on individual modules of the whole program.

Linkers and loaders

In order to actually run the program, the object code data produced by an assembler has to be placed in the memory of the microprocessor system. This process is carried out by a loader program which reads the object file and transfers the data to the appropriate place in the memory. A development system may also provide facilities for programming the object code data into an EPROM device for use in the actual microprocessor board of the project being developed.

When a relocatable assembler has been used an extra step is required since the relocatable modules must first be converted into absolute code. The relocatable object programs for each of the modules of the complete program are linked together by a special program called a 'linker' which allocates addresses to all variables and program instructions as it puts together the individual sections of the program. At the end of this linking stage an absolutely addressed object code file is produced which can be loaded into memory using a normal loader program. The advantage of using a relocatable assembler is that when a change is made in one of the modules or routines in a large program, only the changed routine needs to be reassembled and then all of the modules are linked to produce the new absolute machine code program.

Macro instructions

Some assemblers permit the use of macro instructions or 'macros'. In many programs there will be short sequences of instructions which need to be used repeatedly throughout the program. Of course, the set of instructions could simply be repeated as required but many assemblers allow the short set of instructions to be treated as if they were just one instruction. This composite instruction is called a 'macro instruction' or 'macro'. It may be given a mnemonic name and is written in a statement just as if it were one of the normal instructions built into the CPU.

The macro instruction has to be defined at the start of the program listing. The details vary from one assembler to another but basically a mnemonic name is first specified and then the set of actual instructions making up the 'macro' is defined. The macro definition will also allow variables used in the macro to be specified. This definition sequence tells the assembler what instructions to insert when it encounters the mnemonic for the macro later in the program. Now in the listing, only the macro mnemonic need be used when the set of instructions is required. When the assembler converts the source code listing into machine code it will automatically insert the desired set of instructions in place of each macro instruction.

An important point to note when using macro instructions is that each time an instruction is called it will produce a set of machine code instructions which are stored as part of the program in memory. Unlike a subroutine, which cycles through the same set of instructions in memory, the macro uses up additional program memory each time it is called. Thus although the macro instruction makes the writing of the source code simpler, it still produces the full amount of code in the computer memory.

High level languages

Although many dedicated microprocessor programs are developed using an assembler to produce a final machine code program, this can become a time-consuming and difficult task when a large or complex program is to be produced. The assembly language also assumes a knowledge of the way in which the processor being programmed actually works. As an alternative to assembly language programming it is possible to write the source program in what is referred to as a 'high level language'.

These 'high level' languages generally provide a wide range of facilities and functions not found in assembly languages and do not require a knowledge of the internal operation of the processor before they can be used. Statements generally use English words such as PRINT, INPUT and GOTO as instructions and the variables may be given names such as METRES, HEIGHT and so on. Calculations are defined by writing algebraic expressions such as:

$$A = B * C / D$$

which would cause variable C to be divided by variable D and the result multiplied by variable B. The final result of the calculation is then stored in the memory location allocated to variable A.

The CPU still requires an object program in machine code in order to execute the instructions so, as with an assembler, some form of translation program is required to convert the high level source statements into the final executable code. Unlike assembly code, where each statement translates to one CPU instruction, the high level statement may produce many machine code instructions. The translation program is much larger than an assembler and may typically occupy some 12 to 16 kilobytes of memory.

There are two basic forms of translation scheme used for high level languages which are known as 'interpreters' and 'compilers'. In a compiler the action is similar to that of an assembler in that each statement of the source program is analysed and then converted into a sequence of machine code instructions which will perform the desired actions within the CPU system. Thus, the compiler produces an object code program which may then be loaded into memory using a linker-loader and then executed. In a large program the process of compiling followed by the linker-loader stage can take some time. Each time a small change is made in the source program, the compilation and loading process must be carried out before the program can be executed and this can be annoying when developing or testing a program where many small changes are made in the source version.

An interpreter also takes each source statement and analyses it but instead of producing an object program the interpreter actually executes each statement as it is translated.

Every time the program is executed each statement is translated from the source code and executed before the program moves on to the next statement. The advantage of this is that small changes can be made in the source code, and the program run immediately to see how it works, without the need for a compilation step. This is a great advantage when a program is being developed or debugged since it is possible to execute and test individual statements or segments of the program and gradually build it up until the whole program is working correctly. The disadvantage however is that, because each statement has to be translated during execution of the program, the speed of execution is slowed considerably in comparison with a compiled program.

When a personal computer system is used to provide the microprocessor hardware, it will normally be provided with some form of high level language in which programs can be written and there is little point in trying to write machine code programs on such a machine unless there is some specific reason why the use of machine code is essential for proper operation of the program.

BASIC

Perhaps the most widely used high level language for microprocessor-based systems is BASIC whose popularity is largely due to its almost universal use in personal and home computer systems.

In BASIC the statements consist of English words such as PRINT or INPUT and simple algebraic expressions such as A=B+C. As in an assembler the variables may be given alphanumeric names. The statements are numbered and are then executed in numerical sequence except for certain statements which allow the program to be directed to a particular statement number in much the same fashion as a branch or jump in assembly code.

A major difference in operation between using an assembler and using BASIC is that the assembler produces an actual machine code program whereas BASIC does not. The usual version of BASIC acts as an interpreter. When the program is executed each individual BASIC statement is translated and then executed before the program goes on to the next statement. Usually each BASIC instruction will call up one or more machine code routines in memory which are then executed to perform the actions specified by the BASIC statement. Because the BASIC interpreter has to translate each statement and execute it before going on to the next statement, the program runs at a much slower rate than a machine code program would. Typically, a program in machine code will execute much faster than the same operations executed using BASIC.

The main advantage of BASIC is that there is no need to spend time in assembling and loading the final machine code program before it can be tested. A BASIC program can in fact be written and tested line by line since it is easy to make a change in a statement and then re-run the program to see what happens. This can be a great advantage in developing the program logic. BASIC also has the advantage that the mathematical and input–output control routines are already present and may simply be invoked by calling the appropriate statements. When a microprocessor-controlled system based around the use of a small personal computer is considered then BASIC has many attractions since the programs are much easier to write in this language. Since operations that are critical for timing are often only a small part of the complete program for a system, it is possible to write these routines in machine code and then call them from the main BASIC program as required.

It is possible to obtain versions of BASIC which will act as compilers. Here the BASIC program could be developed and tested using the interpreter version of BASIC and then the source code could be translated into machine code by using the BASIC compiler. This could be an attractive approach for use on a personal computer-based system where the execution speed of the interpreter is not sufficiently high to permit full-speed operation of the program.

As an example of BASIC the following piece of program will calculate and print the numbers from 1 to 30 and their squares.

```
1Ø    FOR N=1 TO 3Ø
2Ø    S=N*N
3Ø    PRINT N,S
4Ø    NEXT N
```

This apparently simple program would represent some tens of statements in assembly code.

FORTH

One interesting high level language, which was originally designed for controlling astronomical telescopes, is FORTH. This language is in fact a sort of cross between an interpretive language like BASIC and a compiled language such as FORTRAN. As in BASIC, the individual statements are interpreted and call machine code routines, but in FORTH complete sections of the program can also be effectively compiled by simply defining them as functions. When the function is defined it produces a sequence of machine code calls or, in some cases, specific machine code instructions and when that function is now called by the interpreter, the computer simply executes the machine code routines specified. This process allows FORTH to execute at about 10 times the speed of a normal interpreter such as BASIC and, in fact, not far short of the speed of a machine code program.

FORTH gives the advantages of an interpreter by allowing rapid editing and modification of the source program whilst retaining high execution speed.

In a typical FORTH system the basic set of program instructions is held as a vocabulary and forms an instruction dictionary. As new functions or instruction words are defined by the programmer these are added to the vocabulary. Each new word is linked to other existing words by machine code calls and, in effect, is threaded through the existing instructions as the new word is executed.

Unlike most other high level languages which tend to use the conventional algebraic form of expression, the FORTH language uses post-fix or reverse-Polish notation where the variables are listed first and are followed by the operator or function designator. Thus to add variable A to variable B we would write:

A   B   +

Note that the variables or constants and the operator are separated by spaces so that the interpreter is able to readily identify the items within the statement. FORTH makes use of a memory stack for holding data that is being processed in a statement. When a variable name occurs, that variable is pushed to the top of the stack. An operator will normally take the top one or two items from the stack, process them and place the result back on the top of the stack. Thus in the above example, A is pushed to the stack, then B is pushed to the stack. When the + is encountered it causes the top two items (A and B) to be pulled from the stack added together and the result placed back on top of the stack.

The FORTH vocabulary will usually include all of the mathematical routines as well as routines for input–output which eliminates the need to write machine code subroutines for these functions. The main problem encountered by programmers using FORTH is the syntax of the language but, once this has been mastered, FORTH can be a very powerful tool in designing the software for microprocessor systems.

FORTH interpreters or compilers are generally available for the more popular personal computer systems such as the Apple machines.

The C language

One language which has become popular with system programmers in recent years is called 'C'. This language has some advantages for writing applications programs since, like FORTH, it combines the flexibility of the assembly language level with the simpler program layout of a high level language. Unlike FORTH the C language is compiled and will produce a machine code object program which may be executed independently of the C language compiler.

In C the basic form of the data used is either single byte characters, in ASCII code, or two-byte data words which are used for binary data values. Like FORTH the C language has a relatively small core of instructions called 'primitives'. For any more complex operations a function is defined and named as in FORTH. These functions may in fact be stored for future use in program libraries and called up during program compilation.

Each statement in C has a similar algebraic-style format to those used in BASIC but has no line number and is terminated by a semicolon instead of a carriage return. This has the advantage that a complex C statement may be split up and printed on separate lines in the listing to give greater clarity. The program is normally structured as a series of blocks of statements each of which may be named. The statements forming each block are enclosed within curly brackets.

The C language was originally written by programmers at Bell Telephone Laboratories for developing system programs and is closely allied to the UNIX operating system. In fact the current version of UNIX was written using C. Although C normally operates under a UNIX operating system a number of C compilers have been written for use on microprocessor systems and will run with operating systems such as CP/M and PCDOS. Most microprocessor versions of C are subsets of the complete C language but the programs produced will usually be compatible with other C compilers.

One important point to consider is that C is not a language for beginners and programmers will need some experience of using other languages if they are to be successful in writing programs using C. One reason for this is that C, unlike most other high level languages, will not check for potential errors. This has some advantages since it will allow the programmer to do virtually anything with complete freedom but this can mean that the program will quite happily self destruct if that is what you tell it to do.

PASCAL
Another high level language which has recently become popular for microcomputer systems is PASCAL. This language was originally developed during the 1970s for use on minicomputer systems and was intended to replace earlier languages such as FORTRAN and to provide a language which was more suitable for writing structured programs.

PASCAL is a compiler-type language which produces object programs in a special format called p code. One of the basic aims was to try to produce a language that could be used on any computer system without having to alter the source program. With other high level languages each different computer manufacturer tends to develop a special dialect of the language and in most cases programs written for one computer will not run on another type of computer unless the source code is modified to match the dialect of the new computer.

This p code program is then translated into executable machine code by a further translation stage. One advantage of this approach is that, in theory, the p code version may be easily transported to another machine using a different CPU and it can still be executed. In practice this advantage has been partly lost because there are now several different dialects of PASCAL and only the basic core of these dialects is compatible on all machines.

Like C the PASCAL language has a block structure in which each program block is a procedure or subroutine and this lends itself to the writing of neatly structured programs. Statements are similar to those in BASIC except that there are no line numbers.

PASCAL is a relatively complex language which can be difficult to learn to use effectively and is not the easiest language for an inexperienced programmer to handle.

Testing and debugging

Once the initial object code for a module of the program has been produced, the next important stage is to test its operations and to remove any errors or 'bugs' from the program.

In order to test a module, in most cases it will be necessary to write some form of test routine which provides data for the program module and allows results to be displayed. In a small program which is totally self-contained, it may be possible to carry out the debugging stage using the actual program itself.

In most cases some small problems are likely to be encountered with the program which might range from a small error in the output results to a complete crash of the program. In either case we need some means of examining the operation of the program in some detail as it is executing. One approach which is generally provided in a development system is the ability to insert 'breakpoints' into the program. The breakpoint allows the program to be halted at a specified instruction and at this point the contents of the various CPU registers and perhaps memory locations may be examined. These results may provide a clue to the cause of the problem in execution in a program. The usual technique for inserting breakpoints is to insert a software interrupt in place of an instruction in the object code. In most systems the object code is held in normal read/write memory so this is easily done. The original instruction code is saved in another part of the memory so that at a later point the breakpoint may be removed and the program restored to its original state.

When the break occurs in execution the contents of the internal registers of the machine will usually be printed out on the display screen. At this point the contents of memory locations may be examined or changed and then the program may be restarted so that it continues with the instruction that had been replaced by the breakpoint. In most systems it is possible to insert a number of breakpoints at different places in the program so that it becomes possible to execute the program a few instructions at a time and examine the state of the results at each stopping point.

Another approach to program testing is to step through the program one instruction at a time and, again, the contents of the CPU registers may be listed at each step. Normally this is done manually by pressing a key to advance by one instruction. A further development is the 'trace' facility. In this operation, the processor can be instructed to go into an automatic step-by-step mode at a particular point in the program and to continue printing out step-by-step results until it reaches another specified instruction in the program. This gives an automatic snapshot of the state of the machine over a short section of the program.

In some systems the breakpoint action can be made to repond to a particular hardware address signal or a particular pattern of data on the data bus and these features can sometimes be useful in detecting faults.

When a high level language, such as BASIC or FORTH, is being used the program action can usually be checked by inserting PRINT statements at strategic points in the program. These statements are used to print out the current values of one or two critical variables and, from the results obtained, it is usually possible to determine where the problem in the software lies. Since it is easy to change a statement or insert extra statements and then try the program again, it is fairly easy to try various corrections until the fault is eliminated.

Test and diagnostic routines

One aspect of software design which is often overlooked is that of including test and diagnostic routines in the software for a system. This can be particularly important when the system being designed is a controller or an instrumentation system.

In a data-logging system some facilities need to be provided for calibrating the system and checking the operation of individual channels. One option that can be built in is the ability to select the input from one channel and display the readings that are being stored in the computer. Now to calibrate the channel a DC voltage calibrator might be applied to the channel input and pre-set inputs may be applied and the corresponding computer readings examined on a visual display terminal. This process allows any zero or scale adjustments in the A/D converter or amplifier system for that channel to be set up. Most data acquisition boards will have pre-set adjustments for setting the scale factor and the zero setting.

Digital-to-analogue converters can conveniently be checked by setting up a simple counting loop, where a count is incremented from 0 to the full-scale limit of the digital-to-analogue converter. The count value is output to the converter and produces a linear analogue ramp at the output. If the routine is made repetitive and run at high speed, the analogue output becomes a sawtooth waveform which can be examined on an oscilloscope. Any problems with missing data bits, monotonicity faults and severe non-linearity can readily be detected by examining the oscilloscope display. In the case of missing bits, the actual bit causing the problem can be found by checking the point on the ramp at which the anomaly occurs. Thus a break at mid-scale would indicate a problem with the most significant bit, whilst a fault at the quarter-scale position would indicate a problem with the next lower bit and so on.

A linear ramp produced from a D/A channel could be fed into an input channel and then the resultant data read into the computer could be output to another D/A, so that the actual analogue input could be compared with a reconstruction of the data received by the computer from the input channel. This test could be used to show up problems of non-linearity in the input channel, assuming of course that the two D/A channels are linear in the first place.

To calibrate an analogue output channel, the output can be stepped between the scale limits by setting up the appropriate digital data and outputting it to the D/A. A further step might be added for the zero position if a bipolar converter is being used. If the steps are made at perhaps 2 to 5 second intervals and repeated continually, the scaling and zero setting of the D/A and its associated amplifier can be checked and adjusted by using a digital voltmeter to monitor the analogue output. In a controller system, a similar calibrated output might be used to check the operation of the valve, motor or other device that is being controlled and any mechanical or electrical adjustments may then be made to obtain the correct operation.

In a controller it is sometimes useful to be able to insert a step input into the loop to check the response of the system. This facility can be built in as a test routine. Further routines will be needed in a controller system to allow the various constants in the controller characteristics to be altered to match its performance to different process conditions. This facility is particularly important when the controller is initially tested, since the running constants of most controller systems are actually tuned in the normal operating environment to give optimum results.

Diagnostic and calibration routines will generally be controlled from a computer terminal unit of some kind, usually with a visual display. If the normal operating mode of the program is a continuous running one, as it would be for a controller, then some facility must be included to allow the terminal to interrupt the normal running mode and switch the program operation to the monitoring or diagnostic routines. This may be done by including a simple test for an input from the terminal each time the main program loop repeats, or it may use an interrupt routine triggered by the terminal input signal. To avoid accidental breaking of the main program flow, it is usually best to test for a particular character code input from the terminal before branching to the test routine. If the chosen code is not detected the main program loop can be resumed with minimum disruption.

When producing the interactive operation with the terminal, the received symbol code will usually have to be sent back to the terminal to produce a display on the screen. This is also a useful check that the terminal link is working correctly and that the processor is responding to the signal from the terminal.

Any messages produced on the terminal display screen will have to be generated by the microprocessor system. These should inform the operator of the action that is being taken by the processor and also prompt the operator to input new commands or data. The system should be designed so that the operator does not need to consult a manual to find out what to do but should always be prompted by the microprocessor. The main limitation to the messages that can be used is the amount of memory available in the microprocessor system.

When a personal computer system is used, it becomes possible to provide much more comprehensive test facilities since most of these machines have graphics display capabilities. Thus, it may be practical to read and store a series of samples from an input channel and then display these as a graph on the screen. It would also be possible to carry out more sophisticated tests such as performing a spectrum analysis on the data or taking a root mean square reading of all the data points.

Documentation

In any microprocessor system design, the documentation of both the software and the hardware is an extremely important part of the project. This is particularly true of the software side of the project since, no matter how clever the programming is, it is likely that at some time in the future some additions or modifications will be required. If the documentation is poor or inadequate then the task of updating the program to cater for new requirements can become extremely difficult, since a new programmer may not understand how the program is supposed to work and even the original programmer may well have forgotten the exact details of why various operations were carried out.

By using the modular design approach and labelling each module with its functional action, the parts of the program that need to be altered can readily be identified. In most cases it may be that only one or two of the modules need to be altered. If an overall flow chart showing the relationship between the modules is produced this can also be helpful, since it will identify any other modules that will need to be altered because of changes made in one of the modules.

Within each module, comments should be included which indicate the function of the individual statements or perhaps of sections of the instructions within the module. These comments should also indicate what data is passed into the module from other modules and what data it must transfer out to other modules. The comments may in some cases be placed on separate source program lines between statements or blocks of statements, or they may be included after the actual statement.

Whilst comments in an assembly language program or in a compiled high level program can be liberally used, since they do not produce object code or slow down the operation of the program, this is not true for interpreter-type programs such as BASIC. In a BASIC program the remarks (REM) statements take up memory space and because they are read by the interpreter will tend to slow down the program operation. By careful choice of variable names, however, plus a few explanatory remarks, it is possible to indicate quite clearly the action of the piece of program without wasting memory space or sacrificing speed. One way of saving memory space is to have one version of the program which includes the remarks and is used as a master copy, whilst another version with all REM statements removed may actually be executed when the program is used. In any case, it is a good idea to have, in addition to the listing for the program, a set of explanatory notes indicating the operation of the program module and defining the variables used within the module.

Chapter Twelve
Hardware Design

Having looked at the process involved in designing and developing the software of the system, we can now consider the factors which are involved in choosing the hardware configuration and the techniques required for testing the hardware system.

The first stage in choosing the hardware is to define exactly what facilities are required from the completed system. A list can be made of these requirements and then a simple block diagram of the overall system can be drawn up. At the centre of the system will be the CPU itself and it might be thought that the type of device used here would be the key to designing the system. In fact almost any of the currently available 8-bit microprocessors will be capable of performing the required computing functions for a typical control or instrumentation application. As a result, the choice of CPU is likely to be governed by factors other than the CPU specification.

Suppose the project is to produce a simple controller system. This might require, say, two analogue input channels to monitor the process and an analogue output to control the process. A monitor display might be required and this would perhaps use 11 or 12 digital output lines. A keypad could be added to allow the system to be set up. The keyboard interface might take up a further 8 digital input–output lines. Other facilities needed might be a counter/timer and perhaps some form of real-time clock which might be provided by the counter/timer device. This gives a set-up similar to that shown in Figure 12.1.

We must also consider the memory requirements for the system. In the case of a controller, it is likely that only a small amount of RAM will be needed since there will not be a lot of data to be stored. A 1K or perhaps 2K RAM should be ample for this application. If the system were to act as a data logger then a much larger RAM might be provided, especially if any significant amount of data analysis is to be performed by the CPU. As far as the program memory is concerned this will usually be provided by a ROM or EPROM device and will have a rather larger capacity than the RAM. Typically a ROM of 2 to 8 kilobytes capacity will be enough for most small projects.

Interfaces to other equipment must be considered when drawing up the

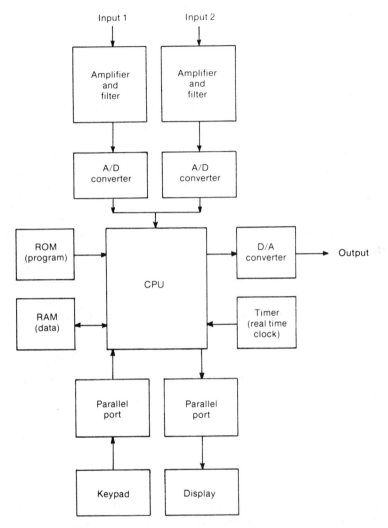

Fig. 12.1 Typical hardware arrangement for a digital controller.

hardware specification. If the project is to link up to other measuring instruments then a GPIB interface will probably be required, although some equipment may use a simple RS232 serial link rather than the GPIB scheme. Some thought must also be given to possible future expansion of the system, or future requirements, since it is usually a lot easier to cater for these at the start of the project rather than try to add them later. This may simply be a question of allocating space for an additional circuit card in the engineered unit.

Once the overall requirements for the hardware system have been defined, the next step is to decide what form the hardware will actually take. There are three basic options available and these are:

1   Use a personal computer system
2   Use ready-built modular cards
3   Design a custom-built system

Of these, by far the simplest and often the cheapest approach is to use one of the popular personal computers, such as the Apple II, Commodore 64 or IBM PC, as the basis around which the system is built. This approach simplifies hardware design since most of the system is already provided in the personal computer itself.

For more specialised systems where a personal computer is not practical, the hardware system may be built up from a selection of ready-made modular circuit cards. These are produced by a variety of manufacturers and the system can be put together by assembling the cards into a chassis frame rather like putting together building blocks. Again, much of the critical hardware design is already built in and the user merely has to perform the overall system design.

The third approach is the most difficult and requires a reasonably high level of in-house expertise. In this case the whole system has to be designed from the ground up and should be based around a CPU device with which the circuit design engineers are familiar. If the system is to be mass produced, or has to be built into some small or specialised package, then this will often be the only real solution. If the computer system is based around the use of one of the single-chip microcomputers then the hardware design may become reasonably straightforward, since it is likely that most of the design effort will involve choosing a suitable configuration for the chip by studying its data sheet or applications manual.

Using personal computers

For data logging and analysis in a laboratory environment, there is little point in custom-designing a microcomputer system from the chip level. This would be rather like re-inventing the wheel. One of the popular personal computer systems can quite easily provide the computing power and, when not being used for data logging, the computer can readily be used for other computing tasks.

Control of a small plant, a machine or a process can also be performed by most of the personal computer systems and will often prove much less expensive than a custom-built control system. Here, however, some additional equipment may be needed to interface the computer to the process being controlled.

A major factor to be taken into account when choosing a personal computer system for use in control or instrumentation work is the ease with which the computer can be interfaced to the real world. Some of the cheaper or less popular models may have very limited possibilities for linking in external signals, or the interfaces may have to be specially designed. Some machines such as the Apple II are particularly good for ease of interfacing. In the Apple II there are seven expansion 'slots' into which may be plugged a variety of interface cards. Thus it is relatively easy to add facilities for an IEEE 488 bus system, analogue input or output, serial or parallel data ports and so on. The interface cards themselves are made by a variety of other suppliers, apart from Apple themselves, so the choice of options becomes very wide indeed.

Other computers, such as the Commodore 64, have the main computer bus brought out to an external connector. A wide range of add-on units may then be connected to the bus to provide facilities such as GPIB, analogue and other inputs and outputs. Once again, because the computer is a popular one, there are many small firms which make interface units and other modules that can be added to the basic computer system.

If the particular interface required is not available then it may have to be designed and built to suit the project in hand. Sometimes it may be possible to adapt one of the standard interface units but, if this is not possible, the hardware design work involved in producing an interface is not likely to present too much of a problem for a good circuit design engineer.

If the system is required to work in real time, and many control or instrument tasks do, then it is worthwhile checking that the personal computer chosen for the project can, in fact, handle interrupts. Some of the simpler machines have fixed built-in interrupt routines which are not readily altered so that it may not be possible to control interrupt operation with the user program. Most of the popular machines, such as the Apple and Commodore types, will allow interrupt handling by the user program and are therefore suitable for real-time tasks.

Another factor to be investigated is the ease with which the computer can use machine code routines and the facilities available for writing routines in machine code. The reason for this is that most personal computers use BASIC as their primary language and, in general, programs written in BASIC are relatively slow in execution so that machine code routines may be needed in order to achieve the required execution speed.

Personal computers generally have much more memory available than the user is likely to need. When the computer system is to be used, say, to analyse data that it has gathered whilst operating as a data logger then larger memory facilities may be required. Some form of backing memory, such as a floppy disk unit, is desirable when the system is used for data acquisition since the disk can be used to store the data acquired during each experiment run. Since the program will almost certainly reside in the main memory, which will usually be a volatile RAM system, it is usual to hold the program on floppy disk and load it into memory when it is to be run.

Using modular cards

The major microprocessor manufacturers, such as Intel and Motorola, produce single-board computers based around their more popular CPU types. An example of such a board is the Motorola M68MM19, or Micromodule 19, which is based around the MC6809 CPU. This is a single circuit board which, in addition to the CPU, contains 2 kbytes of RAM and sockets to take up to 8 kbytes of EPROM devices. There are also serial and parallel I/O ports and a 6840 triple counter/timer built onto the board. As a result this single circuit board provides the basis for a computer system in its own right.

The Micromodule board is compatible with the bus system used in the Motorola Exorciser development system. This means that, for testing, the board could be plugged into an Exorciser system. There are other cards designed to work in conjunction with the Micromodule 19 and these provide a variety of interfaces allowing analogue inputs or outputs, relay drivers and additional memory to be added to the system. All of the cards fit the same bus system so they can readily be connected together to form a complete microprocessor system. A similar range of cards is available based upon the Intel 8080 and 8085 CPUs, although these use a different size card and a different bus system.

Several manufacturers produce a range of modular cards based upon the Eurocard format where the card size is approximately 150 mm $\times$ 100 mm. Again, a wide variety of options and interface facilities can be obtained. A point to watch with these cards, however, is that although the cards may have compatible connectors, the cards from one manufacturer may not be compatible with those from another. This is because some manufacturers adopt different bus layouts on the connector and the power supply lines may be on different connector pins.

If the range of cards available can provide the requirements for the system that is being designed then the appropriate cards can be selected and a system is readily assembled. Many of the card suppliers can also provide modular rack assemblies with the bus pre-wired so that assembly is quite straightforward. Power supplies suitable for use with such rack systems are often available as part of the range of modules.

One slight disadvantage of the modular card scheme is that often, in order to get the facilities required, some cards will contain redundant circuits. These redundant circuits consume extra power and sometimes two standard module cards may have to be used whereas the facilities wanted could have been built into one custom-designed card. In general, the use of two standard cards is a worthwhile trade-off because custom cards can be very expensive to produce.

A data logger system using modular cards might just consist of two cards with one containing the CPU, timer and serial port for a computer terminal whilst the second card would carry the analogue multiplexer and A/D converter. If anti-alias filters were needed, these might have to be incorporated in a specially built card since it is unlikely that the range of standard cards will meet the particular anti-alias filter requirements of the system. A further card might also be added to provide a GPIB interface to other instruments.

Custom design

The third approach to hardware design is to build the circuit up from chip level. This approach may well be dictated if the unit being designed is to be mass produced since the cost of development can probably be absorbed easily when vast quantities of units are made. Another reason for custom design is where the circuits have to be fitted into a small space or the computer unit has to meet some other stringent requirement which cannot be achieved by using standard modular boards. An example of this might be when equipment is being produced for military use where the standard card modules may not meet the high specifications required for military equipment.

For small dedicated controllers a single-chip microcomputer is usually more attractive since it will reduce the component count and enable a smaller computing module to be produced. Here, the circuit board may well be an in-house design arranged to fit in with a particular application. There are, however, some standard cards available which incorporate single-chip microcomputers and these may be useful for one-off systems where the cost of developing a special circuit card is not justified. Of course, a general purpose microprocessor, such as the Intel 8085 or Motorola 6809, could be used but the amount of additional circuitry needed with such devices generally makes them less attractive than the single-chip computer for a custom design. The choice of a particular device will generally be influenced by the user's experience in programming microcomputer systems and obviously one would choose a processor whose program language was familiar. There is little to choose between the popular 8-bit processors in terms of their capability of performing a typical instrumentation or control task.

For custom design projects the best approach is probably to base the design around one of the single-chip microcomputers such as the Intel 8048 or 8051 series or the Motorola 6801 or 6805 types. These are 8-bit devices but for some applications it may be more convenient to use one of the 4-bit microcomputers such as those of the Texas TMS1000 series. For a few applications there may be a need to use a 16-bit processor, such as the 68000, but in general it is likely that most applications needing a 16-bit CPU could be better served by either using a personal computer or modular cards based upon that particular processor.

Most microprocessors are fabricated using NMOS technology, which gives good execution speed and works well on a single 5 V power supply, but the components can use up significant amounts of power and this can present problems in portable equipment. If the equipment being designed is intended for portable operation or for long periods of unattended operation from, say, a battery supply then a CMOS microprocessor or microcomputer should be chosen. In general CMOS devices use very little power and are much less affected by variations in the supply voltage. This can be particularly important where batteries are used as a supply. A typical NMOS circuit will need its supply voltage held to within, perhaps, 5% whereas a CMOS version will operate satisfactorily with supply variations of up to 20%. Although some early CMOS processors were slower than their NMOS equivalents the newer types can usually perform at much the same speed. If a CMOS processor is used it is important to remember that the support devices, such as memories, I/O ports and other interfaces, will also need to be changed to CMOS versions if effective power consumption economies are to be achieved.

With a single-chip microcomputer a large part of the hardware system is contained in the same chip as the CPU so much of the design involves a study of the data or applications sheets for the device to see how it must be configured. These devices do not normally have an external bus system but, generally, the parallel I/O ports on the chip can be configured to operate as a bus system if external interfaces are to be used. Some types do include analogue interface facilities within the single-chip computer so, if analogue input is required, this type of device may prove attractive.

The single-chip computer normally contains some form of ROM for holding the program. This may be either an EPROM, which can be programmed by the user, or it may be a mask-programmed ROM, which will be programmed when the device is manufactured and cannot then be altered. When single-chip microcomputers are used the most popular approach is to use the versions with an on-chip EPROM during the system development stage. This can be erased and reprogrammed as required until the final version has been produced. When only a few units are to be made the EPROM version may be retained so that standard components are used in the system to give lower cost. The EPROM can readily be programmed in-house after each unit has been assembled. If a large production run of units was envisaged then it would be reasonable to consider having the microcomputer produced with a mask-programmed on-chip ROM. For most applications it is likely that only a few systems are required and the EPROM version of the chip is more suited.

The manufacturers of single-chip computer devices usually produce development or evaluation cards which allow a simple system to be set up based upon their particular chip. The prototype system may then be set up and tested using a program stored in a RAM on the development board instead of using the ROM on the microcomputer chip. When the system is working satisfactorily this program may be copied into the on-chip

EPROM and then the microcomputer chip can be transferred to its final circuit board for installation in the unit being produced.

In-circuit emulation

One problem which arises in hardware design is the actual testing of the hardware under the control of the software that is to be used in the final system. The conventional techniques of simply using meters or oscilloscopes tends to be completely inadequate when dealing with microprocessor systems since many of the signals, such as those on data buses, are multiplexed with other signals so that examination of a specific signal using an oscilloscope can become difficult.

One solution to the problems of finding fault conditions in a microcomputer system is that known as 'in-circuit emulation'. The basic principle here is that the microprocessor device itself is removed from the hardware system and is replaced by a probe cable which plugs into the socket that normally holds the processor chip. This cable is connected to a microprocessor development system and the CPU chip within that system now replaces the one in the target hardware. As far as the hardware system is concerned it will still appear to have a microprocessor chip installed. The program can also be held in memory in the development system and it therefore becomes possible to use all of the normal software debugging facilities such as breakpoint insertion and trace operations.

The system may be configured in various ways. For instance, the program may be held in the development system RAM, in which case addresses are not sent to the address bus of the hardware unit when the program instructions are being accessed, although data transfers to the hardware RAM and I/O channels may operate normally. Alternatively, the program may be called from the ROM on the hardware unit so that its operation can be checked.

By using test programs in the development system all of the input–output facilities on the hardware unit can be checked for correct operation. The system may then be run using its own internal program but with the processor function provided by the development system until any possible hardware timing or interconnection problems have been identified and resolved. When the system is working correctly with the emulated processor, the actual CPU chip may be reinserted into the hardware and the whole system should now operate correctly.

One useful feature of in-circuit emulation is that the development system may effectively be used as a logic analyser. Additional probe wires may be connected to selected points in the hardware system and then the operation may be analysed. The system may be triggered either by a particular instruction in the program or by a hardware sync pulse and will then collect perhaps 256 or even 1024 successive samples of the states of selected signals. These may be displayed on the development system monitor as numbers or, in some cases, the system may emulate a logic analyser giving a multitrace oscilloscope-style display. The numerical displays may be presented in binary, BCD, hexadecimal or decimal form to suit the type of data being monitored.

Power supplies

One area of microcomputer system design which is often overlooked and neglected is that of the power supply system. With the ready availability of stabilised power supply units the temptation is to simply choose a supply unit capable of delivering enough current at the required voltage levels and assume that all will be well.

One important consideration is the wiring between the power supply and the actual microcomputer cards. Cables are often specified by a current-carrying capacity rating but it must be remembered that this is based upon their use at mains supply voltages of perhaps 240 volts. All cables have some resistance and will therefore introduce a voltage drop when carrying current. Although the power supply output may be stable, the voltage arriving at a remote card may be seriously affected by voltage drop along the feed cable.

Whilst a drop of perhaps 0.25 V along a cable is unimportant in a 240 V supply, it will cause unreliable operation if it occurs in the +5 V supply for logic circuits. To see the importance of this, consider a typical cable of about 5 amp rating with perhaps 16 cores of 0.2 mm diameter wire. This cable will have a resistance of about 0.02 ohms/metre. If the cable is carrying 5 amps then a length of only 2 metres is sufficient to make the operation of logic devices marginal since the 5 V line will have fallen to around 4.8 V.

In general, it is best to arrange that the power supply is as close to the card being supplied as possible. The main problem is usually encountered with the 5 V logic supply and the best approach is to incorporate a voltage stabiliser on each individual circuit card and then use a partially regulated supply at, perhaps, 8 V to feed all of the cards. Here, voltage drops along the supply cables become much less important provided that there is a sufficiently high voltage to maintain the action of the voltage stabiliser on the card itself.

An aspect of the power supply which becomes significant when the system has to run continuously is the provision of some form of protection against failure of the mains supply. To cause problems in the microprocessor the failure need only be a brief one which might, perhaps, only cause the room lights to flicker momentarily. The result could be a complete crash of the microprocessor system. One solution is to provide complete battery backup for the whole microcomputer so that in the event of a mains failure there is no loss of supply to the processor. An alternative possibility is to provide battery backup to the processor RAM or part of the RAM. In this case, a sensor may be used to detect the mains failure and this is used to trigger an interrupt routine which stores away all current CPU and program states and places any peripheral devices into a safe state before the CPU loses power. In this case, the CPU power supply should have a sufficiently large reservoir capacitor that it maintains the CPU voltage for a few milliseconds to allow the fail-safe routine to complete. On power up, another routine restores the CPU and program status and program operation resumes.

Electromagnetic compatibility

One difficult problem that can be encountered with all microcomputer devices is that of electromagnetic compatibility, or EMC. This covers all aspects of electrical or magnetic interference to other equipment caused by radiation or conduction of signals from the microprocessor and the effects of such interference from external sources on the operation of the microcomputer. In general the more important problem is likely to be that of the microcomputer interfering with the operation of external devices.

In a microcomputer system there are a large number of devices switching currents at high frequencies and these signals are passing along the interconnecting buses and other wiring. The wiring itself acts as an effective antenna and will cause electromagnetic signals to be radiated from the unit. These radiated signals may well extend up to very high frequencies of perhaps 100–200 MHz and can cause severe interference to radio equipment operating nearby. A typical computer can produce very strong signals at distances up to perhaps 20 or 30 metres.

Electromagnetic interference falls into two main categories. Firstly, there is radiated interference produced by electric and magnetic fields generated within the microcomputer unit. This can readily be demonstrated by operating a short-wave or VHF radio in the vicinity of a working computer. The radio will pick up quite severe interference, usually in the form of a whine, buzz or series of beeps, at a number of frequencies throughout its tuning range. The second type of interference is passed through the power supply lines and, perhaps, through other interconnecting lines to other equipment which shares the same power supply.

The microcomputer can itself be affected both by conducted and radiated interference signals. In general, radiated signals are unlikely to affect logic operation unless they emanate from a strong local radio transmitter or from very strong electric or magnetic fields near the computer unit. The more likely problem is that such interference will be picked up by the analogue signal circuits of the unit, such as transducer amplifiers, and perhaps in the analogue-to-digital converter system. This problem can usually be eliminated by incorporating filters in the appropriate circuits.

Problems can be encountered with large transient spikes which occur on the power supply system. Many systems use switching-type power supplies and these will tend to pass any spikes on the mains input straight through to the outputs. If this is a problem then filtering of the mains input leads is usually required to remove the transients before they reach the power supply unit.

There are some standards for the levels of radio frequency interference that may be emitted by microcomputer systems. These normally specify the radio frequency field in terms of volts per metre at some specified distance from the microcomputer. In the American standards, two levels of acceptable radiation are specified. For consumer equipment, such as home computers, the radiated field limit is 100 microvolts/metre at a distance of 3 metres. For industrial equipment the levels are rather lower at 30 microvolts/metre at a distance of 30 metres. The German standards are rather more stringent than those in the USA and specify a maximum of only 50 microvolts/metre at a distance of 30 metres for domestic equipment and 50 microvolts/metre at 100 metres for industrial equipment. In Germany the industrial equipment has to be registered and may be operated only in a specified location.

Index

About the Author

Steve Money is a senior electronics engineer with some thirty
years experience in the field of electronic system design and development. He is currently head of electronic instrumentation at a
small research establishment.

Educated at St. John's College Southsea, he went on to study
electrical and electronic engineering at Portsmouth Polytechnic.
This was followed by a period of some eight years working on the
design and development of radar and guided weapons systems. For
the past twenty years he has been engaged in the design of electronic instrumentation and control systems with a particular inter-
est in digital and computer techniques. For the past five years he
has specialized in the application of microprocessors in instrumentation and control systems.

Mr. Money has written many technical articles for the popular
electronics magazines and has written a number of books on the
subjects of teletext and viewdata, video systems and microprocessors.